Literary and Linguistic Theories in Eighteenth-century France

from *Nuances* to *Impertinence*

EDWARD NYE

CLARENDON PRESS · OXFORD

"This book has been printed digitally and produced in a standard specification in order to ensure its continuing availability

OXFORD
UNIVERSITY PRESS

Great Clarendon Street, Oxford OX2 6DP

Oxford University Press is a department of the University of Oxford.
It furthers the University's objective of excellence in research, scholarship,
and education by publishing worldwide in

.   Oxford New York

Auckland   Cape Town Dar es Salaam   Hong Kong   Karachi
Kuala Lumpur Madrid Melbourne Mexico City   Nairobi
New Delhi Shanghai Taipei Toronto
With offices in
Argentina Austria Brazil Chile Czech Republic France Greece
Guatemala Hungary Italy Japan South Korea Poland Portugal
Singapore Switzerland Thailand Turkey Ukraine Vietnam

Oxford is a registered trade mark of Oxford University Press
in the UK and in certain other countries

Published in the United States
by Oxford University Press Inc., New York

© Edward Nye 2000

The moral rights of the author have been asserted

Database right Oxford University Press (maker)

Reprinted 2006

ISBN 0-19-816012-7

Cover illustration: Charles-François Pannard, 'Le Verre' and 'Le Flacon'
in Théâtre et oeuvres diverses, Paris, Vol. III, 1763

à mes grands-parents

ACKNOWLEDGEMENTS

I AM grateful to the following institutions for the research grants they awarded me: to the Faculty of Modern and Medieval Languages and Literature, Oxford, for a Senior Heath Harrison Prize; to St Cross College, Oxford, for a Paula Soans O'Brian Scholarship; and to St Anne's College, Oxford, for a Kathleen Bourne Junior Research Fellowship. This book began as a doctoral thesis under the supervision of Professor Richard Parish, whose encouragement and insight in my first year were crucial in providing the initial and lasting vision of the research, and Dr Nicholas Cronk, whose expertise, imaginative thinking, and seminal guidance for the subsequent three years were determining factors in the realization of the book. My thanks also to my father, Daniel Nye, and brother, James Nye, who were indefatigable in their proofreading, and thanks also to Dr Kate Tunstall who made important suggestions. Je tiens à remercier Jacques et Josiane Ronget, car sans leurs hospitalité généreuse je n'aurais pu rédiger les chapitres deux et trois. Remaining errors are doubtless my own.

CONTENTS

LIST OF FIGURES

INTRODUCTION

C'est la chose même que le peintre montre; les expressions
du musicien & du poëte n'en sont que des hiéroglyphes.
(Diderot, *Lettre sur les sourds et muets*, 1751; 1965: 84)
Comment se fait-il donc que des trois arts imitateurs de la
nature, celui [la musique] dont l'expression est la plus arbitraire & la moins précise parle le plus fortement à l'ame?
(Ibid: 102)

Coming from the same author and the same work, these two
statements are problematic. In the first, musical expression is
'only' a hieroglyph, and consequently of low artistic standing,
while in the second, musical expression is the most moving, and
presumably, therefore, pre-eminent amongst the arts. Diderot
seems undecided whether the 'hieroglyphic' nature of music
counts for or against it. There is consequently a polemic in the
Lettre sur les sourds et muets which tends to be understated,
because most critics concentrate their attentions on the hieroglyph rather than the Classical idea of imitation. There is also
a polemic more generally in eighteenth-century aesthetics
which is often underestimated for the same reasons. A more
balanced view would do justice to the intellectual tension
between imitation and the hieroglyph by taking more account
of the former.

Enormous intellectual energy is spent by Diderot and many
others on the subject of imitation, because they find that it stub-
bornly resists the best attempts to define what it is. Time and
again the two fundamental questions return: what is imitated,
and how is it imitated? The conventional answer in the eighteenth century to the first question is that art imitates 'nature',
a solution which begs the further question: what is 'nature'?
Contemporaries of Diderot offer three main answers. Firstly,
'nature' may be understood to be whatever is most 'normal' or
statistically frequent. In this sense, the artist's role is to reflect
a detailed mirror image of the reality he perceives. One might
call this kind of imitation 'naturalistic'. Secondly, 'nature' may
be an 'ideal' which is not actually possessed by any individual
or object in reality, but which is an intellectual construct of the

artist's mind. One might call this 'idealization'. Thirdly, lying
somewhere between these two concepts is a view that 'nature'
is what is most characteristic or typical, and this notion of imitation one might call 'typological'. To complicate matters, the
canon of great artists or writers is often assumed to have privi-
leged sensitivity to 'nature', in whatever sense, and so these
writers, too, are worthy of imitation.

As a result, praise for the imitation of 'nature' is an incon-
stant attribute which could be variously accorded to Chardin
for his 'naturalistic' still-life painting, Boucher for his 'idealizing' allegorical painting, or Molière for his 'typological' character portraits. Although this spectrum of aesthetic experience
is very wide, eighteenth-century thinkers find it difficult to
know where to place certain kinds of emotive but 'vague' experiences. Sometimes it is certain kinds of poetry, such as the ode,
which trouble them, or on other occasions, it is instrumental
music like the Italianate sonata. They, like Diderot in the
opening quotations, find it hard to see what, if anything, is imitated in these cases. If it is true that they are non-imitative, then
the solution is either to think of them as unfulfilled aesthetic
experience, or, like Diderot, to refer to them uneasily as different kinds of aesthetic experience altogether. In neither case
is the theory of imitation any clearer, however, because thinkers
make the distinction between 'imitative' and 'non-imitative'
from the feeling that certain kinds of art are anomalous, not
because they are applying clear criteria.

Charles Batteux makes one of the most famous eighteenth-
century attempts to define 'nature' and thus provide the
missing criteria which would make sense of imitation. He proposes a theory of what he calls 'la belle nature'. Diderot,
however, points out correctly that the proposal is no more than
a naming fallacy, because although he qualifies 'nature' with
'belle', he does not explain how one decides what is and is not
'beautiful'. Ever since Diderot made these remarks in the *Lettre
sur les sourds et muets*, Batteux's *Les Beaux-Arts réduit à un même
principe* (1746) is remembered as one of the great heroic fail-
ures of its kind.[1] It is a little unfair, however, that Batteux should
bear the brunt of this criticism, since almost without exception

---

[1] Diderot, *Lettre sur les sourds et muets* (1751; 1965): 88.

all of his contemporaries, not to mention art theorists since Aristotle, would support his basic contention that the arts are imitative.[2] Such is the widespread acceptance of this principle that it would be more equitable to place Batteux alongside Diderot and consider their mutual interests as an indication of wider contemporary concern for the subject. Moving the spotlight away from Diderot and Batteux in this way reveals a host of other thinkers who explore the idea of imitation in many varied and novel ways, and thus demonstrates the particular manner in which the eighteenth century thought about a theory which dominated the history of art at least from the Ancient Greeks until the Romantics.

The thinkers discussed in this book study imitation in language in the hope that some light can be shed on the problems outlined above. They have a remarkable ability to avoid the polemical territory occupied by the different factions of the various 'querelles littéraires', and instead they study imitation in a disinterested, quasi-objective way. It would nevertheless be a mistake to interpret their ideas completely out of context as purely linguistic studies, because they do in fact owe something to contemporary literary debate. Court de Gébelin's etymology, for example, is partly a word history, but also a system of sound symbolism which supports the traditional practice of euphony in poetry and, in addition, an incredibly detailed account of how sound echoes sense to make language a vehicle for naturalistic imitation. Consequently, it is not possible to pin down the subject of these texts as either linguistics or literary criticism, because they are a combination of both. The term which fits them best is 'aesthetic'. Firstly, because these thinkers are non-polemical and take a disinterested approach to controversial issues. Secondly, because, unlike the 'gentleman critic', they take an analytical approach to matters of literary taste. Thirdly, because they manage to apply a high degree of rational analysis without relegating the pleasures of the senses to the 'irrational passions', as Descartes did. And most importantly, they are interested in the pleasures of the senses arising from any object, not only an object of art. That is to say that the 'aesthetic' has as much to do with something as banal as the proportions

---

[2] Aristotle, *Poetics*, 1, 4 (1995): Vol. II, 2316, 2318.

of a door frame, or the feel of varnished wood, or the taste of wine, as it does the elegant composition of a painting. This broad perspective is usually articulated in the eighteenth-century in terms of Sensualism, and is particularly evident in Diderot's definition of beauty as the general perception of 'rapports', wherever they may be found (see Chapter 1.7). The combination of these four characteristics of eighteenth-century discussion mean that 'taste' is no longer an appropriate term for understanding the theory of imitation in the arts.[3]

The term 'literary aesthetics' also distinguishes these texts from another neighbouring *genre*, which is the abstract study of beauty by Crousaz or André, for example.[4] Theirs are works of logic more than aesthetics; they aim at a logical reduction of multifarious phenomena without necessarily saying anything about experience of beauty through the senses, nor the practical issues of representation.

The 'aesthetic' approach to literary issues has more in common with what Alexander Baumgarten meant by this word. He did, after all, coin it himself in his *Reflections on poetry* (1735), from the Greek meaning approximately 'science of sentiment'.[5] All four of the 'aesthetic' criteria above are shared by Baumgarten: interest in response to art but disinterest in partisan literary controversy, analytical approach to 'taste', dissatisfaction with Descartes, and a broad conception of the pleasures of the senses. There are also differences, however, notably that French aestheticians draw on a variety of intellectual sources, from Empiricism to Sensualism and even Cartesianism, in a way which Baumgarten would probably have thought inconsistent. The purpose of retaining the designation 'aesthetic' for the French writers is not to redefine the word so much as to suggest that the origins of the subject are many and varied, and not only traceable to Baumgarten.

Eighteenth-century speculation on language provides an

---

[3] The presence of an 'aesthetic' category in the eighteenth century is all the more conspicuous in comparison to its absence in the seventeenth century. Furetière, for example, assigns 'goût' to the category of 'Morale' (Moriarty, *Taste and Ideology*, 1988: 60).

[4] Crousaz, *Traité du Beau* (1715). André, *Essai sur le Beau* (1741).

[5] The original title of Baumgarten's work is *Meditationes philosophicae de nonnullis ad poema pertinentibus*. For more on Baumgarten, see Cassirer, *The Philosophy of Enlightenment* (1951): ch. VII, vi.

unusually rich number of perspectives on contemporary thought, touching as it does on a wide range of intellectual problems, from the linguistic to the social, the anthropological, the rational, the psychological. No less so the aesthetic. Certain thinkers find that the theory of language is a focal point for a wider discussion of the theory of representation, art, and aesthetics because all are perceived to be manifestations of the same principle of imitation. Theories of language are often written with aesthetic considerations in mind, which means that what looks like a text of only linguistic interest turns out to bear on fundamental issues of representation in the arts. Put another way, we might say that Girard's dictionary of synonyms, or Gébelin's symbolic etymology, or Condillac's origin of language are all abstract poetics. They are other things besides, of course, but there is a common factor uniting a great number of contemporary theories of language: a consideration at some level of aesthetic principles of representation.

The next remarkable feature of the language theories in the eighteenth century is that the complementary relationship between language and aesthetics comes to an abrupt end with the Revolution. The fruitful exchange between theories of language which were not complete without considering aesthetic issues, and vice versa, does not outlast the century. Although there is a great deal of interest in the theory of language and especially in universal language schemes during the last decade of the century, language theorists pay little attention to aesthetic issues. Conversely, literary writers reject the intellectualism of the Enlightenment, and claim instead that literary expression is beyond rational explanation. Several of them call this the principle of 'impertinence'; an emancipation from the rational cohesion and 'pertinence' which was the ordering principle of literary theory earlier in the century. 'Impertinence' contrasts vividly with the injunction throughout the rest of the century to write in a 'nuanced' style. 'Nuances' is a term closely connected with discussions about artistic representation, used to signify that it is possible to demonstrate the detailed structure of an art work which makes it figurative, or imitative of something, and thereby make an appropriate critical evaluation. By charting the progress of this word, and by studying the rise and fall of interest in aesthetics expressed in language theories, we follow the course of the idea of imitation in the arts which is handed down to the eighteenth century from centuries of art history, but which is in its twilight years before the Romantics find new theories to supersede it. The course in question, 'from nuances to impertinence', is a lucid period in the history of art theory when enormous intellectual energy is devoted to discovering what and how art imitates.

THE HISTORY OF 'NUANCES': IMITATION IN THE EIGHTEENTH CENTURY

What is now largely a fashionable word for minutiae was once interestingly implicated in important discussions about the imitative qualities of different kinds of artistic representation. 'Nuances' in seventeenth-century France means largely what it had always meant since its inception in the fourteenth century, that is 'shades of colour'. At some point in the late seventeenth century, however, and mostly in the eighteenth century, 'nuances' comes to mean also 'shades of meaning or feeling', and hence can be used in relation, not only to colour and light, but also to language, style, music, and artistic expression in general. The 1680 edition of the *Dictionnaire de Richelet* runs through a gamut of different trades ('perruquier, lainier, teinturier, fleuriste' and 'tapissier'), each of which uses 'nüances' to mean 'shades of colour', and sometimes more technically a 'colour sampler', or what is called in modern French 'un nuancier'. It then cites a new and figurative meaning to the word: 'ce mot est beau & nouveau dans le figuré. Exemple, l'extrême difficulté ne paraît qu'à penser sur chaque sujet ce qu'il y a de meilleur, à dire, & à trouver dans le langage je ne sais quelles *nuances*, qui dépendent de se connoître en ce qui sied le mieux en fait d'expression (Le Chevalier de Méré, *Conversations*, page 20)'.

The *Dictionnaire de l'Académie* does not pick up on this new figurative meaning until the third edition in 1762. The first edition does, however, provide a useful indication of its origins and associations. 'Nuance' does not have its own entry (it does in the second edition of 1718), but has a subheading under 'nué', along with 'nuage'. 'Nuage' has the figurative meaning: 'les doutes, les incertitudes, les ignorances de l'esprit', so that by the time of the third edition, 'nuance' and 'nuage' are antonyms derived from the same root 'nué': 'nuage' means intellectual obscurity, and 'nuance' means intellectual subtlety. Other dictionaries, notably Trévoux and Furetière, do not give a figurative meaning for nuances, but in practice it is in widespread use all through the eighteenth century in a host of different contexts.

The development of this word is interesting in itself as one more example of a tendency to draw analogies between visual and linguistic representation. In this sense it is an application of the well-known Horatian axiom *ut pictura poesis*, and an interesting addition to the panoply of ways in which words are said to paint pictures and pictures are said to tell stories.

It is also a word which is to prove very useful to those who wish to discuss different kinds of imitation, the naturalistic, idealizing, or typological, because originating as the word does from the sense of colour in the natural world, but coming to mean shades of thought in the mind, it can mean all things to all people. Like much that is important at the time of this turning point in aesthetic thinking during the eighteenth century, 'nuances' is an unstable compromise between different concepts of imitation.

One might say schematically, therefore, that there is a school of thought in the eighteenth century which says that 'imitation' means 'the ability to represent nuances', and that 'nuances' means as much 'shades of colour in the external world' as it does 'shades of feeling in the mind of the artist'. It is as if art theorists cannot make up their mind about the relative importance of naturalistic and idealizing imitation, so they use a word which means both. In the process, they stretch the principle of imitation to increasing degrees, until some in the latter part of the century say with Chabanon that '[il n'y] a pas de nuances', by which he means that music in particular and art in general is not imitative at all (Chabanon, *Observations sur la musique, et principalement sur la métaphysique de l'art*, 1779: 121).

While the tension lasts, 'nuances' is used confidently to suggest that imitative ambitions, naturalistic or idealizing, are a viable proposition. 'Nuances' is a kind of standard bearer for the traditional importance of mimesis in art. There are times, however, when writers voice their doubts about imitation, and wonder whether nuances can ever be captured. Either naturalistic imitation is impossible, because the natural world is too diverse, or idealizing imitation is impossible because our response to art is too complex and subjective. Diderot expresses the first concern when he repeats the conventional wisdom of the time that an artist can derive 819 'nuances' from an original palette of five colours, but also concludes that this is not enough: 'il faut oublier la richesse de la nature et l'indigence de l'art, ou s'affliger' (Diderot, *Pensées sur la peinture*, 1988: 809, 810). Emmerich de Vattel expresses the second anxiety, concerning idealizing imitation, in an essay on literary taste, when he uses the word 'nuances' in a manner very characteristic of his contemporaries in order to express a hope that it is possible to learn discernment, while admitting that it may be beyond our rational abilities to understand our feeling for beauty:

Dans le fonds, la question revenoit à ceci: Avons-nous une idée distincte de tout ce qui fait la beauté & ses diverses nuances? [. . .] Si nous sommes bien éloignés de l'avoir, si le sentiment nous fait apercevoir confusément, quoique très-vivement, mille beautés, mille gradations de beautés, dont il nous seroit impossible de rendre un compte intelligible; il faut convenir que le sentiment va beaucoup plus loin que la discussion. (Vattel, *Poliergie, ou Mélange de littérature et de poësie*, 1757: 19–20)

If it is the case that the nuances of our aesthetic response are too numerous to grasp rationally, then discussing it in such rational terms is a senseless exercise. Most of the time, however, authors like Diderot and Vattel do forget the ultimate impossibility of perfect imitation in order to pursue the idea as a working hypothesis.

The quotation above from Vattel is formulated in Cartesian terms which are an indication of some, but not all of the background to eighteenth-century aesthetics in general, and nuances in particular. Since neither he nor any other of the authors interested in nuances mention Descartes by name, the significance of their terms is debatable, but there is nevertheless much to suggest that a Cartesian rationalist mode of thinking, if not actually a methodology, informs their approach. Vattel seems undecided about what level of understanding it is possible to reach concerning colour. In Cartesian terms, it is doubtless possible to have a 'clear' intuitive and unmistakable awareness of red when we see it, but it is debatable whether we can have any greater understanding than this. If colour and sense impression in general have a hidden formal structure which is too complex for us to unravel all its peculiarities, then it is not possible for us to have what Descartes and Vattel call a 'distinct' idea, because it remains permanently 'confused'. What is at stake is a more or less intellectual understanding of colour, and by implication painting, and even the arts in general, since all involve sense impression: if it were possible to have a 'distinct' idea of colour, then it would join the ranks of abstract subjects like mathematics and philosophy, and we might arrive at a mathematico-philosophical idea of imitation in the arts. If not, and colour is formed of a blurred blending of infinite blendings, then there can be no rational understanding of it. All we can do is open our eyes as wide as we can, because there will never be words or concepts, including 'nuances', to explain the phenomenon.[1]

From Vattel's quasi-Cartesian point of view, 'nuances' is the word for the enumerable peculiarities of sense impression which have to be identified in order to reach a 'distinct' idea of colour, and by his implication, a 'distinct' idea of beauty. In short, the question he asks in the quotation above is whether it is possible to have a Cartesian aesthetics, which seems ambitious if not presumptuous when we consider that Descartes never discussed aesthetics, and indeed specifically excluded sense impression from the realm of 'certain' knowledge. From Descartes's perspective, the concept of 'aesthetics', a 'science of sentiment' is a contradiction in terms, because certainty does not exist in matters perceived by sense alone.

'Nuances' and eighteenth-century theories of imitation probably do have a rationalist background, but it is probably an exaggeration to call it 'Cartesian' in the proper sense of the word. This is not only for the reasons outlined above, that there are incompatibilities between nuances and Descartes, but also because Lockeian empiricism is at least as influential in the French eighteenth century as Cartesian rationalism. It would unquestionably be a misrepresentation of Condillac or Dumarsais, for example, to construe them as Cartesians simply because they use 'nuances'. On the contrary, both are explicitly Lockeian. It is probably better to assume that the intellectual climate in the French eighteenth century is mixed, and that it might be

---

[1] On Descartes's 'clear' and 'distinct' ideas, see *Œuvres* (1964–76): Vol. VII, 22.

just as appropriate, for example, to draw an analogy between 'nuances' and Lockeian 'simple ideas' as it is to make Vattel's Cartesian analogy. Otherwise, the danger is the kind of erroneous simplification for which Chomsky's *Cartesian Linguistics* is often criticized.[2] In the course of this chapter on 'nuances', it will be better to bear in mind the example of Hume's 'missing shade'. He is the archetypal 'honest' philosopher who begins from his strictly empiricist point of view to say that two colours may resemble each other so closely that it is beyond our sensory capability to perceive an intermediary shade. He ends on a rationalist note, however, by saying that it should be possible to imagine the missing shade.[3] The French eighteenth century is equally divided, and it is probably best, therefore, to reduce neither 'nuances' nor theories of imitation to rationalist or empiricist principles. They are a confluence of the two, and consequently capture the spirit of the French eighteenth century caught between French and English philosophical traditions.

Everyone is looking for 'nuances', and it seems worth finding out why. Félibien in colour, Castel in colour and music, Girard in synonymy, Condillac in literary style, Diderot in a theory of beauty, d'Alembert in systematics, and Batteux in the theory of literary genres. Some of their ideas will necessarily be glossed in order to chart a course from the end of the seventeenth century to the end of the eighteenth, but many points will be picked up in more detail in subsequent chapters.

1.1   The 'querelle du coloris'

There is an early, tentative shift of the meaning of 'nuances' from the domain of colour to colour theory during the 'querelle du coloris' in the 1660s and 1670s, when some painters and critics find it theoretically desirable to discuss shades of colour as if they were measurable and subject to clear rules of composition. The debate is long and involved, but

---

[2] Chomsky calls the entire history of 'grammaire générale', from Port-Royal in 1660 to Humbold in 1836 'Cartesian' (*Cartesian Linguistics*, 1966). Aarsleff and Joly disagree (Aarsleff, 'The History of Linguistics and Professor Chomsky', 1982; Joly, 'La linguistique cartésienne', 1977).

[3] Hume, *Enquiry concerning Human Understanding*, Section II.

briefly, Charles le Brun and the 'poussinistes' contend that in order to understand how painting produces the illusion of reality, it is helpful to explain it in terms of 'le dessin', or line, perspective, and the predictable rules of geometry. These are dependable qualities in painting which are much more appropriate to the eternal truths which great art should aspire to than the transient vagaries of colour in nature. Roger de Piles and the 'rubénistes', however, argue on the contrary that colour is essential, because in the real world it is what renders objects visible, and in painting it is the key to the creation of *chiaroscuro* which in turn produces the illusion of three-dimensional reality. In addition, colour is an important part of the aesthetic enjoyment of viewing a painting, even its 'soul', and should not be stigmatized as mere sensuality.[4]

The problem for the rubénistes is that colour is a less rigorous, less rational criterion than line, because it cannot be learnt in the same way; there are no measurable proportions of light and darkness which produce predictable effects of form and distance.[5] On the assumption of the rubénistes that painting is fundamentally the art of using colour, then painting would appear to be more a matter of subjective judgement than determinable processes. The problem with the poussiniste point of view is that too much emphasis on line and the geometric rules of perspective and composition leads to an analytical appreciation of isolated aspects of painting. It may be an obstacle to appreciating the synthesis of the whole which must be important in the basic pleasure which painting affords.

The disagreement between the rubénistes and the poussinistes arises from different responses to a question which will be echoed all through the aesthetic debates of the following century: to what extent is it possible to rationalize art if it is in part, at least, an object of the senses, and is it important to do

[4] For more discussion of 'querelle du coloris', see Lichtenstein, *La Couleur éloquente* (1989), and Teyssèdre, *Roger de Piles et les débats sur le coloris* (1957).

[5] Ruskin says something similar: form is absolute, so that one can say at the moment one draws any line that it is either right or wrong, but colour is wholly relative (see Gombrich, *Art and Illusion*, 1996: 261). The 'querelle du coloris' happens at about the time Locke is writing his *Essay Concerning Human Understanding*, in which there are similar implications to his radical idea of primary and secondary qualities: colour is a secondary quality which is 'in the mind' rather than 'in the world' (Locke, *Essay*, 1690; 1977: 59).

so anyway? The answer is almost always that it is both possible and important, but this requires a conciliatory approach which is not always a common factor of these 'querelles'. Félibien finds a conciliatory path between reason and sentiment in the 'querelle du coloris' in a way which is quite characteristic of the course taken by later linguistic thinkers faced with similar aesthetic issues, and to do this he uses the idea of 'nuances' in a way which is to become typical. His polemical standpoint is more complex than it is possible to summarize in a few words, but essentially, he maintains quite a degree of balance between the rubénistes and the poussinistes, despite his position as secretary to the Académie which one might have thought would cause him to lean in favour of the poussinistes. The balance manifests itself, for example, in the equal praise he accords line and colour in Le Brun's painting, which is a surprising interpretation of a painter whose style had quite clearly come to represent the poussinistes view of the primary importance of line.[6]

He uses 'nuances' in the context of this balance, and more specifically as part of his musical analogies which he uses to bring the subjective qualities of colour under the umbrella of a more rational theory of painting. Roger de Piles, the most notable rubéniste, liked his well-known analogy between a painting and a concert, and would probably have liked the following use of 'nüance' for the same reasons:

De toutes ces couleurs l'on en fait une nüance, les unissant doucement les unes avec les autres, il s'en forme une harmonie comme dans la musique [. . .] De même qu'il n'y a qu'un certain nombre de consonances dans la musique, dont on peut en les assemblant, faire une diversité de modulations & d'harmonies; aussi par le mélange d'un petit nombre de couleurs, il s'en peut faire des espèces sans nombre. (Félibien, *Entretiens*, 1685: V, 27–8)[7]

Félibien suggests that *le coloris* in painting is like harmony in music, and that both are an effect created by very many combinations of a small number of elements. 'Faire la nüance' in Félibien's sense is to make a complex harmony which in fact depends on a finite palette of colours. He suggests that the rules

<hr />

[6] See Teyssèdre, *Roger de Piles et les débats sur le coloris* (1957): 63.
[7] For Félibien's analogy and de Piles's response, see Teyssèdre, *Roger de Piles et les débats sur le coloris* (1957): 63.

for mixing colour may be as determinable as the modulations and harmonies possible in music, which themselves are derived ultimately from a simple and ordered sequence of notes.[8] The comparison is particularly effective for two reasons. Firstly, because in the musical terminology of the time, there already exists the expression 'faire la muance' (from the verb 'muer'), meaning to sing in tonic sol–fa. The Chevalier de Méré, for example, uses 'nuances' and 'muances' interchangeably in different editions of *De la Conversation*.[9] 'Muances', however, becomes increasingly redundant during the eighteenth century, because as Jean-Jacques Rousseau points out in his article 'Muances' for the *Encyclopédie* (subsequently republished in his *Dictionnaire de la musique*), the French are the only nation to adopt the do–re–mi syllables to mean the absolute musical scale. The two systems of notation are less distinct, and 'faire la muance' becomes a less effective image for the reconciliation of absolute and relative values. Perhaps 'faire la nüance', management of 'le coloris', is a better image for later writers on imitation.

The second reason that the analogy between music and colour seems pertinent, is that it is already suggested in the notion of a 'chromatic' scale, and also because there are seven notes in the diatonic scale, and seven colours in the rainbow. This image of the prismatic colours is used by Félibien to suggest that the enigmatic way in which one colour mixes with the next is based on a finite and predictable sequence of seven colours. This would provide an overall principle of harmony from which would derive the intermediary shades of colour. 'Faire la nüance' means, therefore, the way in which the artist creates, in Félibien's words, 'un tendre nouëment' of colour on the canvas from a finite selection of paints in the palette. In the quotation below, Félibien's first step is to compare the colours and intermediary shades of the rainbow to the artist's application of colour on the canvas:

---

[8] For more on colour and musical harmony, see Teyssèdre, 'Peinture et musique: la notion d'harmonie des couleurs au XVIIe siècle français' (1967).

[9] Wandruszka, 'La Nuance', 1954: 237. Méré's *De la Conversation*, Vol. V, 1, 74, uses 'nuance' in the 1668 edition, and 'muance' in the 1671 edition. Wandruszka's article is pertinent, but short on conceptual interpretation. Wandruszka suggests that the earliest incidence of 'nuances' used out of the context of colour is in de Pure, and mentions also an early poetic use of the word by Tristan l'Hermite in 'Le Promenoir des deux amants' from *Les Amours* (1638) (Wandruszka: 237).

Quand un Peintre scait mêler ses couleurs, les lier & les noter tendrement, on appelle cela bien peindre. C'est la partie qu'avoit le Corege [. . .] Ce beau mélange de couleurs [est] dans la jonction, ou nouëment des parties claires avec les brunes. Ce nouëment, interrompit Pymandre, & ce mélange de couleurs qui se fait avec tendresse [. . .] n'est-ce point ce que [. . .] Ovide entende, lorsqu'il parle des couleurs de l'Arc-en-Ciel? [quotation from Ovide] Je ne crois pas qu'on puisse mieux exprimer le passage presque insensible qui se fait d'une couleur à une autre. (Félibien, *Entretiens*, 1685: V, 17)

A few pages later Félibien summarizes the above: 'ce qui se fait si insensiblement qu'on ne s'aperçoit d'aucun changement, ainsi que vous le disiez tout à l'heure, en parlant de la nüance des couleurs de l'Arc-en-Ciel (Félibien, *Entretiens*, 1685: V, 24). Each time the comparison is made between the rainbow and 'le coloris', the implication is that colour in painting is derived from a finite and ordered sequence of colours, and that it is therefore more determinate than we may think. It is as if these writers posit a new level of representation, 'nuances', which is a rationalization of what seems indeterminate by analogy with what is within the grasp of reason. Although the minute transitions between colours cannot be distinguished, the existence of the distinct colours seems to prove that the transitions are there.

A century after Félibien, Diderot draws the same analogy between the nuances of colour in painting and the components of harmony in music, demonstrating the general persistence of the comparison, and in particular the enduring evocative quality of the word 'nuances'. In the following, the music teacher in Diderot's *Leçons de clavecin* is explaining the difference between diatonic and chromatic scales:

LE MAÎTRE. Diatonique, c'est à dire, qui procède en suivant l'echelle ou la gamme des tons et des semi-tons; chromatique, c'est à dire, qui procède par teintes ou nuances.

LE DISCIPLE. j'entends; c'est une métaphore empruntée de la peinture. On a pensé que dans ce genre de musique, les semi tons étaient ce que les nuances ou teintes rompues étaient en peinture.

LE MAÎTRE. Je suis de votre avis. (Diderot, *Leçons de clavecin*, 1971: 158)

The analogy here is reversed, with significant implications in the context of the *Leçons* as a whole. Part of Diderot's intention is to propose an alternative to Jean-Philippe Rameau's established and highly influential theory of harmony which was nevertheless thought by some to encourage too rational an interpretation of music. In his early writings, Diderot is an admirer of Rameau's theories, but he is more critical when he comes to write the *Leçons*. By comparing music to painting, and semi-tones to nuances of colour, he is, in effect, suggesting that we need to understand music in a slightly less rational manner than Rameau suggests. Later in the *Leçons*, Diderot points out that even though the possible harmonies in music are derived from a fixed scale of notes, the sensibilities of the listeners are not fixed at all, and they are bound to react to some extent subjectively (Diderot, *Leçons de clavecin*, 1771; 1969: Vol. XI, 506). Diderot presumably finds the connotations of the word 'nuances' useful in order to suggest that there is an aesthetic of suggestion in music as well as rational theory of harmony.

1.2   Le Blon's invention of colour engraving

The German artist Jakob Christoph Le Blon is inspired partly by Newton's colour theory, which he thinks inappropriate to painting, and partly by the 'querelle du coloris', to invent the red-yellow-blue colour printing process, and the first ever full-colour engravings.[10] He produced multi-colour mezzotint prints by using three engraved plates each inked with one of the three primary colours, which were then overlaid to produce prints which resembled oil paintings so closely that many who saw them did not believe them to be engravings at all. His work was known in England, where he was working, in the 1710s, and in France in the 1720s and 1730s, when he moved to Paris. Such is the interest in his process that he publishes summary details in *Coloritto* (c. 1725), a bilingual English–French text which Fabien Birren describes as 'one of the rarest and most fascinating works in the literature of color'. He continues: 'what now requires cameras, lenses, film, screens, filters, electronic computers, and scanners, Le Blon did by eye and by hand with simple tools, keen judgement and amazing facility [. . .] He had to estimate his

---

[10] For more discussion of Le Blon, see Kemp, *The Science of Art* (1990): 282.

mezzotint (screen) values, and this required skill bordering on genius' (Le Blon, *Coloritto*, 1980: introduction).[11] Contemporaries of Le Blon are similarly impressed. The *Journal des sçavans* of May 1722 thinks that 'cette découverte doit être mise au rang de celles qui distinguent si glorieusement notre siècle'. The *Mercure* of December 1721 is astonished that three colours are sufficient to reproduce 'la couleur naturelle de la chair'. Commentators are impressed, because Le Blon appears to demystify the use of colour in painting; he demonstrates the rational motivation of 'le coloris', in the same way that Brunelleschi demonstrated the geometric rules of perspective three centuries earlier. As such, Le Blon seems to answer the call of the 'rubénistes' in the querelle du coloris, to show that there is a rational basis to colour which makes it as essential to painting as line.

The term 'nuances' arises in these discussions to describe Le Blon's discovery, that from only three 'primitive' colours, natural colour can be reproduced in all its diversity. The reviewers in *Le Journal des sçavans* describe Le Blon's objectives to 'réduire la science du coloris à des règles sûres, & faciles', in order to find colours so 'primitives', that: 'il n'y avoit aucun degré, ni aucune nuance de coloris qu'elles ne fussent capables de produire [. . .] Suivant ces principes, la Peinture pourroit representer les objets parfaitement' (*Le Journal des sçavans*, May 1722). Mondorge, who is one of many to comment on Le Blon's portrait of Louis XV, makes a similar comment: 'Mr. Le Blon [est] convaincu que trois couleurs suffisent pour rendre toutes les nuances que peut fournir la nature', and remarks that the invention would be most useful in the illustration of natural history (Mondorge, *Le Pour et le contre*, 1738: 41). The following year, Prévost writes that the main reason why Le Blon's prints arouse so much curiosity, is that people find it hard to grasp how all the nuances of *le coloris* should depend upon only three colours: '[comment] on pouvoit produire toutes les

---

[11] For more detail, see the introduction to the 1980 facsimile edition, edited by Faber Birren. This edition reproduces one of Le Blon's most impressive, and early prints, 'Narcissus', which is especially interesting because it is not a copy of an existing painting, but an original by Le Blon. Birren points out that Le Blon's invention predates Frederic Eugene Ives's trichromatic printing plates in 1881 by 150 years. Prints by Le Blon are kept by the Bibliothèque nationale in Paris, the Strand Collection of University College London, and the Paul Mellon Collection of the Yale Centre for British Art.

Nuances, que les *Peintres* doivent aux combinaisons multipliées d'un grand nombre de Couleurs' (Prévost, *Le Pour et le contre*, 1739: 266; his emphasis). Viewers find the illusion hard to believe, the similarity between the 'original' oil painting and Le Blon's engraved imitation is perplexing. There is a sense of naive awe to contemporary accounts, as if viewers are rediscovering the mystery of imitation.

Le Blon does not himself use the term 'nuances', perhaps because he is a professional printer who finds technical vocabulary more appropriate. He does, however, make his relation clear to the 'querelle du coloris' as well as to Newton's colour theory. Before taking up printing, he studied painting in Rome under the Baroque artist Carlo Maratti, which may explain the Italian title of his book, *Coloritto*. In the introduction, he claims to have discovered 'le grand secret [. . .] des Coloristes modernes', to have found the formula to the genius of Titian, Rubens, and Van Dyck, even if others have long denied the rational nature of colour: 'quelques uns meme ont declaré qu'il n'y avoit point de Regles sûres pour le Coloris, & quelques uns meme ont pretendu que le Coloris ne pouvoit pas estre reduit à des Regles, jugeant que c'etoit un Talen incommunicable, qui ne se pouvoit pas enseigner, mais une capacité naturelle qu'il falloit porter à sa maturité par une longue pratique'. Le Blon confounds the sceptics, by describing in *Coloritto* how to mix a palette of fifteen colours from the three primary colours. He does not give away the estimated screen values required to reproduce the same palette of colours in a print, but does show a print at its three different stages of creation. Le Blon is keen to point out that Newton's theory of natural light does not work for pigments, and distinguishes between what are now called colour by extraction (light) and colour by addition (pigment and dyes).

Le Blon mastered the process which Roger de Piles said some artists take a lifetime to learn.[12] Although his invention was not a commercial success, his prints can only have increased interest in colour and imitation, and perhaps also in the term 'nuances'. The connotation of rational determination which Félibien gives the term is confirmed by the invention of colour

---

[12] Piles, *Cours de peinture par principes* (1989): 200.

printing, so that the word becomes a powerful blend of organized and limitless reproduction of nature.

1.3 Castel's colour harpsichord and colour weaving

The problem with colour, from the point of view of those who would like to make it more quantifiable, is that it is too much like Zeno's paradox: a spatio-temporal continuum is infinitely divisible. That is to say that beyond Newton's seven intervals in light and Le Blon's three in pigments, colour dissolves into a blur. The rubénistes were therefore at a polemical disadvantage vis-à-vis the poussinistes, who could cite the dependable rules of line and perspective to support their contentions. Analogies with the musical scale by Félibien and others are intended to compensate for this disadvantage by claiming that the 'muances' of music are like the 'nuances' of colour, and that both are ordered according to a fixed scale. The comparison between the two, however, is hard to demonstrate convincingly. The Jesuit priest and polemical scientist Louis-Bertrand Castel takes up Félibien's challenge: 'je venois de lire [. . .] dans M. Félibien, que la peinture seroit toujours fort imparfaite, quant au *Coloris* & au *clair-obscur*, tandis qu'elle n'auroit point ses *Tons* & ses *Modes* déterminés, & une espèce de *Diapason* ou *Gamme de couleurs*, parallèlement aux tons & aux modes, dont la Musique avoit comme de tout tems été en possession' (Castel, 'Nouvelles expériences d'optiques' 1735: 1447). He sets out to find the 'Diapason ou Gamme de couleurs' by further developing Newton's colour wheel, a device for plotting nuances of colour relative to the seven prismatic colours and to white.[13] By doing so, he was able literally to point to the nuances that some believed were not quantifiable.

He achieved this with the 'ruban oculaire', a fabric woven from threads of silk of twelve different colours, passing from blue through shades of each colour, and back again to blue, giving 'un vrai cercle des couleurs': 'un ruban de sept à huit pieds de longueur, qui étoit un vrai cercle de couleurs, mais nuancé au parfait, non seulement par les demis & les quarts de

---

[13] See Kemp, *The Science of Art* (1990): 286. For more general comment on Castel, see Mortier (ed.), *Autour du Père Castel et du clavecin oculaire* (1995).

teinte, mais comme à l'infini ou à l'imperceptible au moins
[. . .] Il me suffisoit d'approcher de la nature, jusqu'à tromper
l'œil' (Castel, *Optique des couleurs*, 1740: 176, 177). Elsewhere,
he calls this 'un cercle des nuances' (p. 173). The 'ruban'
creates a harmonious mix of colours from a finite set of 'primitive' colours, 'un beau désordre' which is nevertheless 'une
pure affaire de calcul', because the transitions depend on gradually increasing and decreasing numbers of threads of each
colour (pp. 170, 179). The nuances are countable threads, and
sufficiently distinct, therefore, never to degenerate into 'un
lavis' or a blur of unspecified colour. It is possible to point to
any part of the woven material and quantify the particular
nuance according to the proportions of different coloured
threads.

The 'ruban oculaire' is therefore a demonstration of quantifiable colour, but as he states in the quotation above, it is also
a *trompe l'œil*, an optical illusion which serves to demonstrate
that we cannot necessarily trust the evidence of our senses,
including the evidence which leads some to claim that colour
is too nebulous to measure. Castel describes some optical games
the viewer can play with the 'ruban'. One kind of illusion is
created by viewing the 'ruban' from different distances. From
a medium distance, the transitions between the different
colours are so refined that the eye can go from one end to the
other without being able to see where exactly the colour has
changed: 'on auroit juré qu'on voyoit toujours la même
couleur' (Castel, *Optique des couleurs*, 1740: 178). From further
away, the viewer sees only the twelve main colours, whereas at
close hand he sees the individual threads which produce the
transitions of colour. One can also look at colours in different
contexts, because the same colour looks different depending
on whether or not it is juxtaposed with others: what appears
yellow seems 'fauve' when placed alongside pure yellow, and
vice versa, what appears 'fauve' seems yellow alongside pure
'fauve'. On another occasion, Castel invites us to look continu-
ously at the colour crimson, until our vision is saturated, so that
when we next look at red, it appears orange.[14]

The 'ruban oculaire' permits colour to escape from Zeno's

---

[14] These colour games are similar to those which Goethe plays in *Zur Farbenlehre*
(1810).

paradox, because we can put our finger on the indivisible nuances, the threads which constitute the different colours. It also shows how the illusions and effects created by colour mixes are derived ultimately from this scale of nuances. Like Le Blon, therefore, Castel has demonstrated a rational basis for the apparent vagaries of colour.

Unlike Le Blon, however, Castel's idea is based on Newton's colour wheel, and it is this principle which leads Castel to venture further than Le Blon in order to construct his famous 'clavecin oculaire', a harpsichord which simultaneously played music and colours. In effect, he develops yet another model of 'nuances', this time more overtly correlated to music, and thereby suggesting more directly that our aesthetic response to music is explicable to some degree by reference to an underlying structural order.

As a consequence, he is an early if not an entirely unwitting contributor to the 'querelle des bouffons', an operatic debate provoked in 1753 by the performance of an Italian touring company whose preference for great swelling arias rather than *récitative* caused discussion as to the relative merits of melody and harmony in music.[15] Jean-Jacques Rousseau, a musical autodidact, challenged the much-respected theory of harmonics conceived by the great Baroque composer Jean-Philippe Rameau and still largely accepted today by musicologists. Rousseau thought that melody was more important than harmony, because it must be derived from the natural ability we have to modulate the voice. Rameau argued that harmony was more important, because musical harmonies are naturally present in all resonating bodies. Hence his theory of 'le corps sonore': if one identifies that the lowest note in a resonating body is C, for example, one can predict that the other notes will be intervals of the chord of C major (specifically, C, E, G in one octave, C and G in the octave above, and E two further octaves above). Rousseau's reply was essentially that Rameau's theory misses the point; the science of physics does not explain the aesthetic pleasure in listening to music, and it is likely to encourage rationalistic interpretations which overlook the fact that music should move us emotionally.

[15] For more detail on the 'querelle des bouffons', see Verba, *Music and the French Enlightenment* (1993).

One of the interesting aspects of this debate is that it was sparked by the quite pragmatic issues surrounding the reception of an operatic performance, but in the end raises the quite fundamental aesthetic question about whether or not it is possible to have a 'science of sentiment', based for example on Rameau's harmonics, or whether in the final analysis being moved by music is not beyond rational explanation. The question is the same as that posed at the beginning of this chapter by Vattel, who wondered whether 'le sentiment va beaucoup plus loin que la discussion', and also the same as the question continually posed by those who use the word 'nuances'.

Castel's confident demonstration of an underlying structure of nuances which create the global effects of colour places him squarely in Rameau's camp. He is writing before the 'querelle des bouffons', of course, but Rameau's theory is older still (his first theoretical treatise is *Traité de l'harmonie réduite à ses principes naturels*, 1722), and Castel considers him 'un homme de génie dans son art' (Castel, 'Nouvelles expériences d'optiques', 1735: 1474). Moreover, his 'clavecin oculaire' is so widely discussed in the eighteenth century that participants in the 'querelle' inevitably use it to support their arguments one way or the other. The 'clavecin oculaire' consisted of a modified harpsichord, on which was placed a large box containing some five hundred lamps. One side of the box had sixty coloured-glass apertures about three inches high. When a key of the harpsichord was pressed, a light shone through the aperture corresponding in colour to the note played.[16] Synchronizing the colours and the notes is no doubt a technical feat in itself, but defining a principle of a correspondence between them seems no less a challenge. The formula Castel devised for this purpose was derived partly from Le Blon's work, and partly from Rameau's harmonics.[17] Like Le Blon, his three 'couleurs prim-

---

[16] This is the description provided by the composer Georg Telemann in Castel, *Optique des couleurs* (1740): 470. Kemp describes copies made in contemporary London (Kemp, *The Science of Art*, 1990: 289).

[17] Castel expresses his admiration for Rameau in his writings on colour, but does not mention Le Blon. He does, however, review Le Blon's *Coloritto*, and acknowledges the innovation in colour printing, while complaining that the book explains nothing (which is partly true, since Le Blon does not give away the secrets of his screen values). Castel also suggests that Le Blon may have plagiarized his own theories (Castel, 'Coloritto, or the harmony of colouring', 1737: 1441).

itives' are red, yellow, and blue, but unlike Le Blon, he abstracts further to a single fundamental colour, blue, which he calls 'la couleur tonique'. Why he should choose blue above yellow and red is not clear, but the idea of a single fundamental colour is analogous with Rameau's theory of the 'corps sonore' in the example above. The debt to Rameau is strongly suggested by the composer Georg Telemann's description of Castel's colour system: 'il y a un son fondamental & primitif dans la nature, auquel nous pouvons, par les régles de l'Art, donner le nom de *ut*: & il y a aussi une couleur tonique originale & primitive, qui sert de base & de fondement à toutes les couleurs, c'est le *bleu*' (Castel, *Optique des couleurs*, 1740: 475). Castel's belief that C ('ut') and the major chord of C are the most natural is also Rameau's,[18] and one wonders if there is an echo of Rameau's theory of the 'basse fondamentale' in Telemann's expression 'qui sert de base & de fondement'.

At this stage, with a fundamental colour blue and three 'primitive' colours, blue, yellow, and red, Castel has the equivalent of Rameau's C major chord. Beyond this are a further nine colours which, together with the three 'primitive' colours, constitute a chromatic scale of twelve. Further still are what Castel calls the 'nuances', which are the harmonies derived from the chromatic scale (see Figure 1). The sequence and choice of 'couleurs chromatiques' are determined by the colours of the spectrum: 'l'arc-en-ciel & le Prisme sembloient me présenter tout ce sistême tonique dans leurs couleurs ainsi déterminées par les Philosophes' (Castel, 'Nouvelles expériences d'optiques', 1735: 1453).

The colour harpsichord is an exceptionally elaborate application of the colour–music correspondence which others have discussed before and since.[19] More specifically, it is a demonstration of the equivalence between musical 'muances' and painterly 'nuances', and as such rises to Félibien's challenge to find the '*Diapason* ou *Gamme de couleurs*' which would put colour theory on a par with musical theory. And yet the colour harpsichord is more than an experimental model of a taxonomic

---

[18] Rameau, *Complete Theoretical Writings* (1968–9): Vol. III, 28.
[19] Others interested in music and colour include Arcimboldo in the seventeenth century, Wagner and Scriabin in the nineteenth and twentieth centuries, and Walt Disney in his film *Fantasia* (see Gombrich, *Art and Illusion*, 1996: 311).

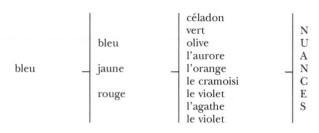

		céladon	
		vert	N
	bleu	olive	U
		l'aurore	A
bleu	jaune	l'orange	N
		le cramoisi	C
	rouge	le violet	E
		l'agathe	S
		le violet	

'couleur tonique'   'couleurs primitives'   'couleurs chromatiques'

Fig. 1. Louis-Bertrand Castel, schematic representation of 'la musique des couleurs'.

theory of colour, like the 'ruban', since it is also evidently a musical instrument, designed presumably for the aesthetic appreciation of its audience. This appreciation becomes doubly definable, firstly in terms of Rameau's theory of harmonics, and secondly in terms of Castel's theory of nuances. The equivalence between them provides mutual support and leaves little room for competing interpretations of musical aesthetics, such as Rousseau's belief in the power of melody to move the listener. In the terms of the 'querelle des bouffons', Rousseau already complains that Rameau's theory of harmonics probably encourages too mathematical an understanding of the aesthetics of music. Castel's seems to corroborate it and further marginalize melody.

The colour harpsichord was probably important to Castel precisely for its affinity with Rameau's musical theory, because it adds a new dimension to what would otherwise constitute only a skeletal taxonomy of colour. Even Newton's colour wheel which was so influential for Castel and others is still only a measuring device with music as its yardstick. In the following quotation, Castel is dissatisfied with previous theories of colour, and wishes that there were a kind of 'spiritual' optics which took account of subjective appreciation rather than only 'des angles & des positions locales'. In effect, he seems to be calling for a psychology of colour:

Le mal vient de ce que l'optique a été fort imparfaite. On n'a connu que des angles & des positions locales pour règles de tous les jugemens de l'œil; au lieu qu'il y a une optique fine, délicate, toute

spirituelle qui dépend & des dispositions naturelles de notre esprit, &
de celles ou le met un certain raport [*sic*] d'objets qui agissent souvent
en même-tems, souvent passagèrement les uns après les autres sur
notre œil. C'est surtout cette succession d'objets mobiles & passagers
que l'optique vulgaire ne conoît pas. Nous n'avons jugé jusqu'ici que
des objets & des couleurs fixes & immobiles dans leurs places. L'harmonie consiste essentiellement dans une diversité mobile. C'est cette
mobilité qui produit la vraye diversité capable de plaire, de piquer, de
passioner. (Castel, 'Nouvelles expériences d'optiques', 1735: 1480)

The angles and local positions of which he complains may be
those which can be plotted on Newton's colour wheel. Interesting and useful as they are, especially to the foundation of
Castel's own theories, they only quantify colour; they do not
explain taste: 'les dispositions naturelles de notre esprit', or the
aesthetic effects of certain combinations: 'la vraye diversité
capable de plaire, de piquer, de passioner'. The point of the
colour harpsichord may be to combine the taxonomic theory
of the 'ruban' with the aesthetics of music, in order to show
how nuances can be moving.

This is partly Diderot's interpretation in the *Lettre sur les
sourds et muets*. His deaf mute is impressed by the instrument,
because it helps him finally understand the nature of music and
language which, of course, he has never heard. He does this by
analogy with the nuances of colours: 'mon sourd s'imagina
[. . .] que chaque nuance avoit sur le clavier la valeur d'une des
lettres de l'alphabet; & qu'à l'aide des touches & de l'agilité
des doigts, il combinoit ces lettres, en formoit des mots, des
phrases, enfin tout un discours en couleurs' (Diderot, *Lettre sur
les sourds et muets*, 1751; 1965: 50). The deaf mute assumes that
each nuance is a component of meaning, like a musical note
or a letter of the alphabet. On this principle, he goes on to
suppose that music must be a mode of meaningful communication, like language, because he notices that 'les signes de joie
ou de tristesse qui se peignent sur nos visages & dans nos gestes,
quand nous sommes frappées d'une belle harmonie' are the
same as those expressed by someone listening to a speaker
(Diderot, *Lettre sur les sourds et muets*, 1965: 51). This is exactly
the kind of implication of the theories of Rameau and Castel
that Rousseau warned against, because it seems a short step
between identifying an underlying harmonic structure and
claiming that this is what music or colour 'means' or 'expresses';

or in the terms of Diderot's deaf mute, that a particular harmony is a 'sign' for a particular emotion like 'joy' or 'happiness'. One senses that Diderot's own views are ambiguous in this respect, and we shall discuss further his interpretation of the colour harpsichord in Chapter 4. Nevertheless, the deaf mute's inference is certainly amenable to Castel, because the harpsichord is designed to marry a taxonomy of colour with the aesthetics of music to give 'une optique spirituelle', or some kind of psychology of colour.

The deaf mute's analogy between music and language springs from the moment he sees the nuances of Castel's colour harpsichord. The delight he subsequently expresses is characteristic of many other commentators in this chapter and in the eighteenth century who think that seeing the nuances is always synonymous with understanding. The delight is also an aesthetic one, because the deaf mute thinks he has finally understood that the moving nature of music derives from nuances. The overall combination in Castel's colour harpsichord of Rameau's harmonics, a taxonomy of colour, and the confident identification of nuances renders it a potent means of explaining aesthetic experience. It is no doubt significant that Diderot, at least, specifies that Castel plays 'des sonates de couleurs' (Diderot, *Lettre sur les sourds et muets*, 1965: 50); the Italianate sonata is instrumental, and it is sometimes felt that the absence of lyrics renders the emotional charge of the sonata harder to explain. Fontenelle, for example, is said to have exclaimed: 'Sonate, que me veux-tu?'. By composing 'des sonates de couleurs', Castel has mixed the most emotionally charged music with the most structured and reasoned theory of harmony, thus effecting a marriage of science and sentiment, and truly, therefore, 'aesthetic' in the proper sense of the word.

Rousseau thinks there is too much science and not enough sentiment in this 'aesthetic': 'que dirions-nous du peintre assés dépourvu de sentiment et de goût pour raisoner de la sorte et borner stupidement au physique de son art le plaisir que nous fait la peinture?' (Rousseau, *Essai sur l'origine des langues, c.* 1754; 1995: 414).[20] Michel-Paul Guy de Chabanon agrees, and

[20] Thomas thinks that this quotation and the subsequent passage is a parody of Rameau's theory of the 'corps sonore' (*Music and the Origins of Language*, 1995: 133).

picks out 'nuances' as the most misleading factor in this aesthetic: 'la Musique n'a pas de nuances non plus pour dif-
férencier la tendresse d'une mère de celle d'une maîtresse ou
d'un ami. Les chants qui conviennent à l'une conviendront de
même aux deux autres' (Chabanon, *Observations sur la musique,
et principalement sur la métaphysique de l'art*, 1779: 121). These
comments by Rousseau and Chabanon are separated by more
than twenty years, but the cultural background is similar.
Rousseau's *Essai* is partly a response to the 'querelle des bouffons' in 1753, and Chabanon's *Observations sur la musique* is
partly a response to a revival of this 'querelle' caused by a controversial performance of Gluck's *Iphigénie en Tauride* in 1779.
The imitative opening scenes of a storm rekindle the debate
about whether music can imitate naturalistically in the manner
Gluck would like, or whether it is only an art of suggestion. Chabanon's comments are thus inspired by the immediate context
of Gluck's opera, but they are also aimed explicitly at Castel's
'clavecin oculaire', which he thinks is 'une invention ridicule
[. . .] une absurde chimère', and more science than sentiment:
's'il eut composé en Musique il auroit cru le temoignage de ses
sens, plus que celui de son esprit & de son savoir [. . .] Il nous
suffit d'avertir le Philosophe qu'il ait à se méfier de sa propre
intelligence' (Chabanon, *Observations sur la musique*, 1779: 8,
11). Even though Chabanon and Rousseau plainly dislike the
theoretical implications of Castel's harpsichord, it is evidently
as emblematic for them of a rational aesthetic as it is for Castel's
admirers. It is no doubt appropriate, therefore, that Castel
should explain his inventions using the word and concept of
'nuances', which seems also to be synonymous with the same
kind of aesthetic.

1.4　Girard and synonymy

The notion of colour predominates in Castel's use of the word
'nuances', but the meaning shifts from colour to semantics in
the course of eighteenth-century discussions of synonymy. Synonymy fascinates thinkers for the same reason that colour interested Félibien: it complicates representation with a sense of
intractable ambiguity or even vagueness, yet it is an inescapable

part of the way we use words. This constitutes a linguistic richness for some writers, like the 'nouveaux précieux' in general or Marivaux in particular, who exploit the semantic nuances between words for comic or expressive effect. For others, however, it is a potential source of obscurity and dilution of the power of expression, because it may be that words strike home more effectively if they are unambiguous. In which case, language is only 'rich' if it contains words like gold coins in a treasure chest, each with a discrete and quantifiable value.

The fascination with colour and synonymy is analogous, and so are the explanations of the way they function. Before even the 'querelle du coloris', Vaugelas compares synonymy with the artist's use of colour in his seminal *Remarques sur la langue françoise*: 'je ne puis assez m'estonner de l'opinion nouvelle qui condamne les synonimes [. . .] Représenter ces pensées-là on se gouverne comme les peintres, qui ne se contentent pas souvent d'un coup de pinceau pour faire la ressemblance d'un trait de visage, mais en donnent encore un second qui fortifie le premier, & rend la ressemblance parfaite' (Vaugelas, *Remarques sur la langue françoise*, 1647: 493–4). Vaugelas claims that the apparent contradiction between the vagaries of synonymy and the necessary clarity of expression already exists in painting, where shades of colour are overlaid to produce a greater illusion of reality.[21] Girard continues this optical theme in synonymy, expressed this time as 'nuances', to show that obscure shades of meaning are part of a clear, rhetorical system of 'idées accessoires' and 'idées principales': 'l'essence du synonyme [est] dans une même idée principale [. . .], sujette à être diversifiée par des idées accessoires, à peu près comme une même couleur paroît sous diverses nuances' (Girard, *Synonymes*, 1737: p. xiii).[22] Girard is making a strong claim for synonymy by placing 'nuances' alongside these rhetorical terms, because by implication, it should be possible to describe and standardize them as much as any other item in the rhetorical repertory. His

---

[21] See Chevalier, 'Note sur la notion de synonymie' (1971): 42.

[22] The *Bibliothèque Raisonnée* gives a brief review of Girard's dictionary, and repeats the same metaphor: 'le but que Mr. l'Abbé GIRARD se propose, est de faire comprendre que presque tous les mots qu'on regarde comme parfaitement SYNONYMES dans notre langue, diffèrent réelement dans leur signification, à-peu-près comme une même couleur paroît sous diverses nuances' (Vol. XIX, Par. II, 1737).

dictionary of synonyms is intended for this purpose, and one might say that Girard did as much for synonymy as Le Blon did for painting by inventing colour printing: both demonstrate in their respective fields that the nuances of expression are as much a matter of theory as they are empirical practice. Both also attenuate Diderot's pessimistic statement that 'il faut oublier la richesse de la nature et l'indigence de l'art, ou s'affliger', because the balance between nature and artist has been redressed: the richness of nature has been circumscribed and the technique of representation has been intellectually and technically facilitated. In this sense, Girard plainly does not accept either of the two concepts of linguistic richness outlined above, that the nuances of synonymy should either be reduced to discrete values like gold coins in a treasure chest of language, or over-used to the detriment of clarity. A dictionary of synonymy provides a middle course between the two by embracing ambiguity while setting boundaries to it; Girard has squared a circle and devised a dictionary of slippery meaning. He uses the idea of 'nuance' to explain that the compromise between these two concepts of 'richness' is inevitable: 's'il n'est question que d'un habit jaune, on peut prendre le souci ou la jonquille: mais s'il faut assortir, on est obligé à consulter la nuance. Eh! quand est-ce que l'esprit n'est pas dans le cas de l'assortiment? Cela est rare; puisque c'est en quoi consiste l'art d'écrire' (Girard, *Synonymes*, 1740: xii). If ideas which the writer wishes to express are always a medley of colours rather than a single 'jonquille' or 'souci', then accurate imitation demands the use of subtle means of expression like synonymy. The use of 'nuance' here is partly a traditional image of words as the dress of thought, and writing as a matter of taste, like choosing a colour scheme to wear. 'Consulter la nuance', however, may also be a reference to widespread use of 'nuances' in various trades to mean a 'colour sampler', or what is now called 'un nuancier'.[23] Girard may have in mind that authors should consult his dictionary of synonyms rather like a craftsman would consult his sampler. Both are attempts to standardize ambiguity. It is probably in this sense that he says his dictionary is another 'art d'écrire'.

Girard more than anyone in the eighteenth century institu-

---

[23] See Richelet's definition in my Introduction.

tionalized synonymy in a way which doubtless contributed to its success as a popular intellectual pursuit and even 'un jeu de société'.[24] The *Encyclopédie* quotes extensively both from his dictionary of synonyms and from his other major work as a grammarian, *Les Vrais Principes de la langue françoise* (1747), and subsequent writers on synonymy acknowledge their debt to him.[25] The success of his dictionary may also have popularized a new sense of the word 'nuances', meaning shades of linguistic meaning rather than only shades of colour, because Girard so elaborates on Vaugelas's analogy between synonymy and painting that he gives the linguistic sense of the word 'nuances' a great deal more intellectual weight.

1.5 Condillac's Art d'écrire

Condillac also wrote a posthumously published dictionary of synonyms, probably before 1760, as part of the *Cours d'Etudes* for the Prince of Parma.[26] It is even more refined than Girard's; each article has a one-word title, compared to Girard's three-word titles, and there are sometimes as many as seventeen synonyms for one entry.[27] His interest in the subject is part of a wider enquiry into semantic analogy as a way to represent the way we think. There are gradations of thought in the way we conceive the world which it is possible to represent by stylistic gradations in the way we write. His theory of style in his *Art d'écrire* is therefore more than a literary treatise; in the context of his thought as a whole, it is the crystallization of his ideas on the possibility of idealizing the imitative relation between

---

[24] See Auroux, 'D'Alembert et les synonymistes' (1984): 93; Hausmann, 'Le *Dictionnaire* de Condillac' (1978): 232.

[25] Dumarsais: 'Monsieur l'Abbé Girard a déjà examiné cette question [. . .] Je ne ferai guère ici qu'un extrait de ses raisons, et je prendrai même la liberté de me servir souvent de ses termes, me contentant de tirer mes exemples de la langue latine. Le Lecteur trouvera dans le livre de M. l'Abbé Girard de quoi se satisfaire pleinement sur ce qui regarde le françois' (*Des tropes*, 1988: 232). Condillac often refers to Girard in his *Dictionnaire des synonymes* (Condillac, *Dictionnaire des synonymes*, 1951: p. x). Modern dictionaries of synonymy usually mention Girard in their introduction.

[26] Condillac, *Dictionnaire des synonymes* (1951). Hausmann thinks that the dictionary was probably completed by 1760 ('Le *Dictionnaire* de Condillac', 1978: 226).

[27] Hausmann, 'Le *Dictionnarie* de Condillac' (1978): 235.

writing and thinking. The 'art' of writing for Condillac, therefore, means something between what we would call in modern terminology 'semiotics' and 'stylistics'.

Condillac's enquiry is wider than Girard's, but they both resort to the same idea of 'nuances' and the same analogy with the art of the *coloriste* painter. Condillac opens a chapter entitled 'Des Comparaisons' in the *Art d'écrire* with an image of thoughts reflecting between each other like the accidents of broken colour in nature which the *coloristes* considered to be an important subject of painterly representation: 'les rayons de lumière tombent sur les corps, et réfléchissent les uns sur les autres. Par-là les objets se renvoient mutuellement leurs couleurs. Il n'en est point qui n'emprunte des nuances, il n'en est point qui n'en prête; et aucun d'eux, lorsqu'ils sont réunis, n'a exactement la couleur qui lui seroit propre s'ils étoient séparés' (Condillac, *Art d'écrire*, 1798: 168).[28] He would evidently agree with Girard that there is 'un assortiment de l'esprit', or a medley of nuanced colours in the mind. The job of language is to do justice to the nuances, and again, Condillac chooses an analogy from painting to explain the stylistic ambition: 'il y a, en quelque sorte, entre [nos pensées], des reflets qui portent des nuances de l'une sur l'autre; et chacune doit à celles qui l'approchent tout le charme de son coloris. L'art de l'écrivain est de saisir cette harmonie' (Condillac, *Art d'écrire*, 1798: 168–9). Condillac goes on to explain that the best stylistic reproduction of this harmony of ideas will depend on discriminating use of figurative language, because it is an aspect of writing which on the one hand can create appropriate semantic patterning, but on the other hand can be abused to create semantic incongruity or discordance. The examples he gives of the most harmonious style are from the canon of great stylists and practitioners of a 'style coupé', such as Fléchier, who construct sentences with a clear sense of logical progression and an effortless impression of continuity between clauses and ideas (see my Chapter 3).

Condillac could have made this point without reference to 'nuances' or to the art of the *coloriste*, especially since his idea is essentially a conventional one, that the model of 'style coupé'

---

[28] Compare Piles, *Cours de Peinture par principe* (1989): 172.

provided by Fléchier, La Rochefoucauld, Bossuet or any other of the great stylists is the best example to follow. The point of using 'nuances' is that it is a new optical analogy which supports the well-worn Horatian axiom *ut pictura poesis*, and thereby places additional emphasis on imitation that the old axiom takes for granted. The particular emphasis he gives is idealization. He internalizes still further the sense of 'nuances' to mean not only the subtleties of language, as Girard suggested, but the subtleties of thought which language represents, or what Girard called 'l'assortiment de l'esprit'. 'Nuances' has retreated a little further from the idea of 'shades of colour', and more towards 'shades of feeling or meaning'. This is interesting for the same reason that Condillac's thought in general is remarkable, because of all eighteenth-century philosophers, including John Locke a few years earlier, Condillac posits the closest relationship between language and knowledge, and as a result one of the most idealizing concepts of imitation. It is not surprising, therefore, that he extends the use of a word which already implies 'making sense of representation'.

1.6   Bièvre's 'calembours'

The Marquis de Bièvre, known to some of his contemporaries as 'le père des calembours', did not invent either the word or practice, but he popularized both to an extraordinary degree. He also made more serious remarks about the 'calembour', language and representation which make interesting reading in the light of Condillac's thoughts above. Both use 'nuances' to explain their methods, but Bièvre is sceptical about the imitative enterprise that it has come to imply, and one aspect of his predilection for excruciating puns is perhaps a desire to poke fun at the philosophers and stylists with their studied 'nuances'.

His first published work is *Lettre écrite à madame la Comtesse Tation, par le Sieur de Bois-Flotté, étudiant en droit-fil* (1770), reprinted four times in two months. He quickly followed it with an ambitious sequel, *Vercingentorixe* (*sic*, 'vers singeant Thor rixe'?), which is a comic 'drame bourgeois' written entirely in Alexandrine 'calembours':

> Oui, barbare,
> Tu croyois m'abuser par ton air *de guitare*,
> Mais plus que toi Sylvie est adroite *en entrant*.
>   (Bièvre, *Vercingentorixe*, 1770: sc. ii)
> Vas, nous savons *de Naple* où tu portes tes vœux
> Pars *de gâteau* cruel, laisse-moi.
>   (Ibid., sc. iv; author's emphasis)

Bièvre's 'calembours' were quite a cultural phenomenon in the 1770s and 1780s, and the critical reaction is sharp, yet mystified. Grimm reviews Bièvre's *Lettre*, and thinks that 'cette plaisanterie misérable [...] n'est pas grâve', but is nevertheless concerned at its popularity:

> Que cette insipide et execrable rapsodie ait fait dans le public plus de sensation qu'aucun des ouvrages publiés dans le cours de l'hîver, qu'on en ait fait plusieurs éditions en très-peu de semaines, et que, pendant plus de quinze jours, on n'ait parlé que de la comtesse Tation, voilà une note d'infamie qui tombe directement sur le public, et dont il ne se relevera pas de sitôt dans mon esprit. (Grimm, *Correspondance*, 1877: Vol. VIII, 504)

The implication is that Bièvre is writing crudely for the undiscriminating masses, but his own comments on the nature of the 'calembour' are more thoughtful than Grimm suspected. Such is Bièvre's reputation as 'le père des calembours' that it is he who is asked to contribute the article 'Kalembour, ou Calembour (Gramm.)' for the *Supplément à l'Encyclopédie* in 1777, which is incidentally the first time the word appears in any dictionary.[29] Here he explains that the crudity remarked upon by Grimm is intentional, and in fact motivated by a particular view of the way in which language operates. 'Nuances', he says, are a figment of the philosopher's imagination, and nature is far too complex to ever be represented convincingly in language: 'toutes les langues du monde fournissent nécessairement une ample matière aux équivoques; la nature est si riche, nous sommes remués par tant de causes, que notre articulation ne peut suffire à distinguer les nuances que nos yeux & notre esprit

---

[29] Leo Spitzer suggests that 'calembour' is first used in 1754 in a comic opera by Jean-Joseph Vadé, and is derived from the same source as the English 'quandary' and 'conundrum' (*Linguistics and Literary History*, 1948: introduction).

peuvent apercevoir; ainsi les kalembours doivent être aussi anciens que les hommes' (Bièvre, 'Kalembour', 1777: 681). There is an imitative deficit between the richness of nature and our ability to reproduce it, so that ambiguity is as old as language itself. 'Nuances', therefore, as used by the likes of Condillac and Girard to explain the subtleties of linguistic representation, are an illusion, an optical analogy invented only to resist the fact that language is a blunt tool. It is consequently far better not to expect it to produce objects of refinement, but instead to enjoy the incongruous words and ideas it brings together through such devices as the 'calembour'.

Bièvre was better known in his time for his bad punning and virtuoso 'bilboquet' technique than his serious considerations on language, but both the ludic and lucid aspects of him seem genuine.[30] Homonyms are, in any case, a serious interest of other contemporary writers on language, such as the Latin rhetorician Pierre Hurtaut, who devised the first dictionary of homonyms in 1775.[31] They are a fruitful way to undermine the theories of nuanced language and style that Condillac and others propose, because they correlate one thing with another, but in the process, they destroy any rational sense. Condillac would say that they are 'analogies' which are 'tirées de trop loins', but they are nevertheless pleasing to contemporaries because they are a kind of *rococo papillotage*. Suzanne Necker encounters both styles among the visitors to her salon in the 1770s and 1780s, and comments: 'Quel contraste! nous aimons les nuances dans les idées, et cependant nous aimons les idées imprévues' (Necker, *Mélange*, 1798: Vol. I, 67). 'Nuances' and the 'calembour' are indicative of different tastes, but also of different intellectual principles: Bièvre does not share Condillac's enormous confidence in the imitative ability of language to capture the nuances of the way we think. Instead, he thinks the 'calembour' is a more realistic, if irreverent idea of what language is capable of doing. It is a reminder of what Diderot

---

[30] See my article, 'Bilboquet, calembour and modernity' (*SVEC* 2000: 08).

[31] Hurtaut also enjoyed a joke at the expense of rhetoricians (including himself!), when he wrote what is announced on the spine as *L'Art de P.* (1751), which it transpires, on turning to the first page, is not another *L'Art de parler*, but *L'Art de péter*, a detailed study of articulated hot air, and a parody of contemporary essays on language.

would rather forget, which is 'la richesse de la nature et l'indigence de la langue'.

1.7 Diderot's article 'Beau'

'Nuances', so far, has been involved in an aesthetic debate about
imitation. It is also used in cognate ways in logic and systematics, because according to a certain school of thought, knowledge imitates nature as much as art does. Diderot's use of
'nuances' in his article 'Beau' lies somewhere between the two,
because he adds it to the traditional array of terms in logic to
solve a problem in aesthetics, which is the existence or not of
an 'essence' of beauty. This confident use of logical principles
to discover knowledge is not peculiar to Diderot, but characteristic of the eighteenth-century attachment to Aristotelianism
in general and encyclopaedic enterprises in particular. The way
Diderot uses 'nuances' here is an example in microcosm of
what we will discuss later: the confident elaboration of systems
of knowledge which are thought to imitate the natural order of
the world.

'Nuances' comes at an important juncture in Diderot's
article: after he has explained that the common factor which
unites all the things we call 'beautiful' is 'les rapports', and
before he then goes on to explain how this transcendent principle accommodates all the particular and subjective ideas of
beauty we can have. 'Rapports' is derived from the Sensualist
principle that consciousness fundamentally means perception
of one's environment, and also the ability to compare one perception with another. Like Condillac, Diderot believes that we
are born with an ability to perceive 'les rapports': 'nous nais-
sons avec la faculté de sentir et de penser; le premier pas de la
faculté de penser, c'est d'examiner ses perceptions, de les unir,
de les comparer, de les combiner, d'apercevoir entre elles des
rapports de convenances et de disconvenance, etc' (Diderot,
'Beau', 1988: 415).[32] As a consequence, the primary judgements which can be made are those of 'longueur, largeur,

---

[32] It may be that Diderot's idea of 'rapports' is less derived from Sensualism than
architecture. See his letter 'A Mademoiselle . . .' which follows his *Lettre sur les sourds
et muets* in the Fellows 1965 edition.

profondeur, quantité, nombre', so that our perception of the world is fundamentally one of 'ordre, de rapports, de proportion, de liaison, d'arrangement, de symétrie' (pp. 416, 417). The feeling of beauty must also be a perception of some kind, and a universal concept of beauty must be fundamental to all beautiful things. The perceptual common denominator which Diderot suggests is 'rapports': 'j'appelle donc *beau* hors de moi, tout ce qui contient en soi de quoi réveiller dans mon entendement l'idée de rapports; et *beau* par rapport à moi, tout ce qui réveille cette idée' (Diderot, 'Beau', 1988: 418). At this point, having established what he means by a universal sense of beauty, Diderot focuses his attention on the problem of subjective taste. How is it possible to explain the existence of a universal 'beau', based on 'rapports', when different people may have different perceptions of the same object, ranging from 'joli', to 'charmant' to 'sublime'? Diderot's answer is that we must think of beauty as like the abstract idea of colour, and of our subjective tastes as like the different 'nuances' of colour that we prefer. Our tastes for different 'nuances' vary, but no one would deny that they all share the concept of colour. Similarly, we may show how the subjective notions of beauty may contribute to an abstract 'beau': 'selon que les rapports et l'esprit des hommes ont varié, on a fait les noms *joli, beau, charmant, grand, sublime, divin* et une infinité d'autres, tant relatifs au physique qu'au moral. Voilà les nuances du *beau*' (Diderot, 'Beau', 1988: 427). This leads him in the remaining part of his article to explain the different reasons why some 'nuances du beau' are preferred to others.

'Nuances' enters the discourse of Aristotelian logical division indirectly, via an analogy with colour, but the fact that it does at all is doubly interesting. Firstly, because the significance of 'nuances' gains in proportion to the conspicuous contemporary importance of Aristotelianism; and secondly, because it illustrates the faith that many eighteenth-century thinkers have in Aristotelian logic, because not content with the traditional terminology, they add more. 'Nuances' here is really a synonym for the Aristotelian notion of a 'particular', and Diderot's phrase 'les nuances du beau' expresses the idea that particulars are instances of a universal, even if it is sometimes hard actually to discover what that universal is. The principle that 'nuances' are manifestations of some higher logical under-

standing is the same principle which is applied in previous aesthetic debates: the mere fact that we can identify 'nuances'
means that we can make some sense of what seems obscure. In
Aristotelian terms, we would say that particulars and universals
are logically dependent on each other. If they were not, and if
particulars could exist without being attached ultimately to
some universal or other, then the world would be a jumble of
particulars, and consequently permanently incomprehensible,
at least in Aristotelian terms. It is this principle which helps
Diderot clarify the 'jumble' of subjective tastes and to define a
universal idea of 'beauty'. The 'rubénistes' in the 'querelle du
coloris' argue partly on the same grounds that there is logic in
colour, because the accidents of broken light in nature which
seem incoherent are actually manifestations of a higher order
of colour. They are related to universal concepts.

Diderot's article 'Beau' is one of his most scholastic pieces of
writing, and it is interesting that he considers 'nuances' to be a
term with sufficient intellecutal rigour to use in this context.

1.8   D'Alembert, Court de Gébelin, and encyclopaedias

Aristotelian logical division is a powerful tool used with more
or less humility by those who wish to explore the way knowledge imitates nature. Some, like Aristotle himself, are cautious,
because they realize that the explanatory value of any system of
classification depends on the criteria for division, and that in
reality, nature is so diverse that some particulars are always likely
to fall through the net.[33] He shares the view which Diderot
expresses at the beginning of this chapter about 'la richesse de
la nature et l'indigence de l'art'.

Aristotle's caution did not prevent one of his most notable
followers, Porphyry, using the principle of logical division to
elaborate a complete hierarchy of categories, ranging from the
most general, 'genus', to the most particular, 'individuum'. The
'Porphyrian tree' has since become canonical in Aristotelian
logic.[34] Neither did Diderot's reservations suppress his energy
and enthusiasm for one of the great eighteenth-century

---

[33] Aristotle, *History of Animals*, 588b 5–17 (1995): Vol. I, 922.
[34] Slaughter discusses and illustrates the Porphyrian tree in *Univeral Languages
and Scientific Taxonomy* (1982): 29.

projects to classify knowledge, the *Encyclopédie*. The Baconian tree of knowledge in Volume I is testimony to his faith in the capacity of the logical mind to understand and represent the subtle gradations of knowledge. And yet 'nuances' appears again in d'Alembert's *Discours préliminaire à l'Encyclopédie* in order to sound a note of intellectual humility. He says that our knowledge of the world will always be incomplete, partly unexplored, like a vast ocean 'sur la surface duquel nous apercevons quelques îles plus ou moins grandes, dont la liaison avec le continent nous est cachée'. Consequently, the tree of knowledge can never be as subtly nuanced as it should be if it really is to reflect nature: 'l'arrangement le plus naturel serait celui où les objets se succéderaient par les nuances insensibles qui servent tout à la fois à les séparer et à les unir. Mais le petit nombre d'êtres qui nous sont connus, ne nous permet pas de marquer ces nuances' (D'Alembert, *Discours préliminaire*, 1751: Vol. I, p. xv). Nuances are again the Aristotelian 'particulars', or Porphyrian 'individua' which are necessarily prior to any formal arrangement of knowledge into categories, but which may nonetheless defy classification. D'Alembert's assumption, like Aristotle's, is that they are really there, concealed by a sea of unknown, but that our knowledge of them is limited. The same principle is used by the 'rubénistes' in the 'querelle du coloris', to argue that colour is, indeed, intelligible, but that its constituent parts are concealed. In both cases, 'nuances' is the word used to lay claim to the ultimate intelligibility of a phenomenon, even if in practice we lack the intellectual tools to demonstrate it.

The intellectual and commercial success of Diderot and d'Alembert's *Encyclopédie* is one demonstration of the contemporary appeal of encyclopaedias. Their enthusiasm is tempered, however, with the circumspection they expressed through the 'nuances' idea. There are other encyclopaedists who throw caution to the wind and indulge more freely in logical division, and their efforts, too, are characteristic of a sometimes zealously Aristotelian era. Again, the 'nuances' idea illustrates their approach.

Antoine Court de Gébelin is one such eager encyclopaedist. His nine-volume *Monde primitif, analysé et comparé avec le monde moderne* (1773–84) has all the breadth of interest and thorough method of Diderot and d'Alembert's *Encyclopédie*, but with an extraordinary taste for speculative analogy.[35] A number of volumes are devoted to etymology, which Gébelin understands in the Greek sense of 'true meaning'.[36] He uses the technique of logical division to inquire into the true meaning of words, beginning with the evidence of modern French, from which he retreats by careful steps until he reaches what he claims to be the single, primitive Celtic root. The result looks more like implausible morphology to the modern eye than any kind of etymology, because an 'origin' for Gébelin is not necessarily a chronological root, but something which is logically derived from the evidence, something higher in the Porphyrian tree than the particulars at the bottom. Gébelin's term for the particulars, the words of modern French, is 'nuances'. Yet again, it seems to signify the confidence that when we can identify the particulars, the essence cannot be far away. He describes his procedure as follows: 'sous une monosyllabe Celtique, mot primitif & radical, [nous avons divisé] en diverses branches séparées par une idée particulière, subordonnée à la générale. A la tête de chaque division, nous avons [marqué] la nuance particulière dont il venoit de se charger' (Gébelin, *Monde primitif*, 1778: Vol. V, p. vii). If we apply these principles to the entry for the Celtic root *BAL*, meaning 'sun', or 'all that is bright, high up, round or beautiful', we arrive at the schematic

---

[35] *Monde primitif* won the 'prix Valbelle' in 1780 (François, *La Grammaire du purisme*, 1973: 248). Before publication, subscribers numbered twelve hundred, compared to two thousand for Diderot's *Encyclopédie*, and it still had an enthusiastic readership as late as 1830. Gébelin was a leading intellectual and Freemason, and founded a public university for the study of primitivist philosophy, the Musée de Paris. The Prussian ambassador had monuments brought to France from China to help the philosopher in his studies (Le Flamanc, *Les Utopies prérévolutionnaires et la philosophie du 18e siècle*, 1934: 115–16). Le Gros, however, describes a harsher critical reception: 'dès 1773, le premier volume fut attaqué dans le *Journal des Savans* [. . .] On a dit & répété dans une multitude d'écrits, que le *Monde primitif* étoit un ouvrage repoussant, rempli de fatras, d'inutilités, de conjectures frivoles, de systèmes imaginaires, &c.' (Le Gros, *Analyses des ouvrages de Rousseau et de Court de Gébelin*, 1785: 209). Droixhe adds his own criticism to that of Grimm's contemporary comments (Droixhe, *La Linguistique et l'appel de l'histoire*, 1978: 367–74). Decker has shown how Gébelin was responsible for generating the cult around Tarot cards by interpreting the newly imported German and Swiss game as an elaborate allegory, an ancient book of wisdom purposely disguised by Egyptian sages as a pack of cards (Decker, *A Wicked Pack of Cards*, 1996).

[36] For other interpretations of the word and concept of 'etymology', see Zumthor, 'Etymologie (essai d'histoire sémantique)', in *Etymologica* (1958).

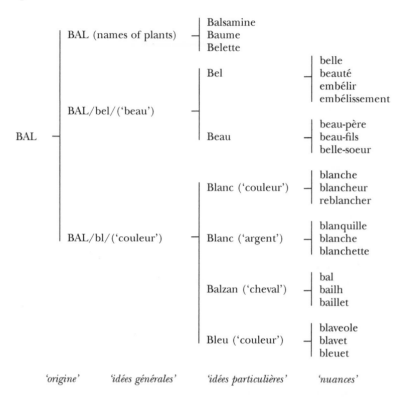

'origine'   *'idées générales'*   *'idées particulières'*   *'nuances'*

Fig. 2. Schematic representation of Antoine Court de Gébelin's etymology; complete derivations for three of the twelve forms of the Celtic root BAL.

representation shown in Figure 2.[37] From the primitive root *BAL* are derived the three 'idées générales' of 'plantes', 'beau', and 'couleur', from these are derived the numerous 'idées particulières', and finally the words of modern French themselves, or 'les nuances'.

Extravagant as this etymology seems, the methods at least are the same in principle as those used by Diderot and d'Alembert to devise the tree of knowledge in Volume I of the *Encyclopédie*. The difference lies in Gébelin's confident approach, because

---

[37] Charles de Brosses, who is discussed more in Chapter 4, gives the same definition of the primitive root 'BAL' (*Traité de la formation méchanique des langues*, 1800: Vol. II, 246).

he seems to gather together effortlessly all the particulars, or 'nuances', into their respective divisions as if the logical net which Aristotle and d'Alembert admitted must have holes could unproblematically unite all the diversity of the French lexicon. In a way, Gébelin is doing the same as Diderot did in his article 'Beau' to demonstrate the existence of an essence of beauty, except on a vast scale, across three encyclopaedic volumes of etymology. Diderot applied the Aristotelian principle that where there are particulars there are bound to be universals, so that if we can demonstrate a common thread running through all our subjective tastes, this will point to the existence of a transcendent sense of beauty. His conclusion was 'voilà les nuances du beau'; perhaps Gébelin's ought to be, according to Figure 2, 'voilà les nuances de BAL'.

'Nuances', then, is a neo-Aristotelian term used to express confidence in logical division. Even on occasions when thinkers say that the nuances are beyond us, like d'Alembert speaking of the tree of knowledge, it is still assumed that they are there anyway, concealed but nevertheless a guarantor that the world of knowledge is made up of discrete units and therefore fundamentally intelligible.

1.9   The theory of genres

If 'nuances' is part of the terminology of systematics and imitation, it is perhaps not surprising to find it in a context which combines both. The theory of genres in the eighteenth-century is often far less problematic than it is in the minds of thinkers before and since, precisely because there is an effortless conflation of these two perspectives, systematics and imitation. Thinkers in this period apply to the letter principles which go back ultimately to Aristotle and Plato that there are three fundamental 'modes' of narration which encompass all possible 'types' of literary expression, or more accurately, all 'types' of literary imitation of nature.[38] The 'modes' are linguistically inescapable, and in this sense 'natural' and imitative, while the

---

[38] On the historical and theoretical background to genres theory, see Genette, 'Genres, "types", modes', in *Poétique* 32 (Nov. 1977): 389–421. The whole of issue 32 is devoted to genres.

'types' are logical divisions within each mode which can be made according to the particular complexion of the particular literary form. A great deal of the confusion and controversy concerning the theory of genres stems from the word itself, because it does not distinguish between 'mode' and 'type', which is the crucial difference between the generative principle and the product. Arguably, the confusion is more a feature of modern debate than eighteenth-century discourse. When the word is used to refer to a specific 'type' of literary expression in the eighteenth century, it is simultaneously metonymic for the process which gave rise to it; thinkers are more aware that 'genres' can refer to principle or product. As a result, reconciling a 'system of the arts' with innovative literary practice is relatively easy: all that is necessary is to establish which mode of narration the new form is closest to, and incorporate it into the spectrum of other types which equally derive from one of the fundamental modes of narration. In the eighteenth century, the space which is made for new literary forms is often called a 'nuance' between existing forms.

'Nuances' (singular or plural) is sufficiently common in this context to suggest confident application of these principles, but maybe also greater need to do so, as the pressure grows to recognize the importance of new or different literary forms. Of all eighteenth-century art theorists, one of the most conservative and therefore the keenest to incorporate new forms into the spectrum of established practice is Charles Batteux. He describes the formal possibilities and dangers of mixing genres:

> Dans nos trois genres ou couleurs de poésie, les nuances peuvent s'affaiblir ou se fortifier jusqu'à un certain point sans sortir de leur espèce; le poète peut se jouer dans l'intervalle d'un extrême et du milieu, nuancer son style, pourvu qu'il ne rompe point l'unité. Mais si en descendant ou en montant, il passait au-delà de ce milieu, marqué par le goût aussi bien que par l'esprit, quoiqu'il conservât la couleur poétique en général, il est évident qu'il perdrait celle de l'espèce, la comédie deviendrait tragique, la tragédie serait épique ou lyrique, c'est-à-dire, que les couleurs et les genres seraient confondus. (Batteux, *Les Beaux-Arts*, 1746; 1989: 201)

'Nuances' is particularly appropriate in the context in which Batteux borrows Horace's term 'couleurs' to refer to the three

Aristotelian modes of narration: lyric (the author has the only voice in the text), dramatic (the characters have the only voice), and epic (author and characters both have a voice). These are the three fundamental ways of telling or representing an 'action', which is the subject, according to Aristotelian poetics, of any artistic imitation.[39] Fontenelle uses 'nuances' in an almost identical way in what Gaiffe calls 'l'échelle de Fontenelle'.[40] Quite what Horace, Batteux, and Fontenelle knew about the science of colour, or whether Batteux and Fontenelle knew of Le Blon's discovery of the three primary colours is hard to tell. In any case, the analogy between colour and the system of the arts suggests the happy marriage of 'mode' and 'type' mentioned above. That is to say that writers are free to experiment with different mixes, as long as the particular 'nuance' they are seeking does not simultaneously span the core characteristics of one mode and the core characteristics of another. In other words, it is neither natural nor probably possible for literary imitation to have two centres of gravity, one which would cause the work to revolve around all the expectations we have, say, of drama, and another around those we have of epic. We can express the same proposition using the contemporary associations that 'nuances' has with the textiles industry, and by thinking of Castel's 'ruban oculaire': any point on the continuum of colour can be a subtle shade of two colours, but it cannot simultaneously be blue and yellow (see Figure 1).

Perhaps this constitutes a 'law of *genres*', not in the prescriptive sense, but in the sense of a natural law or acknowledgement that literary imitation is simply like this. Batteux's 'law of nuances' is analogous with what we might call Rameau's 'law of muances', his Pythagorean theory of harmony in which harmonics are derived ultimately from a law of acoustics.[41] In both cases, even if composers and writers do not realize it, they are working within natural limits. It is in this sense that it is

---

[39] Aristotle, *Poetics*, 2 (1995): Vol. II, 2317.
[40] Gaiffe, *Le Drame en France au XVIIIe siècle* (1971): 449; Fontenelle, *Préface de la tragédie et des six comédies* (1758): pp. xxii–xxv.
[41] For a long and interesting digression on the idea of musical modes and literary genres, see Marmontel, 'Analogie du style' in *Elémens de littérature* (1819): Vol. I, 202–10.

sometimes said that eighteenth-century thinkers 'believed' in genres, with the inference sometimes that they believed in a figment of their intellectual daydreams. What they gave credence to, however, was not the worth of an abstract taxonomy of literary 'types', comprising, for example, comedy, satirical comedy, parodic comedy, and so on, but the determinative force of literary 'modes'. Modern critics who 'believe' in genres tend to do so for similar reasons. Derrida, for example, argues that all texts 'participate' in genres, and that consequently, 'il n'y a pas de textes sans genres'.[42] It is in this context that we ought to interpret André Chénier's ostensibly implacable remarks about the limits of mixing genres; they are meant to reflect an incontrovertible fact of literary life, of 'nature', more than dogma:

> La nature dicta vingt genres opposés
> D'un fil léger entre eux chez les Grecs divisés.
> Nul genre, s'échappant de ses bornes prescrites,
> N'aurait osé d'un autre envahir les limites;
> (A. Chénier, 'L'Invention', 1950: 124)

The way Batteux uses the word 'nuances' in the context of genres is a further instance of its associations with the idea of imitation, and especially with the attempt to give a rational account of imitation. For Batteux's purposes, the word has useful connotations with justifying the existence of something which has a dubious status, like the quantifiable shades of colour in painting. What is dubious in the theory of genres is the place of peripheral forms of literature which may be so radically incompatible with the three fundamental 'modes' of imitation that they cannot be included in the traditional system of the arts. The more important these peripheral forms become in a literary culture, the more the system of arts looks absurd if it excludes them. A good example of this scenario in Batteux's thinking is the manner in which he includes lyrical poetry (meaning poetry of personal expression) into the spectrum of imitative arts, whereas traditionally such poetry is not imitation at all; in Aristotelian terms, it can have no imitative content,

---

[42] Derrida, 'La loi du genre', in *Parages* (1986). For the opposite view, that genres is an artificial taxonomy of unconnected literary types, see Croce, 'History of artistic and literary kinds' in *Aesthetic as Science of Expression* (1922): 436–48.

since it does not represent an 'action', but is more like a prayer or outpouring of sentiment. For Batteux, however, 'imitation' can mean 'imitation of a sentiment', and consequently lyrical poetry finds a place in the system of the imitative arts.[43] Not only is this inclusive notion of imitation characteristic of the declared intention of his book, *Les Beaux-Arts réduits à un même principe*, but it is also symptomatic of shifting literary values which tend to demand that more notice be taken of literary forms which were traditionally considered to be of minor importance. Lyric poetry in particular is set to supplant the literary hierarchy in the following half century and become the most elevated literary form. Batteux's treatment of it is an indication of its growing importance, and his use of 'nuances' is a symptom that he is struggling to make it compatible with imitation. Like others who use the word, it seems to be part of the conceptual armoury employed to bolster the status of something which looks dubious; in this case, the growing appeal of lyrical poetry is justified by incorporating it into the gamut of established literary practice; it has become a nuance in the spectrum of imitative literary types, despite the fact that it is debatable whether it is imitative at all in the traditional sense.

Batteux approaches genres and the 'law of nuances' from an abstract, theoretical point of view. Others raise the same issues in different terms. In the case of Voltaire, it is characteristically expressed as a matter of taste and discernment rather than cold theory. He warns against too much mixing of genres: 'les nuances, à la vérité, sont innombrables, mais les couleurs éclatantes sont en petit nombre' (Voltaire, 'Des beaux-arts', 1751; in Moland 14: 553). He thinks that in practice this means that there are no more than a dozen or so different kinds of comedy.

Diderot is interested in theory as well as practice when he discusses the principles of the *genre sérieux*, sometimes called by other playwrights the 'drame bourgeois'.[44] It is an intermediary genre between tragedy and comedy, such that it is 'sans ridicule qui fasse rire, sans danger qui fasse frémir' (Diderot, *Entretiens sur le Fils naturel*, 1757; 1970: 173). The balance is careful, but variable according to the particular effect sought by the play-

---

[43] Genette, 'Genres, "types", modes' (1977): 402.
[44] Different names for these plays often denote different blends of tragedy and comedy, but for the purposes of argument I will discuss only Diderot's conception.

wright. When in the *Entretiens* 'Moi' asks Dorval where he would place *Le Père de famille* on the dramatic scale, he replies: '*Le Fils naturel* a des nuances de la tragédie; *Le Père de famille* prend une teinte comique' (p. 209). The *genre sérieux* fails if the balance is not right: 'les nuances empruntées du genre comique sont elles trop fortes? L'ouvrage fera rire et pleurer; et il n'y aura plus ni unité d'intérêt, ni unité de coloris' (Diderot, *Entretiens*, 1757; 1970: 176). In other words, the emotional content or 'intérêt' can be so ambivalent that the audience are confused and the play loses its dramatic impact.[45] For this reason, he thinks that there is less artistic merit in Shakespearean tragicomedy, because we move abruptly from laughter to tears: 'vous voyez que la tragi-comédie ne peut être qu'un mauvais genre, parce qu'on y confond deux genres éloignés et séparés par une barrière naturelle. On n'y passe point par des nuances impercep-tibles. On tombe à chaque pas dans les contrastes, et l'unité disparaît' (Diderot, *Entretiens*, 1970: 174). Tragicomedy breaks what we might call the 'law of nuances', by infringing the 'bar-rière naturelle' between comedy and tragedy, or in Batteux's terms, it simultaneously spans the core characteristics of one genre and another. In practical terms, the 'law' is broken when scenes of pure comedy and pure tragedy are freely juxtaposed, presenting the spectator with 'contrasting' representations of a single action, thus not necessarily leading to a convincing rep-resentation of the action.

Diderot's plays were never successful, but he is convinced of the principle of an intermediary genre. 'Nuance' is a term which suits Diderot's purpose in this context for the same reasons that it suited others on different occasions. For Diderot, it is important to express the significance he attaches to the new genre, while at the same time allowing for continuity with tra-ditional theatre. The *genre sérieux* was never designed to break the mould of traditional theatre, but the amount of time which Diderot devotes to writing plays and discussing the underlying theory suggests he nevertheless accorded a significant status to it. 'Nuances' is a way of expressing this process of incorpora-tion into tradition, because it is meant to suggest that the plays exist in their own right, but are related to existing theatre; by

---

[45] See my discussion of the 'drame' and the meaning of 'intérêt' in Chapter 3.

analogy with Castel's 'ruban oculaire', we might say that we can see clearly how one 'nuance' is related to the others on a continuum of colour.

Conclusion

'Nuances' has such a wide currency in such a wide number of contexts because of the prevailing interest in imitation. D'Alembert remarks upon this in one of his many perspicacious observations on the nature of the times: '[l'esprit philosophique] dans les belles-lettres [. . .] a entrepris d'analyser nos plaisirs et de soumettre à l'examen tout ce qui est l'objet du goût' (d'Alembert, *Réflexions sur l'usage et sur l'abus de la philosophie dans les matières de goût*, 1766; 1805: Vol. IV, 413). Part of this interest is doubtless an inheritance from Aristotle who said that man is the most imitative creature in the world, and that pleasure in art must, therefore, be largely a response to its imitative content (Aristotle, *Poetics*, 4; 1995: Vol. II, 2318). But the composite meaning of 'nuances' is a measure of eighteenth-century anxiety with an old idea. It covers all kinds of imitation, from the naturalistic imitation of Le Blon's colour engravings, to the idealizing imitation of Condillac's theory of language, as if in order to maintain the standing of a venerable theory it is necessary to stretch it to increasing degrees. Batteux is criticized by Diderot and many since for his elastic view of imitation which includes even lyrical poetry, but his attempt is really quite characteristic of the era. Diderot himself does it in the *Lettre sur les sourds et muets*, or at least he problematizes the issue when he imagines Castel playing sonatas on his colour harpsichord. He thus mixes Rameau's rationalist theory of harmony with Fontenelle's apocryphal exclamation on feeling inexplicably moved by an Italian sonata: 'sonate, que me veux-tu?', and we are left to wonder whether Castel's instrument can be a model of both aesthetic experiences at once.

As well as a composite meaning, 'nuances' is multipurpose and applicable to all the arts, which goes some way to answering the 'how' question of artistic imitation: one art does it like another. It is a circular argument: one demonstrates how the arts are imitative by saying that they all imitate in the same way, and yet it is pretty much a universal ambition of eighteenth-century art theorists, including Diderot whose ultimate concern in his *Lettre sur les sourds et muets* is declared at the end of the full title: 'l'expression particulière aux beaux-arts'. The very fact that 'nuances' means approximately the same thing when applied to music, painting or writing is a demonstration of the synaesthetic equivalences sought between the arts in order to support the theory of imitation.

Lessing eventually foils these intellectual ambitions in his *Laocoön* (1766) by arguing persuasively and in retrospect definitively that it is the differences between the arts which matter more than the similarities. Nevertheless, the currency of the word 'nuances' is an indication of the prevalence and vitality of an extended sister-arts theory embracing all the arts, not only poetry and painting. If we forget this in favour of Lessing and the 'winners' in the history of aesthetics, we underestimate the strength of a current of intellectual ideas which produced such interesting theories as Diderot's hieroglyph (see Chapter 4).

'Nuances' is also a lexical football kicked backwards and forwards between those who do and do not have faith in the idea of imitation. Chabanon, speaking of music in particular and 'the arts inspired by the muses' in general, says that there are no nuances and no way of rationalizing, on the principle of imitation or otherwise, the way we are powerfully moved by art. When the word is used in this manner, it becomes less the vehicle of a consensus around the theory of imitation, and more the subject of 'querelles littéraires' which are the subject of the next chapter.

PRECIOSITY AND ITS DISCONTENTS

Some authors stretch the idea of typological imitation so far that they are accused by others of preciosity. Writers like Marivaux and Houdar de La Motte cultivate the art of synonyms, rhetorical devices or figurative language with the intention of drawing a typical or characteristic picture of human nature, and argue that there is a fundamental 'clarity' of imitation in doing so. Opponents such as Voltaire argue that this art actually leads to semantic obscurity, and that nothing comprehensible is imitated at all. There are different priorities in either case which come to the fore in the first half of the eighteenth century in the controversy surrounding the 'nouveaux précieux'. The styles of Marivaux, La Motte, and others is likened disparagingly by contemporaries to the seventeenth-century preciosity which Molière derides in *Les Précieuses Ridicules*. It is probably fairer to the so-called eighteenth-century inheritors of preciosity, however, to say that they have an intellectual intention to clarify the inchoate which is quite unlike the social ambitions of their predecessors. They contend that it is essential to fragment language and manipulate the resultant 'nuances' of expression in order to represent accurately the intricacies of human nature. Rather like Roger de Piles in the seventeenth century 'querelle du coloris' who argued that there are important reasons why the painter should render the broken, transitory effects of colour in nature, the 'nouveaux précieux' think that there are intricate reflections of thought which are worth imitating in literary style. It is these 'nuances' of thought which they wish to translate into the 'nuances' of writing, rather in the same way that Condillac suggested in Chapter 1: 'il y a, en quelque sorte, entre [nos pensées], des reflets qui portent des nuances de l'une sur l'autre; et chacune doit à celles qui l'approchent tout le charme de son coloris. L'art de l'écrivain est de saisir cette harmonie' (Condillac, *Art d'écrire*, 1798: 168–9). Condillac is not a 'précieux', of course, but we will see in Chapter 3 that his theory of literary aesthetics encompasses an astonishingly wide

range of styles. Nevertheless, Condillac's image of 'nuances' is
close to the way other modern critics explain preciosity: '[la pré-
ciosité] se détourne des synthèses, fragmente ses concepts,
comme des cristaux qu'elle détacherait d'une pierre, polissant
une facette menue, puis une autre, pour faire rebondir de l'une
à l'autre un rayon de lumière qui jaillit en éclair' (Bray, *Anthologie de la poésie précieuse*, 1946: introduction). There is a literary
tradition of preciosity, from the 'poésie courtoise' of the trou-
badours, to 'le marivaudage' in the eighteenth century, to the
hermetic language of Mallarmé and the 'fin de siècle' Symbol-
ists, each in their own way chipping away at the reality which
language may cause us to take for granted. Voltaire stands for
a different tradition which believes that there is a danger in
refining literary expression to the point where we destroy its
integrity and meaningfulness.

Both sides in this controversy seek reliable criteria to establish the difference between proper literary expression and artificial refinement. One solution is to look to the practice of great
authors in order to arrive at an idea of 'usage'. The suitability
of such a criterion, however, is dependent upon the degree of
respect accorded to past writers, and in an era such as the first
half of the eighteenth century when issues from the 'querelle
des anciens et des modernes' are still very much alive and excit-
ing controversy, 'usage' is itself a matter of debate, and therefore not an appropriate point of reconciliation. Instead, what
is needed is a paradoxical notion of 'usage' which actually
excludes reference to literary practice; in other words, a more
abstract study of language which is nevertheless a practical contribution to the literary debate. This is provided by a trio of
writers who are the subject of this chapter: Gabriel Girard, who
composes the first vernacular dictionary of synonyms, César
Chesneau Dumarsais, who is the first to study figurative language in isolation from other aspects of rhetoric, and Pierre-
Joseph Olivet who writes one of the most systematic accounts
of French prosody. The first two studies, on synonyms and
tropes, are what one might call 'containment theories' for preciosity, because they recognize the expressive potential of these
devices, but at the same time circumscribe limits to their use.
The last of these three studies, on prosody, is a counterweight
to precious style, because it reinforces a more conventional

poetic mode of expression. All three studies together are a further example of how the principle of literary imitation is stretched to include new and old styles of writing.

2.1 Marivaux and two kinds of 'clarté'

Marivaux uses precious language to create what is sometimes described in retrospect as a psychological dimension to his novels. He is criticized by conservative contemporaries for his verbalism, or what became known as 'le marivaudage', because his language seems to stretch the limits of comprehensibility to the point where it appears detached from reality, but he has counter arguments which are interesting not only as reflections on his own style, but also on the intentions of the 'nouveaux précieux', and of preciosity in general. His major contention is that his language is inevitably complex in order to represent properly the complexity of his ideas. This is compatible with his own understanding of 'clarity', but he acknowledges that there are two schools of thought which may be mutually exclusive; the first depends mostly on being understood: 'dans son sens étroit, c'est une exposition de nos pensées qui fait que tout le monde les aperçoit, les entend dans le même sens. Il n'est pas nécessaire, pour être clair, d'avoir exprimé tout ce que vous pensez; mais il est nécessaire que ce que vous exprimez soit entendu de tous également'. The second school of thought is more sensitive to the problem of finding literary expression for inchoate ideas:

Dans toute son étendue, et par rapport à l'auteur, c'est l'exposition nette de notre pensée au degré précis de force et de sens dans lequel nous l'avons conçue; et si la pensée ou le sentiment trop vif dépasse toute expression, ce qui peut arriver, ce sera pour lors l'exposition nette de cette même pensée dans un degré de sens propre à la fixer, et à faire entrevoir en même temps toute son étendue non exprimable de vivacité. (Marivaux, 'Sur la Clarté du discours', 1988: 52)

Marivaux is stylistically inclined much more towards the second principle of 'clarté'. It places him in the precious school of thought, because he believes that language is sometimes incapable of giving proper representation to ideas, and that the sensitive writer is inevitably led to fragment and reconstruct it. His ambition is to convey a meaning which is almost ineffable, 'à faire entrevoir toute son étendue non exprimable de vivacité'. His style of writing requires proportionately more patience from the reader in order to discern the 'pensée non exprimable', but there are also rewards. In his novels, his character portraits often begin with a conventional physical description, but subsequently resolve themselves into a semantic nexus of words, and finally inspire a lively image. In *La Vie de Marianne*, for example, the image is sometimes more important than actually giving a name to the character:

> La mère de la demoiselle pouvait en avoir cinquante ou cinquante-cinq [ans]; petite femme brune, assez ronde, très laide, qui avait le visage large et carré, avec de petits yeux noirs, qui d'abord paraissaient vifs, mais qui n'étaient que curieux et inquiets; de ces yeux toujours remuants, toujours occupés à regarder, et qui cherchent de quoi fournir à l'amusement d'une âme vide, oisive, et qui n'a rien à voir en elle-même.

Her eyes are animated only because she has nothing on which to focus within herself. Marivaux extends the analogy of active eyes to an active but vacuous mind:

> Car il y a de certaines gens dont l'esprit n'est en mouvement que par pure disette d'idées; c'est ce qui les rend si affamés d'objets étrangers, d'autant plus qu'il ne leur reste rien, que tout passe en eux, que tout en sort; gens toujours regardants, toujours écoutants, jamais pensants. Je les compare à un homme qui passerait sa vie à se tenir à sa fenêtre; voilà l'image que je me fais d'eux, et des fonctions de leur esprit.
> (Marivaux, *La Vie de Marianne*, 1997: 316)

The first, and physical, description we have of this character is 'des yeux vifs', which might suggest intellectual vivacity; the final, metaphorical image we have, is of an intellectual bystander with no ideas of her own. The occasion for this image, and the pivot between the physical and psychological description, is the subtle distinction between 'des yeux vifs' and 'des yeux curieux'. They are analogous, in that both suggest animation, but the first implies an inquiring mind, while the second has the connotation also of a meddlesome mind capable of little else than spying on others. Many of Marivaux's more involved psychological insights derive, like this one, from apparently trifling nuances of meaning between analogous expressions. If they appear precious and obscure, then it is because Marivaux is seeking to make them 'clear' in his second sense; he is more concerned with the accurate expression of ideas, than he is with the easy transparency of his language. He sometimes apologizes for his long psychological character portraits, but justifies them according to this kind of 'clarté': 'c'est encore leurs pensées que j'explique, et je soutiens que je les rends comme elles étaient' (Marivaux, *La Vie de Marianne*, 1997: 115).

The smallest nuances and the most unassuming synonyms can occasion the most earnest reflection, making the narrative quite unpredictable. Marianne's reflections on her own condition, for example, lead her to discuss the existential difference between 'être' and 'vivre':

A voir quelquefois ce qui se passe dans notre instinct là-dessus, on dirait que, pour être, il n'est pas nécessaire de vivre; que ce n'est que par accident que nous vivons, mais que c'est naturellement que nous sommes. On dirait que, lorsqu'un homme se tue, par exemple, il ne quitte la vie que pour se sauver, que pour se débarrasser d'une chose incommode; ce n'est pas de lui dont il ne veut plus, mais bien du fardeau qu'il porte. (Marivaux, *La Vie de Marianne*, 1997: 184–5)

This deft use of language provides psychological insight which constitutes a verbal exploration of character, but in fairness to Marivaux's detractors we might say that it calls for an intellectual response from the reader rather than an emotional one. This gives rise to certain difficulties of interpretation, because Marianne's lucid self-analysis on some occasions sits oddly with her tearful abandon on others. The contrast between the two is sometimes so great that Marianne comes across at least as a scheming character, if not a hypocritical one, instead of the innocent victim of circumstances which ostensibly she is.[1]

However debatable, 'le marivaudage' in these cases is at least intended to express a significant idea. There are other times, however, when Marivaux's predeliction for punning leads him to play with semantics mostly for comic effect, and in these instances, he has a weaker claim to the idea of 'clarté'. The mixture of punning and preciosity which is usually meant, by

---

[1] For a structuralist interpretation of the semiotics of Marivaux's style and character portraits, see Bennington, 'Les Machines de l'Opéra' (1982).

'le marivaudage', by contemporary and modern critics alike, leaves Marivaux open to the criticism that his principle of clarity is a sham, and that psychological insights in his novels are no better than his frivolous punning elsewhere.

In the opening scene of *La Seconde surprise de l'amour*, for example, Lisette is trying to raise the spirits of her brooding mistress:

LA MARQUISE. Eh! laissez-moi, je dois soupirer toute ma vie.
LISETTE. Vous devez, dites-vous? Oh! vous ne payerez jamais cette dette-là; vous êtes trop jeune, elle ne saurait être sérieuse.

It is the pun on 'devoir' which maintains the dialogue when Lisette would otherwise obey her mistress and leave the stage. Or again, in the opening scene of *L'Ile des esclaves*, the pun is part of the new egalitarian language of master and servant to replace the old 'langue d'Athènes'. Sometimes Arlequin addresses his master with the familiar 'tu', on other occasions, he refuses his master's attempts at reconciliation:

IPHICRATE. Eh! ne sais-tu pas que je t'aime?
ARLEQUIN. Oui; mais les marques de votre amitié tombent toujours sur mes épaules, et cela est mal placé.

The issue of 'clarté' does seem uppermost in Marivaux's mind in this instance; the pun is part of the comedy of reversed roles, and is a theatrical device to encourage us to take sides with the funnier of the two characters.

Marivaux obviously has an interest in explaining the connection between the punning and preciosity, but it is perhaps his neglect of the question which is partly responsible for the pejorative connotations even today of the term 'marivaudage'. Like 'preciosity', it has a bad name. Perhaps he thought the joke was on his critics if they could not appreciate a pun for what it is worth, a moment's laughter, instead of treating it in sober earnest. Even if it is not an issue for Marivaux, however, it is a matter which will concern Dumarsais when he writes *Des tropes* in 1730, and analyses semantics in such a way as to elucidate the relation between punning and preciosity, and in the process finding an answer which potentially reconciles Marivaux with his critics.

2.2 *Houdar de La Motte's idea of poetry and prose*

In the early eighteenth century, the criterion of *usage* comes under scrutiny in what some critics have called 'la querelle des vers'.[2] The debate is a mark of the enduring controversy between the anciens and the 'modernes', but with a greater focus on the importance of form in art, and in particular of versification in poetry. La Motte has the questionable merit of posing the most significant questions in this debate, without always finding the most felicitous answers. As we shall see later, Voltaire admires him for his independent thinking, but despises the kind of poetry which he advocates in practice.

La Motte's principle is that the distinction between prose and poetry is artificial, and based only on an inherited system of convention which causes us to identify poetry with the formal requirements of versification, and prose with the absence of regular form. It is according to the same simple dichotomy that Molière's 'bourgeois gentilhomme' discovers by deduction that he is speaking prose, because 'tout ce qui n'est point prose est vers, et tout ce qui n'est point vers est prose' (Molière, *Le Bourgeois gentilhomme*: Act II, Sc. v). The equivalent principle causes Vaugelas, Le Bossu, and Bouhours expressly to forbid the use of verse forms in prose, in case the result should be a monstrous amalgam of two distinct forms of expression.[3] In contrast, La Motte objects to a division based solely on the presence or absence of versification, since the nature of 'poësie' lies elsewhere: 'j'ai donc dit que la Rime & la mesure n'étoient point la Poësie [. . .] La Poësie, qui n'est autre chose que la hardiesse des pensées, la vivacité des images & l'énergie de l'expression, demeurera toujours ce qu'elle est, indépendamment de toute mesure' (La Motte, in *Œuvres*, 1754: Vol. I, 553). Since 'poësie' is arresting ideas, powerful imagery, and stirring language, it is arguably as suitable in prose as it is in verse. In which case, versification is irrelevant to 'poësie', and it is immaterial whether an ode, an epic, or a tragedy is written in prose or in verse. In consequence, La Motte sets out partly to demonstrate that there

---

[2] Lote, *Histoire du vers français* (1992): Vol. VII, 143.

[3] Vaugelas, *Remarques sur la langue françoise* (1647): 266–77; Bouhours, *Doutes sur la langue françoise* (1675): 266–67; Le Bossu, *Traité du poëme épique* (1675): 22.

can be 'poësie' without versification, and partly to show how the two can in fact coexist, on condition that there is less relative importance attached to versification than convention would sometimes allow.

Unless this condition is met, there is a danger that the rigours of versification will stifle the expression of 'poësie'. Ideally, there would be a balance between fixed and free verse, which would satisfy our taste for a certain shape and regularity of expression, without inclining towards a feeling of monotony. La Motte thinks that this delicate balance between 'symétrie' and 'variété', upon which depends 'l'harmonie du vers', is often lost by poets who are too eager to conform to the formal constraints of traditional versification: 'l'homme est ami de la symétrie; mais il l'est encore plus de la variété. Il faut donc, pour le satisfaire, lui présenter des proportions exactes, mais lui en offrir toujours différentes. Les vers ne satisfont qu'au premier goût' (La Motte, in *Œuvres*, 1754: Vol. I, 563). Formal composition is pleasing, but insufficient in itself. It is for this reason that La Motte prefers the varied metrics and interlacing rhyme of the ode to the rigid and predictable form of the Alexandrine. His tacit and sometimes explicit assumption, is always that versification is an instrument at the service of the poet's message, and should be sufficiently adaptable to facilitate, rather than impede expression. Versification has some intrinsic value as a skilful demonstration of 'la difficulté vaincue', a display of formal virtuosity, but it encourages the reader to feel a sense of admiration more than beauty; like d'Alembert's image of a dancer in shackles, the constraint may be admirably overcome, but it is in the end a hindrance.[4] La Motte was himself an accomplished dramatic poet, and he does not dismiss versification *per se*; rather he asks that we consider carefully the reasons for our enjoyment: 'je conviens que le charme [de la rime] est réel pour bien des gens; & j'y suis si sensible moi-même, qu'il m'arrive souvent d'admirer en vers ce que je ne saurois qu'approuver en prose. Il ne s'agit que de la vraye cause de cette illusion: je l'attribue, pour la plus grande partie, à la surprise agréable qui naît de la difficulté vaincue' (La Motte, in *Œuvres*, 1754:

---

[4] D'Alembert, *Suite des réflexions sur la poésie, et sur l'ode en particulier*, in *Œuvres* (1822): Vol. IV: 300.

Vol. I: 554). Form in art is difficult and desirable, but it is not
the only, and perhaps not the most important objective. Artifice for its own sake quickly appears gratuitous and ridiculous,
like the 'bouts rimés', acrostics and verse games which La Motte
thinks were invented partly in mockery of poetic convention.
These displays of technical virtuosity are in the end puerile and
futile 'badinage', which try to make a virtue out of a difficulty:
'faire passer des grains de millet par le trou d'une aiguille étoit
sans doute le fruit d'un exercice opiniâtre; & cependant la mer-
veille, à cause de sa puérilité, ne mérita à son Auteur d'autre
recompense qu'un boisseau de millet, pour pouvoir continuer
son badinage' (La Motte, in *Œuvres*, 1754: Vol. I: 568–9). La
Motte is clearly sceptical about the benefits of versification, and
believes that more attention ought to be paid to his conception
of 'poësie'. He is led as a result to experiment in a number of
ways which serve to illustrate what he means by 'poësie', and
what place there is left in his scheme for versification.

La Motte first formulates these ideas in 1707, when he publishes his *Discours sur la poësie en général,* in which he expresses
his desire, much repeated in subsequent writings, to consider
the nature of poetry, 'la poësie en général', in abstraction from
the models provided by distinguished poets. His indifference to
tradition makes him a 'moderne' in the eyes of his adversaries,
but it derives less from a polemical agenda than from a spirit
of intellectual inquiry. In this light, his infamous transposition
into prose of the first scene of Racine's *Mithridate* looks as much
like an exploration into the relative merits of 'poësie' and versification, as it does a vituperative blow against an established
literary figure. His belief is that the essential beauty of Racine's
language is retained in the prose, and that those who disagree
are not accustomed to recognizing beauty where it really lies,
which is in the mastery of 'poësie', or: 'la justesse des pensées,
liées entr'elles par le meilleur arrangement, la convenance des
tours qui expriment des sentimens proportionnés à la nature
des choses dont on parle, & le choix des expressions les plus
propres à faire passer exactement dans l'esprit des autres
les idées qu'on veut leur donner' (La Motte, *Comparaison de la
premiere Scéne de Mithridate, avec la même Scéne réduite en prose*, in
Œuvres, 1754: Vol. IV, 408). There would be little that is new
in this inventory, were it not for the fact that 'les tours, les

sentiments proportionnés, le choix des expressions' are intended as a substitute for versification, not only as a complement. His purpose is to give priority to the rhetorical expression of ideas more than the formal arrangements of verse, with the consequence that he is later criticized on both counts for his precious literary style and his dull, listless verse. In the following, I shall consider first his preciosity, then his verse.

Desfontaines's *Dictionnaire néologique* (1726) is a compendium of those new expressions and figures of speech which he feels have most offended contemporary sensibilities, and as such, it is a great help in identifying La Motte's stylistic innovations. He is the author most cited in the dictionary, and arguably the subject of Desfontaines's parodic short story about a bouffon character called Pantalon-Phœbus, who entertains with frivolous word play, and who is described in the preface to the dictionary as '[un] grand marieur de mots, l'un de l'autre étonnés'.[5] All the following examples are taken from Desfontaines's dictionary, and ultimately from La Motte's odes, fables, and translation of Homer's *Iliade*.

La Motte is fond of surprising and challenging his reader with the device of catachresis, by 'marrying' words which we would otherwise not expect to find together. Sometimes he uses an unexpected adverbial expression, such as 'chargé d'âge':

> Un Renard grand Docteur, mais déja chargé d'âge,
>   Ne pouvant plus comme autrefois,
> Assiéger les oiseaux, ni chercher loin ses droits,
>   De la ruse essaya l'usage.
>   (La Motte, 'Le Renard et le prédicateur',
>   Livre V, Fable 3, in *Œuvres* 1754: Vol. IX:
>   271–4)[6]

'Chargé d'âge' conjures up a more vivid image of the burden of years, weighing down the old fox, who has come to rely more on mental than physical agility. Sometimes, the adjective comes in an unexpected position, to give a fresh, vivid sense to a commonplace expression; we expect 'honneurs funèbres', like 'oraisons funèbres', but instead we find 'funèbres honneurs' and 'funèbres jeux':

---

[5] See the statistical analysis of Desfontaines's *Dictionnaire*, in Deloffres, *Marivaux et le Marivaudage* (1971): 40.

[6] See Desfontaines, *Dictionnaire néologique*: 'chargé d'âge'.

Allons . . . mais quoi! Patrocle est privé de nos pleurs,
Et sa dépouille attend les funèbres honneurs;
(La Motte, *Iliade*, Bk II, in *Œuvres*, 1754: Vol. II,
298. See also p. 302.)[7]

The inversion of noun and adjective in 'funèbres honneurs'
gives a metaphorical sense to the conventional meaning of
'burial rites', a sense of horror and foreboding that a turning-
point has been reached, that Hector has killed Patroclus, and
that Achilles will now inevitably join the battle. On other occasions, La Motte uses verbal phrases such as 'boire l'espoir à
pleines coupes':

La nuit se passe au Camp, ou cependant les troupes
Boivent dans les festins l'espoir à pleines coupes
(La Motte, *Iliade*, Bk XI, in *Œuvres*, 1754: Vol. II,
272)[8]

The taste of victory and hope for the future mingle in the same
celebrations. Contextual assistance with this interpretation is
provided by 'dans les festins', which tempers some of the shock
value of catachresis by providing a dependable, literal meaning
to 'boire' before its figurative meaning emerges. La Motte uses
the same strategy for the expression 'faire bourse commune de
la gloire':

Pour chercher sûrement fortune,
Nombre de braves Chiens se liguerent entr'eux.
De gloire & de butin faisons bourse commune,
Leur dit, monté sur la Tribune,
Un Dogue, Orateur vigoureux.
(La Motte, 'Les Chiens', Livre 4, Fables 4,
in *Œuvres*, 1754: Vol. IX, 212–14)[9]

The cynical politician will appeal at once to the pride and to
the material greed of his fellows. Another favourite device of La
Motte and the 'nouveaux précieux' is the oxymoron, which
is a kind of concentrated catachresis. Desfontaines comments
upon 'une fille effroyablement belle', 'une piece horriblement
admirable', and 'un Tableau plaisamment formidable'. He cites
La Motte:

[7] Ibid.: 'funèbre'.   [8] Ibid.: 'boire'.   [9] Ibid.: 'bourse'.

> Apollon veut expressement
> Que l'on soit rustique avec grace
> Et populaire élégamment
> (La Motte, 'L'Eclipse', Livre
> II, Fable 12, in Œuvres, 1754:
> Vol. IX, 131–4)[10]

The wit required to formulate a meaningful oxymoron, and subsequently the effort required by the reader to decipher the intention of the author, has an intellectual appeal for La Motte. Desfontaines, however, comments with some reserve: 'il faut avoir un peu d'esprit pour entrer dans ce Laconisme expressif' (Desfontaines, *Dictionnaire néologique*. 'Compter'). In addition to catachresis and oxymorons, La Motte makes a great deal of use of metonymy. Sometimes it is metonymy of cause and effect, as when the gardener gives in to the seductive rhetoric of the bramble, plants it in his garden, whereupon it quickly smothers all the other plants: 'Fruits, potager, tout meurt; les fleurs deviennent foin' (La Motte, 'Le ronce et le jardinier', Livre I, Fables 9, in *Œuvres*, 1754: Vol. IX, 75–6).[11] 'Deviennent foin' is a metonym for 'flétrissent' which emphasizes the inevitable and precipitous consequences of yielding to rhetoric. Sometimes La Motte uses metonymy of concrete and abstract meaning, such as when he says that it is human nature to flatter ourselves, 'de sourire à son néant':

> Qu'est-ce que l'Homme? Aristote te répond
> C'est un Animal raisonnable.
> Je n'en crois rien; s'il faut le définir à fond,
> C'est un Animal sot, superbe & misérable.
> Chacun de nous sourit à son néant,
> S'exagere sa propre idée:
> Tel s'imagine être un Géant
> Qui n'a pas plus d'une coudée.
> Aristote n'a pas trouvé notre vrai nom,
> Orgueil & petitesse ensemble
> Voilà tout l'homme ce me semble
> (La Motte, 'Le Bœuf et le Ciron', Livre I,
> Fable 13, in *Œuvres*, 1754: Vol. IX, 84)[12]

The expression captures the moment of cheerful complacency in the face of our own inadequacies. La Motte uses metaphor

---

[10] See Desfontaines, *Dictionnaire néologique*. 'plaisamment'.   [11] Ibid.: 'foin'.
[12] Ibid.: 'néant'.

in equally innovative ways, when he expresses a spiritual kind of inheritance with a metaphorical use of the expression 'avancement d'hoirie':

> Coypel, digne héritier d'un Apelle nouveau
> Qui, recuëillant sa sublime industrie,
> T'es fait donner ta part de son peinceau
> En pur avancement d'hoirie;
> (La Motte, 'La Magicienne', Livre I,
> Fable XVI, in Œuvres, 1754: Vol. IX,
> 90–2)[13]

There seems to be a spiritual, almost a familial bond between the greatest painters, so that they are inspired by and inherit the genius of past masters.

These constructions, metonymy, catachresis, oxymora, and metaphor, are some of the 'tours, choix des expressions' and 'sentiments proportionnés à la nature des choses' which La Motte thinks are essential to 'poësie'. They merit the esteem which we accord to any author's experiments with language and sensitivity to what is meant by 'literary expression'. In addition to their experiment value, some of his compositions, particularly the odes and fables, have rightly been praised for their creative variety and vividness.[14] The practice of this kind of 'poësie', however, comes at the expense of other qualities which we might expect of poetry, so that La Motte's longer verse often sounds dull and lifeless. He enjoys the ode, the fable, and the eclogue for their varied form, the relatively effusive style traditionally tolerated, and also quite simply their brevity. They seem to be less offensive to his taste for 'variété' before 'symétrie'. More controversial is his treatment of tragic drama and epic, his prose version of Œdipe and his quite radical adaptation of Homer. All have important consequences for his general conception of poetry.

La Motte's idea of 'poësie', then, is to pepper his prose or verse with inventive micro-rhetorical structures like metonymy, metaphor or catachresis, and there is little room for extended imagery and lyricism. It is partly for this reason that his adaptation in 1714 of Homer's Iliade is controversial, because it loses sight of Homer's original style, and becomes a self-indulgent exercise in La Motte's own poetic ideas. Some of the most

---

[13] Ibid.: 'avancement d'hoirie'. [14] Finch, The Sixth Sense, 1966: 66.

100062 PRECIOSITY AND ITS DISCONTENTS

recognizable and lyrical features of Homer, such as the long paratactic constructions and the hypotyposis are edited out. In effect, the task of versifying Homer becomes easier in some respects, since La Motte is less confronted with the problem of rendering lyrical descriptions from the synthetic grammar of Greek into the analytical grammar of French. In contrast, Anne Dacier's translation in 1699 is much more faithful to the lyricism of the original, and it is perhaps her respect for Homeric style which causes her to choose prose over verse.[15] La Motte, on the contrary, spends little time worrying about the constraints of the Alexandrine, because he considers it little more than a procedural matter which the poet is obliged to follow in order to satisfy the conventional demands of the art. Versification has very little relevance to his idea of poetry. He demonstrates by composing a five-act tragedy in prose, Œdipe, and grudgingly transposing it into verse, complaining that he has to do so only because most audiences would not understand a prose tragedy, and because most actors would not know how to deliver prose on stage. He objects to verse partly for reasons of verisimilitude:

N'est-il pas, j'ose le dire, contre nature, qu'un Héros, qu'une Princesse asservissent tous leurs discours à un certain nombre de sillabes; qu'ils y ménagent scrupuleusement des repos reglés; & qu'ils affectent, jusques dans leurs passions les plus impétueuses, le retour exact des mêmes sons qui ne peut être que le fruit d'une recherche aussi puerile que pénible? Que cette mascarade du discours est étrange! (La Motte, *Discours à l'occasion de la Tragédie d'Œdipe*, in *Œuvres*, Vol. IV, 1754: 392)

The conventions of rhythm, caesura and rhyme are manifestly incompatible with moments of high passion, when it seems absurd and unnatural that the characters should express themselves in the contrived language of verse. At these moments, the audience is distracted from the action on stage, and feels more

---

[15] For a comparison of their different styles, see particularly the description of Achille's shield in Dacier, *L'Iliade*, 1712, Bk XVIII: Vol. III, 126–36; and La Motte, *L'Iliade*, 1754: Bk IX, 274–5. The technical merits of each *Iliade* are discussed by Mazon, who dislikes La Motte's treatment of Homer: '[il] lui enlève toute couleur et toute vie et lui donne l'aspect d'une momie ratatinée et dessechée' (*Madame Dacier et les traductions d'Homère en France*, 1936: 15). The 'querelle homérique' which Dacier and La Motte provoked is discussed by Naves, who points out also that La Motte, unlike Dacier, did not read Greek (*Le Goût de Voltaire*, 1938: 23, 29–44).

a sense of admiration for the poet than sympathy for the characters. La Motte's second objection to versification is that it
inhibits the subtleties of 'poësie'; and that prose is better
adapted to his kind of literary language: 'on pourrait toûjours
donner à un raisonnement sa gradation et sa force, au lieu que
le caprice des rimes contraint souvent d'y mêler quelques foib-
lesses, ou quelque inutilité' (La Motte, *Discours à l'occasion de
la Tragédie d'Œdipe*, in *Œuvres*, Vol. IV, 1754: 394). There is an
admirable brevity in La Motte's 'poësie'; it seems to thrive on
saying as much as possible in as few words as possible. In verse,
however, he finds that there is a degree of redundancy in
expression, according to the requirements of rhythm or rhyme.
His third objection to verse is that traditionally it has placed too
much emphasis on euphony and the suggestiveness of certain
sounds, when in fact there is no objective justification for any
relation between sound and meaning: 'les sons d'une langue
sont indifférens, du moins pour ceux qui n'en sçavent point
d'autres ils ne nous plaisent ou ne nous choquent, que par le
sens que nous y attachons; car enfin ils ne sont que l'occasion
arbitraire de nos idées [. . .] Il ne tiendroit qu'à nous de faire
un beau mot de celui de *porc*, & un mot désagréable de celui
de *coursier*' (La Motte, *Discours sur Homere*, in *Œuvres*, 1754: Vol.
II, 114–15). Again, the task of translating Homer in verse, and
of versification in general, is simplified if no attention is paid
to the sound qualities of the language. This particular simplification of the traditions of versification is an enormous under-
estimation of Greek and Latin verse, and from the point of view
of many of La Motte's contemporaries, it is also a missed opportunity in French verse (See Chapter 4).

Despite these reservations, La Motte writes a great deal in the
Alexandrine, but on the principle that there is little more to
versification than a certain number of conventional operations
which can be carried out on prose. He claims that it is personal
taste which brought him to write *Œdipe* first in prose, and only
later to transpose it into verse, but it is probably also a desire
to provoke his adversaries with an illustration of how simple and
mechanical these operations can be. If we are generous to La
Motte, it will be useful to consider one of the most emotionally
charged scenes of the play, when he would argue that the
natural passion of prose contrasts most vividly with the

contrived dullness of verse. The alterations which he makes in order to versify his 'original' prose version demonstrate what he takes to be the art of versification.

In the last scene of Act III, Oedipus realizes he is the murderer of his own father, the King, and Jocasta recognizes her incestuous marriage with her own son, Oedipus.[16] Jocasta is the first to speak when their mutual guilt is revealed. In the prose, she interrupts Oedipus: 'Arrêtez', while in the verse, La Motte feels obliged to employ what he calls the appropriate 'expression épique': 'Ah!'.[17] Similarly, 'ma mort' and 'demander' in the prose become 'mon trépas' and 'conjurer d'accepter' in the verse. He finds the *expressions épiques* a useful formal device for adding a hemistich where phrases in the prose are too short; 'cette horrible menace', 'leur barbare courroux', 'ce terrible mystère', 'mes mortelles allarmes' are convenient verse 'fillers' which are absent in the prose version. There are times when he obviously takes care over the formal composition of his verse. He takes advantage of the compositional possibilities when Oedipus realizes that he is the murderer of his wife's husband, which is expressed in the prose: 'le coupable meurtrier de son époux'. In the verse, sound and words are reflected in a chiasmus with just the kind of formal virtuosity which he argues is a distraction from the drama: 'Qu'un Epoux tout soüillé du sang de votre Epoux!' More often he neglects formal composition. His caesura is sometimes grammatically awkward: 'Vous ne me voyez plus//que comme un parricide', and sometimes semantically awkward: 'Mais, j'y consens, aux Dieux//venez demander grace'. Neither does he pay much attention to the sound of his verse. There is a clumsy repetition of nasal sounds in: 'Mais, Madame, malgré ce pardon magnanime'. There is also a harsh repetition of 'r' sounds just when Jocasta is trying to reassure Oedipus of her enduring love: 'Respectez vos vertus: respectez mes regrets'. The significance of metrics and euphony will be considered more fully in Chapter 4, but it is sufficient here to recognize the little importance that La Motte attaches to them. Neither does he devote much attention to his rhyme scheme, which is either 'rime pauvre', or else uninventive: 'allarmes/larmes, ombre/sombre, trépas/pas'.

---

[16] See Appendix for the relevant passages from each version of La Motte's *Œdipe*.

[17] For La Motte's reference to 'expressions épiques', see his *Suite des Réflexions sur la tragédie, où on répond à M. de Voltaire*, 1754: 439.

These are the operations which transpose prose into poetry, which create an artificial separation between the two, and which are sustained by cultural prejudice and literary convention. La Motte's strategy seems to be a *reductio ad absurdum* of the formal conventions of poetry, since his critics will argue later that it is untrue that poets use versification merely as an extra layer of composition, and that in fact, versification is an organic part of invention, inseparable from other aspects of literary language. They contend that formal constraints are in themselves inspiring, and that they are one element in a crucible of poetic creativity which produces beauty in art.

2.3 Criticism of preciosity

Part of the problem with preciosity from the point of view of its detractors is that it seeks more to surprise and reveal than it does to persuade or convince. In effect, it is criticized for not satisfying rhetorical expectations of how writing should function. Contemporary critics complain that La Motte and Marivaux are too 'philosophical', or 'tiring' because readers expect to be convinced rather than teased with ambiguous nuances of meaning. They interpret the nuances as inadequate inspiration which fails to develop into lyricism, like the sparks of genius which will not quite burst into flame. It is in this sense that Bernis complains that La Motte's 'poësie' lacks lyricism, and is more 'philosophical' than poetic:

> La Motte a peu senti la flamme
> Dont bruloient ces chantres divers;
> Les vains éclairs de l'épigramme
> Brillent trop souvent dans ses vers.
> Plus philosophe que poëte,
> Il touche une lyre muette;
> La raison lui parle, il écrit;
> On trouve en ses strophes sensées
> Moins d'images que de pensées
> Et moins de talent que d'esprit.
> (Bernis, 'Ode IV. Les Poëtes
> lyriques', 1825: 246–7)

He distinguishes sharply between the poet and the philosopher, because it is not the poet's vocation to provide intellectually taxing 'pensées', but to compose pleasing and lyrical 'images'. The difference between 'pensée' and 'images' in the contemporary imagination is a question of degree; 'images' are created by a felicitous concord of like ideas, whereas 'pensées' are incongruous combinations of distant ideas which, in the contemporary terminology, are 'tirées de trop loin'. Critics are aware that some of the most beautiful images derive from unexpected associations, but they are aware, also, that the same mechanism leads to obscurity if taken to excess. One solution suggested by Gamaches is to use figurative language sparingly, and only when there is no equivalent in non-figurative language: 'les expressions figurées ne doivent être employées qu'avec ménagement; on ne doit s'en servir qu'au défaut des mots propres' (Gamaches, *Les Agrémens du langage*, 1718: 124). He realizes himself, however, that figurative language is much more than a supplement to non-figurative language; it does in fact generate it: 'l'usage convertit souvent les termes figurés en mots propres' (p. 125). As a result, there is a risk that conditions restricting the use of figurative language also restrict the generative principle of language itself. Gamaches is one of many who propose a fine line between the two, between those images which he considers 'tirées de trop loin' and those which are within the bounds of acceptability. When he considers La Motte's style, he finds his images 'invraisemblables' and illogical, because they do not meet his standards of congruity: 'si une expression figurée manquoit de justesse, si les deux objets qu'elle unit ne pouvoient aisément s'ajuster ensemble, alors elle fatigueroit l'imagination, & feroit sur elle une impression desagréable' (Gamaches, *Les Agrémens du langage*, 1718: 102–3). Voltaire, too, discourages the 'tiring' use of figurative language, and likewise urges discernment (ironically with an analogy!): 'on aime à s'arrêter dans une promenade pour cueillir des fleurs; mais on ne veut pas se baisser à tout moment pour en ramasser. [La Métaphore] doit être employée avec ménagement' (Voltaire, 'Connaissance des beautés et des défauts de la poésie', in Moland 23, 1879: 356–7). His attitude to La Motte is ambivalent because he admires the independent thinker but despises the precious poet; he sometimes praises 'l'homme d'esprit et de talent', while on other occasions he dislikes his idea of 'poësie' (Voltaire, 'Anciens et modernes', in Moland 17,

1878: 226). He comments on La Motte's adaptation of the *Iliade*: 'au lieu d'echauffer son génie en tachant de copier les sublimes peintures d'Homere, il voulut lui donner de l'esprit; c'est la manie de la plupart des Français; une espèce de pointe qu'ils appellent un *trait*, une petite antithèse, un léger contraste de mots leur suffit [. . .] Ce n'est plus qu'une sentence triviale et froide' (Voltaire, 'Epopée', in Moland 18, 1878: 568). He finds the nuances of preciosity cold and unfeeling, lacking the sensibility that is his own primary concern in drama, for example, when he says that the imperative is to be moving: 'le grand point est d'émouvoir et de faire verser des larmes' (Voltaire, 'Réponse à M. de Lindelle', in Moland 3, 1877: 197).[18] In contrast, preciosity appeals more to the intellect than the heart. The tears which Marianne cries in Marivaux's novel, for example, are too ambivalent to be compellingly moving. It may be unfair to compare Marivaux's novels with Voltaire's plays, since different genres are surely accompanied by different expectations. Nevertheless, sensibility and preciosity seem to have quite different aesthetic intentions, and the difference illustrates Bernis's distinction between 'images' and 'pensées', between language which is intellectually and emotionally engaging.

Versification is, however, one formal and perhaps intellectual aspect of literary language which Voltaire does accept, even embrace, because it enhances poetic expression. La Motte argued to the contrary, that versification is merely an extra layer of composition which appeals because it is difficult, but that it is not essential to poetry. Those, like Voltaire, who disagree with him consider that formalism is in fact integral to creativity, and that it cannot be discarded without forfeiting the very nature of aesthetic pleasure. The analogies they propose in support of formalism are intended to illustrate the mutual dependence in art of form and inspiration, and the consequent nonsense of trying to distinguish them. Montaigne's image of the trumpet is often cited directly or it is adapted: 'tout ainsi que la voix, contrainte dans l'étroit canal d'une trompette, sort plus aiguë et plus forte, ainsi me semble il que la sentence, pressée aux pieds nombreux de la poësie, s'eslance bien plus brusquement

---

[18] See, e.g., the tearful scenes in Voltaire's *Zaïre*, IV, 2; *Mérope*, III, 4.

et me fiert d'une plus vive secousse' (Montaigne, *Essais*, I, p. xxvi, 1969: 193–4). Art amplifies the natural capacity for expression, and arouses a more intense response. Louis Racine accounts for formalism with a similar idea that versification 'channels' poetic inspiration, and also with the characteristic neoclassical notion that art 'perfects' nature: 'la Nature inspire d'abord la rapidité du stile, & la hardiesse des figures: l'art vient ensuite, & pour rendre le stile poëtique encore plus rapide, & en même-tems plus harmonieux, le resserre dans les bornes de la versification, & la versification ne fait que perfectionner l'ouvrage de la nature' (L. Racine, *Réflexions sur la poësie*, 1750: Vol. V, 53). Montaigne's trumpet analogy becomes a favoured means of expressing the principle that art is invariably a perfection of nature. Voltaire and Gaillard quote Montaigne directly,[19] and La Faye seems to adapt his analogy, with an image of versification as words under pressure, like water pushed to greater heights by hydraulics:

> De la contrainte rigoureuse
> Où l'esprit semble resserré,
> Il acquiert cette force heureuse
> Qui l'élève au plus haut degré.
> Telle dans des canaux pressés,
> Avec plus de force élancée,
> L'onde s'élève dans les airs;
> Et la régle qui semble austere,
> N'est qu'un art plus certain de plaire
> Inséparable des beaux Vers
>   (La Faye, 'Epitre sur les avantages
>   de la rime', *c.* 1725)

Voltaire paraphrases these lines in the introduction to his *Œdipe*, republished in 1730 in response to La Motte's own *Œdipe*. Elsewhere, he provides also his own analogy of the ideal harmony between the intellectual restraints of form, and the free rein given to inspiration: 'comment le raisonnement peut-il gouverner l'enthousiasme? [. . .] C'est un coursier qui s'emporte dans sa carrière, mais la carrière est régulièrement tracée' (Voltaire, *Connaissance des beautés et des défauts de la poésie*,

---

[19] Voltaire, 'Art dramatique', in Moland 17 (1878): 418; Gaillard, *Poëtique françoise* (1749): 2.

Moland 23, 1879: 61). Art is a marshalling of natural energies, like a racehorse guided round a track; it makes no sense to suggest that there can be a race without first taming and training the horse. There may be an allusion to a similar idea in Voltaire's poem 'Le Mondain', which is written ostensibly in praise of worldly luxury, but perhaps also in praise of the luxury of versification. He uses the metaphor of champagne to imply that in poetry words are confined like bubbles in a bottle, all the better to delight when the cork flies out and the wine gives a wonderful fizz.[20] Voltaire dislikes La Motte's poetry because, although it has the sparkle of preciosity, it loses the tension provided by good versification. Voltaire might say that La Motte is all bubbles and no bottle, which means that in the end his poetry goes flat. His style is parodied by Voltaire in *Le Temple du goût*, when La Motte asks to enter the elite circle of great writers:

> Ouvrez, messieurs, c'est mon Œdipe en prose,
> Mes vers sont durs, d'accord, mais forts de choses
> (Voltaire, *Le Temple du goût*, in Moland 8, 1877:
> 564)

The caesura is awkward, there is an internal rhyme, 'd'accord/forts', and an unattractive repetition of 'r' and 'd' sounds. His request is denied, and he remains outside the temple with other critics of versification like Perrault and Chapelain. Dacier, too, criticizes La Motte for his dismissive attitude to versification. In an echo of Horace's axiom *miscuit utile dulce*, she thinks that the sound of verse is at least as important, if not more important than the meaning of verse: 'l'oreille séduira souvent l'esprit, mais il arrivera rarement que l'esprit séduise l'oreille' (in Naves, *Le Goût de Voltaire*, 1938: 51). Poetry seduces by a harmony of suggestive sounds which reinforces normal semantics, and perhaps expresses something in addition which Voltaire calls 'les mouvements lents ou impétueux de l'ame' (Voltaire, 'Langues', in Moland 19, 1879: 566). These comments by Dacier and Voltaire are isolated and unsubstantiated

[20] Voltaire, *Le Mondain* in Moland 10 (1877): 87: 'Cloris, Eglé, me versent de leur main | Un vin d'Aï dont la mousse pressée, | De la bouteille avec force élancée, | Comme un éclair fait voler le bouchon;'. A good contemporary image, since champagne had always been a flat wine until approximately the time Voltaire wrote this poem, in 1736, when attempts were made to design bottles strong enough to resist the pressure (personal communication, Nicholas Cronk).

by any extended argumentation; as Voltaire contends in the preface to *Œdipe*, the real answer to literary controversies is not to respond with more disputation, but to write a better play. Nevertheless, Olivet later perceives a need to develop them into an elaborate treatise on prosody which is intended to refute La Motte's claim that versification is artificial.

2.4   Fénelon's compromise

There is very little compromise between the two sides in this debate. Voltaire's party often regard La Motte as a traitor to the tradition of dramatic verse for which he was famous in his time. La Motte and Marivaux, on the other hand, both seem to enjoy provoking their adversaries with a lively disrespect for tradition. The only voice of reconciliation which is heard to any extent is Fénelon's. His prose epic *Télémaque* in 1699 achieves an astonishing success throughout the eighteenth century, partly because the relationship between the young Télémaque and Mentor, his tutor, appealed to contemporary moral sensibilities, perhaps also because of the christianization of Classical legend, and in addition because it manages to reconcile some of the formal expectations of traditional poetry with the demands of the 'modernes' for freer composition.[21] Already in its time it is called a prose poem, because it breaks the traditional injunction against using verse forms in prose, but it does so in such an appealing manner that even the most traditional critics acknowledge its merit. Voltaire, for example, dislikes the connotations of 'poème en prose', but is pleasantly intrigued by the idea of 'une prose cadencée' (Voltaire, 'Des beaux arts', in Moland 14, 1878: 544). Fénelon, unlike La Motte, is allowed into the inner sanctum of Voltaire's *Temple du goût*, on condition that he removes any reference on the title page to 'poème en prose' (Voltaire, *Le Temple du goût*, in Moland 8, 1877: 577). La Motte, too, admires *Télémaque*, and claims that it is partly the

---

[21] Finch points out that there were 173 editions of *Télémaque* by 1800, 253 by 1820, a total of 87 imitations, 8 transpositions, in whole or in part, into French verse, 7 translations, in whole or part, into Latin verse, and a quantity of tragedies, operas, ballets, and 'héroïdes', inspired by portions of its subject matter (Finch, *The Sixth Sense*, 1966: 45, 318–19).

inspiration for his own *Œdipe en prose*. He regrets that he is obliged, partly through his own cowardice, to do to his prose what no one would dream of doing to Fénelon's (La Motte, *Discours à l'occasion de la tragédie d'Œdipe*, 1754: 396). When Fénelon comments directly on the issue of form and versification, he tends to compromise between the positions of La Motte and Voltaire. He recognizes that poetry cannot simply be equated with versification: 'toute l'Ecriture est pleine de poësie dans les endroits même où l'on ne trouve aucune trace de versification' (Fénelon, *Lettre à l'Académie*, 1970: 62–3). He does not, however, think that the solution is to cultivate a precious taste for novel images: 'je veux un beau si naturel qu'il n'ait aucun besoin de me surprendre par sa nouveauté'; and he illustrates his point by saying that there is nothing novel about a ray of sunshine, but it will always be beautiful (Fénelon, *Lettre à l'Académie*, 1970: 78). The compromise he suggests is to 'mettre nos poëtes un peu plus au large [. . .] pour leur donner le moyen d'être plus exacts sur le sens et sur l'harmonie' (p. 67). The extra latitude which he proposes is evident in *Télémaque*. Marmontel later remarks on the suggestive euphony of his style: '[la lettre "l"] semble communiquer sa mollesse aux syllabes dures qu'elle sépare: "On fit couler des flots d'huile douce et luisante sur tous les membres de mon corps". L'l, si j'ose le dire, est elle même comme une huile onctueuse, qui, répandue dans le style, en adoucit le frottement' (Marmontel, 'Harmonie du style', 1819: 16). There is a second feature remarked upon as much by modern critics as Voltaire, when he notices a certain 'prose cadencée' in *Télémaque*. It is difficult to read passages such as the description of Calypso's cave, or of Télémaque's shield, without becoming aware that there is a certain rhythmic regularity in his prose.[22] The style owes something to the Homeric tendency for long description, paratactic constructions and asyndeton, but any influence from Greek does not disturb the reader's impression of refined French composition.

[22] For Calypso's cave, see Le Brun's edition, 1995: 34; and Télémaque's shield, 1995: 288. Clayton divides the first passage into regular verse (*The Prose Poem in French Literature of the Eighteenth Century*, 1936: 208–9); Lote does the same for the first page of *Télémaque* (*Histoire du vers*, 1992, Vol. VII: 138). Grammont points out, however, that the exercise is deeply problematic on linguistic grounds (Grammont, 'Le rythme et l'harmonie chez quelques prosateurs du XVIIIe siècle', 1938).

Fénelon's contribution to debates about literary language is not, however, the only search for reconciliation; there is a body of linguistic theory which is just as innovative in its way, and perhaps a better mark of the particular significance of preciosity in this period. Olivet's *Prosodie*, Girard's *Synonymes*, and Dumarsais's *Des tropes* adopt Fénelon's principle that there should be more latitude accorded to literary expression, but the object of their studies is also to prescribe the precise limits of this latitude. The result is a compromise between conflicting doctrines; like La Motte, for example, they do not refer to the canon of great authors in order to justify their literary theories, and yet like Voltaire, they think that there are indeed objective standards.

When the ideas of these three thinkers are considered in their contemporary context, they seem a remarkable reflection of the controversy surrounding literary language. Girard writes the first vernacular dictionary of synonyms, Dumarsais writes the first specialized work on tropes, and Olivet's description of French prosody is unparalleled in its detail. Together, they are a gauge of the contemporary interest in the problem of literary language, and also the best illustration of why it is sometimes said that the 'querelles littéraires' of the late seventeenth and early eighteenth century had such a profound aesthetic influence on the eighteenth century. Naves says of the 'querelle' involving La Motte: 'à la bien examiner dans son temps et dans son milieu, elle n'est autre chose qu'une crise du classicisme français, ou plus exactement l'apparition et la prise de conscience progressive des contradictions internes de ce classicisme' (Naves, *Le Goût de Voltaire*, 1938: 8).[23] The linguistic theory of the early eighteenth century is a sign of this 'prise de conscience'.

In itself interest in the nuances of synonymy, catachresis, or extended metaphor is not peculiar to these linguistic thinkers, or indeed to the *nouveaux précieux*. One thinks of La Bruyère's *Les Caractères*, where psychological insight is often derived from close synonyms.[24] Or Fontenelle's extended metaphors in *Lettres*

---

[23] For similar comments, see also Lote, *Histoire du vers français* (1992): Vol. VII: 82, 143; Mercier, 'La Querelle de la poésie au début du XVIIIe siècle' (1969): 20, 45.

[24] See, e.g., La Bruyère, *Les Caractères*, II, 17 (1990): 101.

galantes, a work which was in vogue in the first half of the eighteenth century.[25] Others before Voltaire and Gamaches have advised tasteful caution with the use of metaphors.[26] The supposed clarity of literary language is the concern of any writer who is sensitive to the tension between literary convention and invention, and these questions of preciosity and formalism will always be contentious. The peculiar aspect of the early eighteenth century, however, is the degree to which literary debate is accompanied by quite innovative linguistic theory. Naves is probably right to say that the abstract discussion of literature, of 'la poësie en général' which La Motte and others encouraged, leads debate away from practical issues of 'taste', and more towards what we call in retrospect issues of 'aesthetics' (Naves, *Le Goût de Voltaire*, 1938: 104). The purpose of the rest of this chapter will be to consider the involvement of linguistic theory in the light of these literary debates.

2.5   *Girard's compromise:* Synonymes françois

Girard's dictionary of synonyms is the first of its kind, and perhaps the first neoclassical 'art d'écrire' in which there is no reference to the authority of named authors. Since, in this sense, it reads very much like a modern dictionary, it is easy to overlook the fact that in the eighteenth century, literary references would have been conspicuous by their absence.[27] In their place he proposes a notion of the 'valeur' of words, or 'le plus ou moins d'énergie, d'étendue, de précision, de composition, ou de simplicité que les idées peuvent avoir' (Girard, *Synonymes françois*, 1718; 1737: p. xiv). The word 'valeur' is deceptively close to the recurrent contemporary idea of language as a treasure chest and words as gold coins which can be counted out like so many tokens; Vaugelas, Bouhours, and Cordemoy all use this image to describe the 'richesse' of language. Girard's

---

[25] See, e.g., Fontenelle, *Lettres galantes*, Lettre VI (1961): 47. Daniel Delafarge points out that there were five editions of *Œuvres diverses* between 1701 and 1715, three *Œuvres complètes*, in 1715, 1724, and 1728, and that the *Lettres galantes* is included in all of them (Fontenelle, *Lettres galantes*, 1961: preface).

[26] Bouhours, *Entretiens d'Ariste et d'Eugène* (1771): 73.

[27] Girard's dictionary is considered sufficiently 'modern' to appear in the bibliographies of most current dictionaries of synonymy.

dictionary, however, is founded on a different principle, that what matters is not that language uses tokens, each with a discrete value, but that it is a system of related values.[28] Synonyms are a prime example of this, and Girard proposes, therefore, that instead of counting out the gold coins from the treasure chest that we weigh them carefully in relation to each other. He points out that this is the only legitimate way of studying synonymy, because it is based on semantic resemblance, not complete identity. There can never be synonyms in the absolute sense: 'si on la suppose [la synonymie] parfaite, ensorte que, dans quelque circonstance & dans quelque occasion que ce soit, il n'y ait pas plus de choix à faire, pour le sens [. . .] qu'il n'y en a, pour le goût, entre les gouttes d'eau d'une même source, [. . .] alors je dis qu'il n'y a point de mots synonymes dans aucune Langue' (Girard, *Synonymes*, 1737: pp. xii–xiii). Synonymy does not fit into a rigid iso-structural theory of one word for one meaning, or in Saussure's terms, one 'signifiant' for one 'signifié', which tends to be the implication of the 'treasure chest' idea of language. On the contrary, synonymy is the phenomenon of more than one 'signifiant' for each 'signifié', with the consequence that relative value is more important than absolute value when defining meaning. Accordingly, Girard replaces the image of the treasure chest with the image of the 'nuancier', the shades of colour which are related to one main colour: 'je n'entens point par *Langue* un amas général & monstrueux de tous les mots [. . .] L'essence du Synonyme [est] dans une même idée principale, mais sujette à être diversifiée par des idées accessoires, à peu près comme une même couleur paroît sous diverses nuances' (Girard, *Synonymes*, 1737: p. xiii). 'Nuances' makes an interesting addition to the Aristotelian epistemological and rhetorical terminology of 'idées accessoires, idée principale', because it takes on a degree of Aristotelian logic and precision, but nevertheless remains a word for the indeterminate feeling we have that certain shades of colours are related to a single principal colour. The combination of 'nuances', with its subjective connotations, and 'idées accessoires, idée principale', with their epistemological rigour,

[28] Droixhe thinks that Girard's notion of 'valeur' is an important stage in the evolution from rationalism to structuralism ('L'Orientation structurale de la linguistique au XVIIIe siècle', 1971: 22).

is a way of suggesting that the slippery notion of synonymy complies with certain formal arrangements. The balance between the two implies that synonymy is not a frivolous exercise in preciosity, but that it cannot afford, either, to be a self-indulgent exercise at the whim of the writer. This curious blend of the objective and subjective informs the whole of Girard's methodology, because he has evidently a great talent for typology, but also a kind of psychological insight which would not look out of place alongside the character portraits of Marivaux or La Bruyère. His entry for 'Attraits, Appas, Charmes', for example, begins with a basic distinction: 'il me semble qu'il y a quelque chose de plus naturel dans les *attraits*; quelque chose qui tient plus de l'art dans les *appas*; quelque chose de plus fort & de plus extraordinaire dans les *charmes*.' The entry becomes more involved as he continues his distinction: 'le cœur de l'homme n'est guère ferme contre les *attraits* d'une jolie femme; il a bien de la peine à se defendre des *appas* d'une coquette; & il lui est impossible de résister aux *charmes* d'une beauté bienfaisante'. Later still, Girard seems more interested in the psychological and moral apparatus underpinning the synonyms than the synonyms themselves:

Je ne sai si ce que je vais dire sera goûté de tout le monde, mais je sens cette distinction, que je livre au jugement du lecteur [. . .] La vertu a des *attraits*, que les plus vicieux ne peuvent s'empêcher de sentir. Les biens de ce monde ont des *appas*, qui font que la cupidité triomphe souvent du devoir. Le plaisir a des *charmes*, qui le font rechercher par-tout, dans la vie retirée comme dans le grand monde, par le philosophe comme par le libertin, dans l'école même de la mortification comme dans celle de la volupté; c'est toujours lui qui fait le goût & qui décide du choix.

There is something surprising about an exercise in lexicography which engages in moral conjecture, but the speculative nature of some of his entries is part of the purpose of the dictionary to test the nuances to the limit to see what they reveal. In this way, he reconciles a lexicographer's vision of language with that of the precious writer, because an ideal of clarity and distinct meaning is reconciled with the practice of cultivating nuances. He neither denies the slippery nature of synonyms, nor allows them to escape completely the bounds of lexicography, and thus devises in effect a dictionary of slipper-iness. He satisfies the precious writer, because his dictionary is about how best to manipulate language, but also traditionalists, because by nature a dictionary no longer leaves the manipula-tion to the subjective whim of the author.

Other writers express an interest in synonymy, but none carries his ideas to the lengths of Girard's dictionary. Fénelon points to the essential problems in the opening pages of his *Lettre à l'Académie*, and Pons says he intends one day to write his own dictionary.[29] Girard's *Synonymes* was by far the most suc-cessful of its type, re-edited several times by Girard himself, republished throughout the eighteenth century, and largely responsible for his election to the *Académie française* in 1744. Part of the reason for the success of his dictionary must be that he made preciosity palatable for a wider audience. Voltaire thinks that it is 'un livre utile de définitions' (Voltaire, 'Esprit', in Moland 19, 1878: 15), and some of his definitions in the *Dictionnaire philosophique* seem close enough to Girard's to suggest direct influence or at least indirect inspiration (com-pare for example Voltaire's three articles 'Finesse', 'Fierté' and 'Gloire' with Girard's definitions). Diderot's *Encyclopédie* articles 'Adresse' and 'Attention' are also almost identical word-for-word to Girard's, and in another article, 'Agréable, gracieux, considéré', Diderot refers to Girard by name. Similarly the arti-cles 'Vénération, respect' and 'Tolérer, souffrir, permettre' in the *Encyclopédie* by Jaucourt refer directly to Girard. The success of his dictionary may owe something to the less polemical, more conceptual manner in which he approaches the contentious question of preciosity and synonymy; a 'prise de conscience' of the issues that appealed more broadly than the partisan exchanges of the 'querelles'.

2.6 *Dumarsais's compromise:* Traité des tropes

Dumarsais's *Traité des tropes* (1730) is a curious and original work for a number of reasons. The title declares an interest, not

---

[29] Fénelon, *Lettre à l'Académie* (1970): 31; Pons, *Dissertation sur les langues en général* (1738): 172.

in rhetoric, nor in figurative language, but in a smaller category still called 'tropes'. The currency of the word in the eighteenth century may owe something to Dumarsais's treatise, since the word is not attested by the *Académie française* until 1740, and Dumarsais himself illustrates its obscurity by telling the story of the man who thought that 'Histoire des Tropes' was the story of a tribal people (Dumarsais, *Des tropes*, 1988: 59). The second striking aspect is the large number of categories of tropes which Dumarsais lists, but which he makes no real attempt to present in any systematic order. Soublin points out that the contemporary standards are Cicero and Quintilian, who enumerate between eight and thirteen categories, and Beauzée in the *Encyclopédie* who reduces them to only three. In comparison, Dumarsais's list of thirty tropes, his 'brique-à-braque de collectionneur', is quite unparalleled and never imitated (Soublin, '13→30→3', 1979: 41–2). The third surprise is to find an inventory of categories which includes such unconventional tropes as 'allusion, onomatopée' and 'euphémisme', and also grammatical rather than rhetorical categories such as 'équivoque, hypallage', pronouns and prepositions.

It is clear from Dumarsais's unconventional approach that he is not primarily interested in *dispositio*, which is the part of rhetoric which provides a taxonomy of language, nor is he primarily interested in making value judgements with respect to correct style. His specific concern is defined in the long title to his treatise: *Traité des tropes, ou des différents sens dans lesquels on peut prendre un même mot dans une même langue*. He studies the system of association which allows meaning to be transferred between words, with the consequence, pointed out by numerous modern critics, that *Des tropes* is as much concerned with semantics as it is with rhetoric.[30] Any mechanism whereby words change their meaning, whether by simple wordplay (such as 'allusion') or grammar, are included in *Des tropes*, to the exclusion of those rhetorical devices which have no semantic implication (such as parataxis, asyndeton, prosopopoeia). Dumarsais's interests are very narrow from the point of view of traditional rhetoric, so much so that Genette identifies his work

---

[30] Todorov, *Théorie du symbole* (1977): 88; Genette, *La Rhétorique restreinte* (1970): 159.

as a crucial stage in 'la restriction généralisée' of modern rhetoric, because he emphasizes the principle of analogy to the exclusion of almost all the Classical categories of discourse (Genette, *La Rhétorique restreinte,* 1970: 158–9).

There are a variety of reasons for this contraction of interest which have partly to do with the pre-eminence of John Locke's philosophy of language, and partly to do with debates about preciosity in literary expression. In the first case, the radical influence of Lockeian epistemology on the eighteenth century is often remarked upon by modern critics,[31] but it is also notable that his influence is largely unacknowledged by writers in France until Condillac does so in his *L'Origine des connoissances humaines* in 1746.[32] Dumarsais makes no mention of him in *Des tropes* or in his other linguistic writings. Nevertheless, Locke's principles permeate his method. Locke assumed, in essence, that the origin of knowledge lies in the mental manipulation of sense impressions, forming first simple ideas, and thereafter complex, or abstract ideas. By implication, language does not have a primary role in the genesis of knowledge, only the nominal role of designating ideas which already exist. Consequently, the primacy of ideas over language means that it is inappropriate to analyse language in isolation, according to, for example, the principles of rhetorical *dispositio.* Rhetoric is only of secondary importance relative to ideas. Although Dumarsais does not name Locke, there is a chapter in *Des tropes* entitled 'Sens abstrait, sens concret' which is the clearest indication of his influence. Some of the statements in this chapter bear the hallmark of Locke's Sensualism and Associationism: 'les impressions que nous recevons des objets, et les réflexions que nous faisons sur ces impression par l'usage de la vie et par la méditation, sont la source de toutes nos idées' (Dumarsais, *Des tropes,* 1988: 228). There is some evidence to suggest, therefore, that Dumarsais's novel approach to tropes derives partly from the unacknowledged influence of a generally prevalent contemporary interest in Lockeian language theory.

There is another obvious and acknowledged source of inspiration, however, which is the controversy surrounding precios-

---

[31] See e.g. Hazard, *La Crise de la conscience européenne* (1961): 221–31.
[32] Pierre Coste is the first to translate Locke's *An Essay Concerning Human Understanding* in 1700.

ity. Dumarsais takes a non-partisan view, arguing that preciosity is not a new phenomenon: 'on peut dire que chaque siècle a pu avoir ses critiques et son *Dictionnaire néologique*. Si quelques personnes disent aujourd'hui, avec raison ou sans fondement, *qu'il règne dans le langage une affectation puérile: que le style frivole et recherché passe jusqu'aux tribunaux les plus graves,* Cicéron a fait la même plainte de son temps' (Dumarsais, *Des tropes,* 1988: 187–8). There will always be a conservative reaction to novel literary style, and Dumarsais says that his intention is neither to agree nor disagree with the value judgements of Desfontaines's *Dictionnaire néologique.* His aim is rather to take note of and consider dispassionately the phenomenon itself: 'une critique sage, exempte de passion et de fanatisme, est bien plus utile' (Dumarsais, *Des tropes,* 1988: 187). He can allow himself this impartial approach because he is one of the first to believe that tropes are intrinsic to language, and not simply a rhetorical ornament or supplement when ordinary language is lacking: 'dans tous les temps et dans tous les lieux où il y a eu des hommes, il y a eu de l'imagination, des passions, et idées accessoires, et par conséquent des tropes' (Dumarsais, *Des tropes,* 1988: 187). He is certainly the first to make this belief the guiding principle of all his linguistic theory. Consequently, he does not wish to identify their proper use with any dominant literary convention: 'nous nous servons de tropes, non parce que les anciens s'en sont servis; mais parce que nous sommes hommes comme eux' (p. 187). There ought, therefore, to be a way of transcending usage, of finding an abstract, conceptual way of discussing tropes: 'les règles ne doivent point être faites sur l'ouvrage d'aucun particulier; elles doivent être puisées dans le bon sens et dans la nature' (p. 187).

These intentions help to explain the features of *Des tropes* which seem surprising in comparison with other treatises on rhetoric. Firstly, in order to focus more precisely on the issue of preciosity, 'clarté' and making sense, Dumarsais writes only on tropes, that is, only on figures which affect sense. Secondly, in order to understand preciosity in the wider context of semantics, he expands the traditional inventory of tropes to include any way in which words change their sense, whether it be by grammar or wordplay. Thirdly, since he is primarily interested in the phenomenon of transferred sense, he spends very little time defining a hierarchy of tropes which would, for example, subordinate metalepsis and synecdoche to the major category of metonymy. Instead, he presents them as 'un brique-à-braque de collectionneur', in which new tropes such as 'allusion' or 'équivoque' are coequal with established categories such as catachresis or metaphor. He does, in fact, briefly discuss the question of hierarchy in a chapter entitled 'De la subordination des tropes', but thinks that it is largely an irrelevant issue.

It may be useful, therefore, to read *Des tropes* in the light of contemporary literary debates. La Motte's keen use of catachresis, for example, may be one reason why it is Dumarsais's longest entry, and why his treatment is particularly detailed. The controversial nature of catachresis may also have encouraged him to suggest a Sensualist explanation which transcends literary debates. According to his theory, it is undoubtedly a fundamental and profoundly natural trope, because it is involved in the basic semiotic process of language acquisition. It is essentially what a child does when it learns to associate the object 'bread' with the word *bread* by a habitual correlation of the respective visual and aural mental impressions. It only becomes problematic, according to Dumarsais, when for a host of reasons, the mental association is more ambiguous than this. Notwithstanding this risk, however, he is unwilling to distinguish emphatically between abuse and proper usage, on the principle that he is more interested in the phenomenon than the relative merits of catachresis. He displays the same restraint when he discusses prepositions, on the basis that abuse and usage are two aspects of the same process: 'chaque préposition a sa première signification; elle a sa destination principale, son premier sens propre; et ensuite, par extension, par imitation, par abus, en un mot, par catachrèse, on la fait servir à marquer d'autres rapports' (Dumarsais, *Des tropes*, 1988: 90). It is his objective interest in any semantic process, 'extension, imitation' or 'abus' which distinguishes his opinions from those of his contemporaries who had a greater tendency to make value judgements, and this has led some modern critics to contend that *Des tropes* is the first study of modern semantics.[33] Dumarsais

---

[33] Todorov, *Théorie du symbole* (1977): 88; Genette, *La Rhétorique restreinte* (1970): 159; Soublin's introduction to *Des tropes* (1988): 11–12.

assumes that the phenomenon of catachresis is so pervasive and historically so deeply rooted in language, that it would be difficult to criticize its modern, most recent manifestations. He describes how even the most innocuous phrase such as 'dans le doute' is a catachretic construction, based on the primary meaning of 'dans', which relates to a physical place, for example 'dans une maison' (Dumarsais, *Des tropes*, 1988: 90). The effect of grammaticalizing tropes in this way is to place catachresis in a much broader, semantic context than would traditionally be the case, and by implication to discourage the tendency in literary 'querelles' to indulge in easy value judgements.

It also implies that, if Dumarsais allows such latitude to traditionally the most powerful trope, perhaps also he is prepared to consider those semantic devices which are not traditionally considered tropes at all. Two of these new categories are called 'allusion' and 'sens équivoque, sens louche', both of which include wordplay. Dumarsais explains each by reference to related semantic phenomena, with two consequences. Firstly, there is no intrinsic difference between wordplay and other tropes; secondly, it is possible to make an objective judgement of 'good' and 'bad' wordplay according to certain principles which he proposes. There might be a reason, therefore, to accept some but not all of 'le marivaudage', which, as we pointed out earlier, otherwise seems to be an amalgam of comic punning and serious semiotics.

Dumarsais succeeds in understanding 'allusion' in an unusually wide semantic context by taking advantage of the double meaning of the term. It has partly the traditional sense of 'jeu de mots', and partly the modern sense of 'indirect reference'.[34] It suggests to him that perhaps the criterion for a proper 'jeu de mots' ought to be that it relates to a meaning outside the text, that it refers to a definite extra-textual 'idée accessoire'. On this assumption, a 'jeu de mots' would be part of the same semantic phenomenon as allegory or proper nouns in a poem, which also connote extra-textual meaning. Hence, there is

---

[34] Soublin notes Dumarsais's novel use of 'allusion' in her edition of *Des tropes* (1988): 280 n. Cherrier means it only in the sense of jeu de mot in the re-edition of his *L'Homme inconnu* in 1722, entitled: *Polisonniana, ou recueil de Turlupinades, Quolibets, Rebus, jeux de mots, Allusion* [. . .].

nothing intrinsically incorrect in wordplay, since it operates according to the same semantic principles as certain other literary forms. The only pertinent criterion is that the 'jeu de mots' should connote a clear extra-textual meaning. On this principle, he rejects 'jeux de mots' if they are based only on a resemblance of sound, such as the 'calembour', but allows those which play on ideas at the same time, such as the following pun on 'laurier' in a request to the King to relinquish any claim to the author's island in the Rhône:

> Qu'est-ce en effet pour toi, grand monarque des Gaules,
> Qu'un peu de sable et de gravier?
> Que faire de mon île? il n'y croît que des saules:
> Et tu n'aimes que le laurier.
> (Dumarsais, *Des tropes*, 1988: 153)

The verse is an example of what his contemporaries might have called 'esprit', or clever punning. The distinction between 'calembours' and 'esprit' is not new, but Dumarsais's innovation is to base it on something other than an indeterminate idea of 'taste'. Instead, it is justified by a specific semantic mechanism which Dumarsais has defined as 'allusion', and hence also by its place in a semantic framework alongside other figures like 'allegory'.

The question of the 'calembour' arises in another new category called 'sens équivoque, sens louche', which includes all those constructions whose meaning remains ambiguous, however much they are studied. They are aspects of language which are 'louche', because the intellectual eye is sent in two semantic directions at once, like looking at someone who is cross-eyed: 'louche est ici un terme métaphorique; car, comme les personnes louches paraissent regarder d'un côté pendant qu'elles regardent d'un autre, de même, dans les constructions louches, les mots semblent avoir un certain rapport, pendant qu'ils en ont un autre' (Dumarsais, *Des tropes*, 1988: 200). In this category, Dumarsais places homonyms and homophones, which were the basis for many of the 'calembours' of Marivaux and Bièvre, but also a number of grammatical forms. The use of the third person pronoun, for example, very quickly becomes ambiguous, if there is more than one proper noun in the context. There are also elliptical styles which are grammatically misleading, as in the following verbal ellipsis from Corneille: 'L'amour n'est qu'un plaisir, et l'honneur un devoir', which is ambiguous unless we instinctively read 'et l'honneur EST un devoir' (Dumarsais, *Des tropes*, 1988: 201). By being classified together with these other examples of 'sens louche', the 'calembours' are rescued from the lowly status of a stylistic anomaly and explained, instead, as part of a common semantic feature of language which even Corneille uses.

Dumarsais's method is very much that of the systematic observer, noticing a correlation between phenomena which others, critics in the 'querelles', treat in isolation. *Des tropes* is a 'prise de conscience' in the manner of Girard's *Synonymes*, but in this case with regard to the issue of figurative language. As such, it lends credence by its very title to the *précieux* emphasis on tropes, but provides also a semantic containment theory to counter the wilful excesses of some authors.

2.7 *Olivet's compromise:* Prosodie

Olivet's procedure in *Traité de la prosodie françoise* is recognizable from Girard's *Synonymes* and Dumarsais's *Des tropes*. He too considers a particular issue arising from literary debate, and scrutinizes the theoretical implications more than the practice of great authors. Olivet's particular interest is the value of versification, its origins in the French language, and its relation to versification in Classical Latin and Greek poetry. *Prosodie* is an astonishingly detailed description of the sounds of the French language, more detailed even than Bernard Lamy's account in Book III of *L'Art de parler* (1675), and a kind of manual and manifesto for its use in poetry. It thus contradicts La Motte's contention, that versification is a non-essential and purely conventional aspect of poetry, but it does so only by trying to come to terms with an issue which had long troubled those who sought to understand why versification is important in French poetry.

The poetic model since the Renaissance had been the metrics of Latin and Greek poetry, and the traditional answer to critics like La Motte would be that respect for the Ancients demands that French poetry, like Classical poetry, should be versified.

The problem with this answer is that French is patently unsuited to Classical metrics; there is no comparable system of long and short syllables which can be marshalled into metrical feet, and even if there were, the word order of French is sufficiently fixed to inhibit metrical versification. Nobody seriously denied in Olivet's time that French can only have a syllabic versification, although there were attempts in the eighteenth century to write in Homeric hexameters.[35] Nobody denies that there is a difference, but neither can anyone suggest why, therefore, French should be versified. Imitation of Classical culture seems to lead to intellectual paralysis; much as some would like to justify the specific merits of French versification, they cannot because they are held back by their attachment to Classical models.

Olivet's compromise, and his escape from the paralysis, is to retain the importance in Classical versification of marshalled sound, but to examine the French language in particular to discover what poetic tools it can offer. He discovers a syllable system which is not as clear-cut as Latin, but in which there are nevertheless noticeable syllable patterns, categorized as 'brève, très-brève, long, très-long', and 'douteux'. He is aware that it is not possible to prescribe rules for the subtleties of French prosody as it is for more rigorous Classical prosody, and so instead he appeals to the sensitivity of the listener's ear: 'rien n'est déterminé, ni préscrit, cela est vrai. Tout est donc arbitraire; cela est faux. Ici nos Métaphysiciens auroient beau se récrier: ils ont à faire à un Juge qui en sait plus qu'eux, & qui même pousse l'orgueil encore plus loin qu'eux. Quel est-il? l'oreille' (Olivet, *Prosodie*, 1737: 337–8). Olivet thus compromises with La Motte by appealing less to established practice and traditional rules of versification, and more to the poet's ear. After listening with his best poet's ear, however, Olivet disagrees with La Motte, because he hears a gamut of refined distinctions which constitute in themselves the principles of euphonic versification which La Motte found so unacceptable.

Olivet makes a long list of syllables of different lengths and vowel quality, twenty-eight pages in total. He finds them from wherever he can; sometimes they are pronunciations which are

---

[35] See e.g. Turgot, *Sur la Prosodie de la langue française et la Versification métrique*, which includes the poem 'Invocation à la muse d'Homère' (Turgot, *Œuvres*, 1810: Vol. 9, 50–61).

almost obsolete in his time, sometimes on the contrary, they are very modern. He maintains, for example, the distinction which disappears some time in the mid-eighteenth century, between final masculine syllables with and without 's', so that 'sac' is shorter than 'sacs', 'cour' is shorter than 'cours' (the reverse distinction is maintained in modern French 'œuf/œufs').[36] In another case, he adopts the eighteenth-century innovation that /e/ in the tonic syllable, before a consonant and mute 'e', should be relatively open, so lengthening the syllable. Thus, 'alène' is longer than 'haleine', 'lesse' is longer than 'laisse', 'scène' is longer than 'Seine'. It also means that, strictly speaking, 'verre' and 'verd' do not rhyme.[37] The entry for each syllable is long and detailed, like the following for 'an':

Très-bref dans ruban, turban, bouracan, pélican, carcan, encans, ouragan, relan, élan, ortolan, merlan, brelan, talisman, Pan, timpan, trépan, cran, écran, cadran, safran, bougran, tan, orvéitan, Parmesan. Un peu moins bref dans les mots suivans, parce que l'A y est plus ouvert: an, ban, ocean, roman, vétéran, tyran, van, faisan, artisan, courtisan, partisan, paysan, alezan, bilan, plan, charlatan. Tous les pluriels, longs: romans, courtisans. Au milieu de mot, il allonge la syllabe: blanche, danse, chante &c. (Olivet, *Prosodie*, 1737: 298)

Olivet's justification for the intricate and linguistically questionable nature of his exercise, is that French has to make the most of oratorical prosody, since there is no way it can match the linguistic prosody of the Ancients. Oratory is, of course, a more subjective art than Classical prosody, but Olivet thinks that the question is often wrongly posed. It is not a matter of whether French can equal Classical prosody, but whether it has its own native devices: 'il suffit d'examiner philosophiquement, si c'est un mérite à une langue d'être *chantante* par elle-même, & si ce n'est pas assez qu'elle soit de nature à recevoir toutes les inflexions de voix, qui peuvent lui être commandée par la raison, ou par la passion' (Olivet, *Prosodie*, 1737: 279). In effect, he turns a perceived failing of French into a virtue, because it is not constrained like the Classical languages by a fixed linguistic prosody. French prosody is a more adaptable device, better able to follow the ebb and flow of emotions, and perhaps

---

[36] Seguin, *La Langue française au XVIIIe siècle* (1972): 43; and Brunot, *Histoire de la Langue française* (1932): Vol. 6.2, i: 988.   [37] See ibid., 978.

it would be inhibited by the fixed nature of Classical prosody: 'une prononciation variée pour obéir à des syllabes matérielles, sera-t-elle plus mélodieuse, qu'une prononciation variée pour obéir aux mouvemens de l'ame? Comment faisoient les Grecs, lorsqu'il arrivoit, [...] que l'accent prosodique se trouva en contradiction avec l'accent oratoire?' (Olivet, *Prosodie*, 1737: 279). 'L'accent oratoire' is the expressive part of the voice, the manifestation of emotion, often called in the eighteenth century 'l'accent de la passion'. Olivet shares some of the principles of those in the 'querelle des bouffons' who claim that French is more suited to musical arrangement than Italian, because French has no fixed tonic accent, and hence does not so inhibit musical expression. In both cases, the major concern is the expression of sensibility, which in opera is thought to be primarily the role of the music, and in language is the role of oratorical accent.[38]

Olivet believes, therefore, that there can be a distinctive kind of French versification, based on the combination of a refined linguistic prosody and a relatively free oratorical prosody. The two would seem mutually incompatible, in the sense that linguistic prosody is intrinsic to the language, while oratorical prosody is a modification of language in order to reflect sense. And yet they come together in what Louis Racine is later to call 'l'harmonie imitative'.[39] Olivet demonstrates with a verse from Boileau's *Le Lutrin*:

> Et lasse de parler, succombant sous l'effort,
> Soupire, étend les bras, ferme l'œil, & s'endort
> (Olivet, *Prosodie*, 1737: 325)

'Soupire' has the oral quality of a sigh, with a short syllable followed by a long syllable. The action of extending the arms is at first abrupt, and then slow and continuous, like the short /en/ of 'étend', and the two long syllables in 'les bras'. Sleep overtakes us quickly with the three short syllables in 'ferme l'œil', and deeply in the two final long syllables of 's'endort' (Olivet,

---

[38] See Cannone, *Philosophies de la musique* (1990): 52.

[39] Louis Racine: 'l'harmonie du discours consiste donc en deux choses: dans l'arrangement des mots, ce qui j'appellerai *l'Harmonie Mechanique*; & dans le rapport de cet arrangement avec les pensées, ce qui j'appellerai *l'Harmonie Imitative*' (*Réflexions sur la poésie*, 1750: Vol. V, 108–9).

Prosodie, 1737: 326). 'L'harmonie imitative' works by a strategic, or oratorical use of the gamut of refined distinctions which Olivet defines in *Prosodie*. He says that it cannot be prescriptive, but that it is up to the poet to make appropriate use of the intrinsic prosodic system of the French language. The best poets will do this almost without thinking: 'ce que je croirois volontiers, c'est que la Nature, quand elle a formé un grand Poëte, un grand Orateur, le dirige par des ressorts cachez, qui le rendent docile à un art, dont lui-même il ne se doute pas' (Olivet, *Prosodie*, 1737: 327). The idea, expressed here, that the formal conventions of poetry are effortlessly overcome by true genius, is not new, but the notable feature of Olivet's *Prosodie* is that it goes much further than before in trying to demonstrate those features which risk being taken for granted. It is designed to reveal the 'ressorts cachez', to go behind the scenes of poetic performance and account for the beauty of artifice. In the process, it does not entirely abandon the linguistic model of Classical versification, because Olivet still insists on describing French in terms of long and short syllables, but it does consider how best to adapt it to the nature of French versification; in Olivet's words, how best to 'digest' Classical poetics.

Like the works of Girard and Dumarsais, it is a careful analysis of a contentious issue arising from literary 'querelles', and it later transpires, a direct reply to La Motte's belief that versification is artificial. In the 1767 edition of *Prosodie*, Olivet admits that it was La Motte's idea that 'l'harmonie dans le discours n'étoit qu'une chimère' which led him to write his treatise: 'il étoit temps, & plus que temps, de réveiller le souvenir de la prosodie, & de l'harmonie' (Olivet, *Prosodie*, 1767: preface). His *Prosodie*, therefore, is a less neutral contribution to debate than the works of Girard and Dumarsais, but nonetheless, a sensitive investigation of a troubling issue; the poetic quality of the French language. If, as is La Motte's contention, poetry is associated too closely with features such as versification and rhyme, which plainly do not occur in normal French, then poetry seems an artificial construction. Voltaire makes a related comment at the end of the preface to his *Œdipe*, republished in 1730 to counter La Motte's *Œdipe*. He implies that English is a stress-timed language, unlike French which is syllable-timed, so that there is a natural rhythm in English which means that it can more easily be said to be intrinsically poetic: '[il] se fait sentir des syllabes longues & brèves, qui soutiennent encore l'harmonie sans besoin de rimes' (Voltaire, Œdipe, 1730: preface). If French verse can be shown to be an extension of natural devices in the language itself, like metrical rhythm is of the English language, then the French language can be said to be 'poetic'. Olivet engages with this question, and tries to show how versification is a way of maximizing the natural expressive potential of the French language.

In retrospect, it may be that his attachment to the Classical tradition, 'digested' or otherwise, holds back the progress of poetic theory in France, because he has not understood what Scoppa was the first to point out in 1811, that the natural 'poetry' of French is based on a tonic accent at the end of each syntactic unit.[40] The way to maximize its expressive potential in verse would be to abandon the traditional Alexandrine, that is, to dislodge the hemistich as the basic rhythmic unit, and to compose in Romantic 'alexandrin trimètre', or indeed in post-Romantic 'vers libéré', which would allow the poet to assemble irregular combinations of syllables according to the desired accentual rhythm. But these solutions are not available to the eighteenth century. Olivet and contemporary thinkers have to agree with Rousseau when he says that 'le français n'a pas d'accent', and look elsewhere for the natural poetry of French (Rousseau, Discours sur l'origine des langues, 1995: 390–1). The search is troubling, and the French have perhaps been 'intermittently embarrassed by this question for a long time' (Scott, French Verse-Art, 1980: 27–8). And yet the troublesome nature of the question encourages interesting innovation, such as the peculiarly French idea of the prose poem which bridges the gap between prose and verse, or in the present case, the idea of 'l'harmonie imitative' which bridges the gap between Classical and French prosody. Olivet and La Motte are both responsible for highlighting these ideas, La Motte with his prose poems and Olivet with his prosody, but there is a degree of right and wrong in both of their theories. Scoppa's discoveries mean that La Motte is mistaken to argue that poetry is entirely artificial, but they mean also that Olivet has misunderstood exactly how the

---

[40] Scoppa, Les Vrais Principes de la versification (1811).

French language is poetic. Olivet does, however, recognize the threat posed by La Motte's ideas to poetry, and attempts for the first time to 'prove' 'l'harmonie imitative' in what Alexis François has called one of the most ambitious enterprises of the century.[41]

Conclusion

Girard, Dumarsais, and Olivet are manifestly operating in an intellectual atmosphere which disregards more and more the idea of inherited convention, and demands instead a greater understanding of the principles of literary expression. It is worth remembering in this respect that they are writing shortly after the period Paul Hazard has called 'la crise de la conscience européenne', and that poetry comes to symbolize for many the attachment to doctrine and the denial of human nature and reason.[42] In these circumstances, 'usage' is an unsustainable criterion for good writing, because it is apt to incline towards blind obedience to convention and artistically paralyzing respect for past authors.

An alternative criterion which is much discussed by modern critics is 'taste', derived from a compound of those universal human values of sensibility and reason which appeal so greatly to an era trying to liberate itself from weight of doctrine. And yet 'taste' seems radically inappropriate to the works of these three writers. No matter how cultivated, it still implies some of its primary sense of 'spontaneous sensation', and it suggests also the kind of direct involvement with practical issues which is contrary to the theoretical intentions of Girard, Dumarsais, and Olivet. In the contemporary terminology, theirs is a genuine 'philosophical' enterprise, bound up indirectly with literary debate, but reaching out to more speculative goals. It is for this reason that they are all innovative in their way, and all quite curious, eccentric even. Girard's *Synonymes* is a logician's nightmare, a hall of mirrors where all words refer to other words,

---

[41] François says that Olivet's *Prosodie* is: 'un des plus beaux rêves, une des plus remarquables entreprises du siècle' (*Les Origines lyriques de la phrase moderne*, 1973: 29).

[42] Hazard, *La Crise de la conscience européenne* (1961).

and from which meaning never, in theory, escapes. Dumarsais's *Des tropes* is a motley assortment of new and old tropes, a curiosity shop of unexpected items in unpredictable places. Olivet's *Prosodie* is a minute anatomy of sounds, far beyond anything Molière's preceptor could imagine in *Le Bourgeois gentilhomme.* Eccentric or speculative, there is something in this approach which is less suited to the idea of 'taste', and more akin to a theoretical exploration of literary aesthetics. It derives, perhaps, from the rise of the 'philosophe' to a position of cultural dominance in the eighteenth century, at the expense of the 'homme de goût', the gentleman critic who despises their rational systems and theoretical methods.

The hybrid nature of these three abstract but literary studies on language makes them peculiarly conducive to reconciling the demands of literary conservatives with those of the 'nouveaux précieux'. They appeal to precious curiosity in new ways to fragment and manipulate language, but also to the conservative desire to see established boundaries. They are, in effect, containment theories for literary invention. The next chapter will deal with the same problem of allowing for both convention and invention, this time in the works of Etienne de Condillac, whose thoughts on language bring a great deal of reconciliation to these matters.

3

CONDILLAC'S IDEA OF 'NATURE'

Condillac is rarely given the credit he deserves for the range of
his interests, with the result that his recurring subject of inquiry
is often overlooked. His theories of knowledge, literary style,
psychology, and language are often treated in isolation, whereas
in fact, by his own admission, they are all different perspectives
on the same central issue, which is the representation of ideas.[1]
He acknowledges this in the long preface to the grammar he
writes for his tutee, the young Prince of Parma:

Tout ce qui je lui ai enseigné sur la génération des idées, sur les opérations de l'ame, sur la grammaire et sur l'art d'écrire, se réduit, pour
le fond, à un très-petit nombre d'idées qui se prêtent continuellement,
et qui ne sont l'objet de différentes études, que parce qu'on les con-
sidère sous différens points de vue. Qu'est-ce que la Grammaire? C'est
un système de mots qui représente le système des idées dans l'esprit
[. . .]; et l'Art d'Ecrire n'est que ce même système, porté au point de
perfection dont il est susceptible. En faisant successivement ses études,
on ne fait donc que revenir continuellement sur un même fond
d'idées. (Condillac, *Grammaire*, 1798: cxxxvii)

Condillac finds that an unavoidable issue in his recurring interest in the representation of ideas is artistic imitation, and this
becomes most apparent when we do justice to the range of his
interests and consider a number of his works in parallel with each
other: *Essai sur l'origine des connoissances humaines* (1746), the *Art
d'écrire* (published 1798), the *Grammaire* (published 1798) and
the *Traité des sensations* (1754; *La Langue des calculs* will be discussed in Chapter 5). What emerges from this global view of his
theories is an overriding concern with intellectual continuity,
from the origin of thought in sensation, to its most complex
development in modern literary style. The consequence of
this perspective is to reconcile many different and potentially

---

[1] On Condillac's theory of knowledge, see Marcos, 'Le Traité des sensations
d'Etienne Bonnot' (1986); on style, see Branca, 'L'Art d'écrire de Condillac'
(1980); on psychology, see Knight, *The Geometric Spirit* (1968); on language, see
Auroux, *La Sémiotique des encyclopédistes* (1979).

conflicting opinions about imitation in the arts. At its most emblematic, he expresses this in terms of a 'first' and a 'second' nature; different understandings of the 'nature' that art should represent are not isolated from each other but, on the contrary, they are simply different points on a continuum from the most primitive to the most advanced. They are different in some ways, but not discontinuous. Condillac's answer to the troubling question 'what does art imitate' is therefore the broadest conception of nature probably of any of his contemporaries.

Most of the discussion in this chapter will centre around the *Essai sur l'origine des connoissances*, and the *Art d'écrire*. They are quite different in some respects, because the first is an abstract study of epistemology and the second is a practical discussion of literary style. They come together, however, in their shared terminology and concepts, and it is this middle ground which we may call Condillac's aesthetic thought. He traces the intellectual progress of man, from the perception of raw sensation to the rational organization of ideas, through the key concepts of 'attention', 'intérêt', 'langage d'action', metaphor, and 'liaison des idées'. These concepts are interesting, not only because they illustrate Condillac's aesthetics, but also because contemporary literary writers make them the basis of their own aesthetics. The dramatic theory of Diderot and Beaumarchais is based partly on notions of 'intérêt' and 'langage d'action'; Rousseau is fascinated with figurative language; Diderot's art criticism depends partly on 'attention' and 'liaison des idées'; and Buffon also proposes a theory of 'liaison des idées' in literary style. It would be misleading to suggest that Condillac directly inspires their aesthetics, but his thinking does offer a remarkable synthesis of a wide range of ideas, and hence it is a potent model of reconciliation between otherwise dissimilar views. His theories are another example of how far the idea of imitation can be stretched to accommodate a variety of approaches.

3.1 Semiosis

Condillac first imagines how the origin of knowledge depends on a number of natural faculties inherent to any living being:

L'exercice des opérations de leur ame a été borné à celui de la perception et de la conscience, qui ne cesse point quand on est éveillé; à
celui de l'attention, qui avoit lieu toutes les fois que quelques perceptions les affectoient d'une manière plus particulière; à celui de
la reminiscence, quand des circonstances, qui les avoit frappés, se
représentoient à eux avant que les liaisons qu'elles avoient formées
eussent été détruites; et à un exercice fort peu étendu de l'imagination. (Condillac, *Essai*, 1798: 260)

The *sine qua non* of the primitive mind is that it is conscious that
it perceives the outside world, it is aware that it feels. It must
also, therefore, be aware of changes in perception, when it feels
differently, and this awareness Condillac calls 'attention'. When
perceptions change so quickly as to be almost concurrent, it is
possible for the mind to compare past with present, which he
calls 'reminiscence'. When perceptions are not concurrent, the
'imagination' has a limited ability to recall past perception and
compare with the present. Condillac looks to these fundamental faculties to understand the origin of all language, art, and
knowledge, and his intentions are consequently more ambitious than Charles Batteux, his contemporary, who deals only
with the origin of the arts, or John Locke half a century earlier
who discusses only the origin of knowledge and language.[2] The
hypothesis seems reductionist, but in the context of Condillac's
guiding principle of continuity, it is perhaps better understood
as radically developmental.

Among this primary group of intellectual faculties, it is 'attention' which is the most important instrument of change. It is
the ability to focus on a perception, on a change in perception,
or on past and present perception which makes possible a comparison and begins the long process of cognitive development.
The first step in this process is the formation of an idea when
man perceives simultaneously a need of some sort, like thirst,
and a means with which to satisfy it, like the sight of water.
'Attention' to both perceptions causes a temporary association
in the mind, which is the 'idée' that water quenches thirst, and
which lasts only as long as the thirst and the water are both perceived. The next time the man feels thirsty, his 'imagination'
may recall the image of water, and his 'attention' may form the

---

[2] Batteux, *Les Beaux-Arts réduits à un même principe* (1746); Locke, *An Essay Concerning Human Understanding* (1690).

same association as before, except that this time, both perceptions are in his mind; his 'imagination' directs his 'attention' to
a recalled image, and he is in effect free to form all the 'idées'
he wishes. This control over 'attention' is desirable, since
without it, we are at the whim of present experience: 'l'ame
[...] ne va donc d'un objet à l'autre qu'autant qu'elle est
entrainée par la force de l'impression que les choses font sur
elle' (Condillac, *Essai*, 1798: 85). When, on the contrary, it is
possible to fix our attention at will, Condillac compares the consequent act of 'réflexion' to studying a painting:

A la vue d'un tableau, par exemple, nous nous rappelons les connoissances que nous avons de la nature, et des règles qui apprennent
à l'imiter; et nous portons notre attention successivement de ce
tableau à ces connoissances et de ces connoissances à ce tableau, ou
tour-à-tour à ses différentes parties [...] Cette manière d'appliquer
de nous-même notre attention tour-à-tour à divers objets, ou aux différentes parties d'un seul; c'est ce qu'on appelle *réfléchir*. (Condillac,
Essai, 1798: 88–9)

This is the first of many occasions when Condillac draws on
analogies with art to explain his theory of knowledge, and each
time he does this it suggests that he understands the perception of art as a cognitive process related to cognition in general.
These analogies mean that we can fruitfully compare his theories of language and knowledge to his ideas about art in order
to understand his own aesthetics. On this principle, one implication we can draw from the quotation above is that there is
a cognitive reason why neoclassical artists and commentators
claim that art should represent 'la belle nature' rather than
simply 'nature', in other words, why artists should idealize their
subject. The relation between Condillac's concept of cognition
and 'la belle nature' is clearer if we compare Condillac's statements to those of Sir Joshua Reynolds, whose speeches to the
English Royal Academy in the 1770s and 1780s are to all intents
and purposes definitive statements of neoclassical aesthetic
values. Reynolds describes the artist's objective as follows:

The beauty of which we are in quest is general and intellectual: it is
an idea that subsists only in the mind; the sight never beheld it, nor
has the hand expressed it: it is an idea residing in the breast of the
artist, which he is always labouring to impart, and which he dies at last
without imparting; but which he is yet so far able to communicate,

as to raise the thoughts, and extend the views of the spectator.
(Reynolds, *Discourses on Art*, IX: 171)

The reason that 'sight never beheld' beauty is not because it is
an unknown quantity, but because no individual can possess all
the qualities necessary to be the epitome of beauty. Only the
artist can construct an ideal image from his various observations. This process of mental construction of a general ideal
makes a great deal of sense in terms of Condillac's idea of
'réflexion'.[3] Just as language is only truly language when the
speaker is able to manipulate mentally signs in what Condillac
calls 'réflexion', so art is perhaps only art when it is not a direct
representation of nature, but nature distilled and refined by the
artist. Condillac does, in fact, describe mental manipulation of
signs as essentially a creative act in which the power to create
and destroy them is invested in the speaker/thinker: 'l'effet de
cette opération est d'autant plus grand que par elle nous dis-
posons de nos perceptions, à-peu-près comme si nous avions le
pouvoir de les produire et de les anéantir [. . .]. Elle me paroîtra rentrer dans le néant, tandis qu'une autre m'en paroîtra
sortir' (Condillac, *Essai*, 1798: 92). To recall a perception
instead of waiting for nature to make its impression on us is
almost like creating that perception, because the mind can
recall and discard it at will. In these terms, all representation,
including art, is predominantly a mental activity which takes
place in 'le néant' of the mind, and is only indirectly related to
objective, physical reality. From the point of view of a theory of
art, Condillac's concept of cognition makes the abstractions
and idealizations involved in 'la belle nature' look like an aspect
of the highest mental faculty of 'réflexion', and therefore the
culmination of an intellectual evolution which led man away
from dependence on nature.

3.2   *Empathy in the origin of language*

After the genesis of knowledge, the linguistic story begins with
the two children alone in the desert, each able to direct their

---

[3] Condillac is thinking here in Lockeian terms. Locke uses an example with
similar implications for a theory of art in *An Essay Concerning Human Understanding*, IV, vii, 9.

'attention' at will and manipulate their ideas, but neither having yet learnt language. In order to do so, they must learn to direct each other's 'attention' as well as their own, so that they both perceive the same object at the same time. Condillac says that mutual control of 'attention' may have begun with a simple gesture towards an apple, which would prompt one person to understand 'give me the apple, I am hungry'. One gesture has this composite meaning, and relies more on 'sentiment' to be understood than any rational process: 'sentant passer dans son ame des sentimens dont il n'étoit pas encore capable de se rendre raison, il souffroit de voir souffrir ce misérable. Dès ce moment il se sent intéressé à le soulager, et il obéit à cette impression, autant qu'il est en son pouvoir' (Condillac, Essai, 1798: 262). The hungry child will get his apple. There is no need for intellectual understanding at this point, because the communicants are already disposed to empathize, to imagine the needs of the other. Rousseau later calls this characteristic 'pitié', and Condillac here uses 'intérêt', which often means in the eighteenth century 'emotion, passion' or 'sentiment'.[4]

Communication at this stage is a matter of shared 'sentiment' more than representation of ideas, of shared subjectivity which is revealed in the quotation, 'il souffroit de voir souffrir', as if the communication of 'hunger' requires that both interlocutors should feel the same appetite. For Condillac, this ability to share 'sentiment' is a feature of early language which never loses its significance, even in modern questions of language and art. Yet again, there is a clear link here between his theories of knowledge and language, and his ideas on artistic and literary style. We see this, for example, in the Art d'écrire, in which he makes the same assumption as he did in the Essai that 'senti-

---

[4] For 'pitié', see Rousseau, Discours sur l'origine et les fondemens de l'inégalité parmi les hommes (1964): 154. For 'intérêt' see Marmontel's article 'INTERET' in the Supplément à l'Encyclopédie: 'affection [de] l'ame qui lui est chère, & qui l'attache à son objet [. . .] C'est l'attrait de l'émotion qu'il nous cause, ou le plaisir que nous éprouvons à en être émus de curiosité, d'inquiétude, de crainte, de pitié, d'admiration &c.' (Vol. III, 628); see also the preceding article 'INTERESSANT', translated from Sulzer's Allgemeine Theorie der schönen Künste (1771–4): 'l'intéressant est la propriété essentielle de tous les objets esthétiques, [l'objet intéressant] excite l'activité intérieure de l'ame' (Vol. III, 628). Cerutti uses the word in the same sense in his title: De l'intérêt d'un ouvrage (1763); Batteux also in Les Beaux-Arts (1989): 128–9; and Beaumarchais in Œuvres (1988): 135 n.

ment' is communicated by the 'langage d'action' of gesture or facial expression, except this time with reference to modern literary style: 'quel est le visage le plus propre à l'expression? C'est celui qui, par la forme des traits et par les rapports qu'ils ont entre eux, s'altère suivant la vivacité des passions et la nuance des sentimens. [Le style] a son modèle dans cette action [. . .] Il est parfait, s'il est la traduction exacte' (Condillac, *Art d'écrire*, 1798: 283). The object of the painter's art is to capture the same sort of 'langage d'action', or the natural expressiveness of the body, in order to reproduce what Condillac calls the genuine 'caractère', or 'l'âme' of the subject: 'tout [dans l'homme] est l'expression des sentimens: un mot, un geste, un regard les décèle, et son ame lui échappe [. . .] Ce langage est l'étude du peintre [. . .] L'homme de génie ne se borne donc pas à dessiner des formes exactes. Il donne à chaque chose le caractère qui lui est propre. Son sentiment passe à tout ce qu'il touche, et se transmet à tous ceux qui voient ses ouvrages' (Condillac, *Art d'écrire*, 1798: 281–2).

Condillac proposes the same Sensualist principles of language in his theory of the origin of language as he does in his theory of the art of writing: the substance of expression, or what he calls here 'caractère', is conveyed by shared sentiment, whether it be between artist and viewer or between the two children in the desert learning to speak.[5] In both cases expression involves a kind of non-rational ability to 'touch'. It is possible and desirable, therefore, that the original language of 'sentiment' should still inspire literary style, that the writer should express his feeling of being 'touched': 'réflechissez donc sur vous-même, Monseigneur: comparez le langage que vous tenez lorsque vous parlez des choses qui vous touchent, avec celui que vous tenez lorsque vous parlez des choses qui ne vous touchent pas; et vous remarquerez comment votre discours se modifie naturellement de tous les sentimens qui se passent en vous' (Condillac, *Art d'écrire*, 1798: 2).

There are many passages in the *Art d'écrire* and the *Essai*, like the ones above, which share the same fundamental principles. Between the two, there is a common interest in language and sentiment, in the subjective, contemplative aspect of language,

---

[5] See Stevens, 'The Meanings and Uses of *caractère* in Eighteenth-century France' (1989) for other uses of the word.

and in the imperative to 'touch'. There is another aspect to Condillac's linguistic theories, however, which places much more importance on custom, habit, and eventually the conventional rules of art and language. The two different perspectives make an interesting balance between potentially conflicting aesthetic demands. The continuum of intellectual development which he tries to show means that his ideas on language and art do not stop with the 'langage d'action'. There is, instead, 'une révolution continuelle des choses' which means that we distort his aesthetic ideas if we do not take into account later developments.

3.3   From 'nature' to 'second nature' in language

Habit and sentiment are never far apart in the awakening of the senses and the birth of language, because there can be no learning process without their mutual dependence. This is because man gains complete control over the signs of 'langage d'action' when they have become so habitual that the object in nature, for example the apple, is no longer necessary in order to express the sentiment 'I am hungry, give me an apple'. In effect, a convention has liberated man from contingent circumstances, he has abstracted from particular events, so that conventional linguistic signs are related by analogy to their natural counterpart; *Ah!* when one steps on a pin 'is like' *ah!* when there is no pin present and we merely want to express pain. Once this is understood, it is possible to invent further conventional signs by the same process of analogy. In time, the process leads almost to arbitrary linguistic signs, that is, those which are only remotely connected to original expression of sentiment and which have almost completely lost touch with their natural counterparts. Like Chinese whispers, analogies of analogies eventually lead language a long way from the first natural signs. Although there is clearly a gradual loss of natural sentiment in this process, Condillac says that language gains by becoming more and more analytical. Greater precision is possible because the signs of language are not so much composite meanings like 'I am hungry, give me an apple', but more an analysis of thought, a sequential version of the impressions that we seek to express in natural language.

It is difficult to say what is and is not 'natural' in this process, since from the very moment that 'langage d'action' is used at will rather than prompted by circumstances it loses its absolute connection with natural sentiment. In other words, 'langage d'action' is a vinculum between natural and conventional linguistic signs, since it is closest to nature yet reliant on convention to achieve the full status of a language. Thus, habit and sentiment are interdependent; there is no clear division between nature and convention, only a gradual masking of natural signs behind the institutional signs of modern language. There is little point in talking of 'nature' in this case, since it implies a hiatus, a radical distinction between the primitive and the institutional which does not suit Condillac's perspective at all. For this reason, he talks of 'nature' and 'seconde nature', rather in the same way that the Sophists in Ancient Greece sought to reconcile 'physis' and 'nomos' to explain how it is possible to 'teach' virtue, or in the same way that medieval philosophers talked of a 'habitus' to explain how the principles of philosophical analysis can be learnt so well that they become a *secunda natura*.[6] The idea of a second nature has the advantage of acknowledging the importance of learnt behaviour without denying the role of 'first' nature; it implies difference without discontinuity. Consequently, it expresses better the idea that institutional signs are not unnatural as such, and that there is a filiation by analogy and habit with the first tentative linguistic expression. The filiation is essential, as Condillac illustrates with his well-known example of the statue which he gradually brings to life in order to demonstrate the course of cognitive development: it achieves consciousness by 'une habitude de donner son attention, une autre de se ressouvenir, une troisième de comparer' and so on, so that habit is a necessary component of enlightenment (Condillac, *Traité des sensations*, 1798: 86).

---

[6] The burning issue of fifth-century Greek ethics was the part played by natural disposition and training respectively in the production of virtue, that is, the relative importance of *nomos* (custom or convention, crystallized by law), and *physis* (divine and unalterable nature). In order to avoid the antithesis of *physis* and *nomos*, it was sometimes said that it is possible to change a man's disposition, so that virtue becomes for him a 'second' nature (Guthrie, *A History of Greek Philosophy*, 1965: Vol. II: 494–5). The idea of a *habitus* is used by Thompson, to explain that the good taxonomer learns the principles of analysis so well, that they become a second nature (Thompson, 'The Philosophical Foundations of Systematics', 1952: 5).

This means also that there is no necessary contradiction between the 'artificial' conventions of modern language and art, and the 'natural' expression of 'sentiment', because modern sequential language differs from the first kind of impressionistic language, and yet it is related, like a second nature: 'ces langues [. . .] sont devenues pour nous une seconde nature' (Condillac, *Grammaire*, 1798: 16–17). It is related because it is possible to cultivate what Condillac calls 'la liaison des idées', which is a way of mimicking the natural order of experience in the composition of a sentence. Literary style, then, reflects in an important way the origin of knowledge in the senses; both are composed of a chain of connected events. In the *Essai*, Condillac describes the 'liaison des idées' which contributes to the formation of knowledge: 'à un besoin est liée l'idée de la chose qui est propre à le soulager; à cette idée est liée celle du lieu ou cette chose se rencontre; à celle-ci des personnes qu'on y a vues; à cette dernière, les idées des plaisirs ou des chagrins qu'on en a reçus, et plusieurs autres [. . .]. De toutes nos connoissances il ne se formeroit qu'une seule et même chaîne' (Condillac, *Essai*, 1798: 67–8). In the *Art d'écrire*, he proposes that literary style can be modelled on a similar 'liaison des idées', so that there is a clear logical progression. He illustrates with a model sentence from a sermon by Fléchier:

C'est alors que dans le doux repos d'une condition privée, ce prince se dépouillant de toute la gloire qu'il avoit acquise pendant la guerre, et se renfermant dans une société de quelques amis choisis, s'exerçoit sans bruit aux vertus civiles, sincère dans ses discours, simple dans ses actions, fidèle dans ses amitiés, exacte dans ses devoirs, réglé dans ses désirs, grand même dans les moindres choses. (Condillac, *Art d'écrire*, 1798: 153)

The natural order of 'sentiment' is reproduced in the hierarchical arrangement of ideas, so there are 'idées accessoires' which are intimately related to an 'idée générale'. In this sentence by Fléchier, the 'idée générale' is the phrase: 's'exerçoit sans bruit aux vertus civiles', on either side of which there are the 'idées accessoires', first of the circumstances of virtue, then the qualities of virtue. The object of this style is to bring out a feeling of inevitability in the progression of ideas, a feeling of the natural and logical dependence of ideas as the reader is led scrupulously from one to the next. It is an effect which relies partly on the use of parataxis and the most simple co-ordinator 'et' to give the appearance of uncomplicated structure and minimal stylistic interference by the author, but is intended by Condillac to demonstrate how style can be 'natural', in the sense that it is related to the order of sentiment.[7]

Since stylistic composition can be said in some sense to be 'natural', the general implication in his literary theory is that there is a place for conventional form in the arts, that versification, rhyme, or metre are part of the (second) nature of poetry without which it would be deformed and 'unnatural'. It is therefore an illusion to think that prose is free of artifice when in reality the artifice is only concealed: 'l'art entre donc plus ou moins dans ce que nous nommons naturel. Tantôt il ne craint pas de paroître, tantôt il semble se cacher [. . .]. Si quelquefois il disparoît dans la prose [. . .], ce n'est pas qu'on écrive bien sans art, c'est que l'art est devenu en nous une seconde nature' (Condillac, *Art d'écrire*, 1798: 385). If all art is a 'second nature', there is no reason in principle to reject its formal aspects such as versification in poetry, for example. It is always debatable that some forms are too artificial, but the argument from nature cannot be invoked. By extension, if artifice characterizes all forms of art, it would seem reasonable that they should distinguish themselves from each other by more or less artifice. The distinctive feature of poetry would be to employ more artifice: 'le poëte doit écrire avec plus d'art [. . .] ce qui caractérise [la poësie] c'est de se montrer avec plus d'art et de n'en paroître pas moins naturelle' (Condillac, *Art d'écrire*, 1798: 380).

In effect, Condillac has reached the same conclusion as his more traditional contemporaries, that poetry is only poetry if it is versified (Condillac, *Essai*, 1798: 350), but not for the first time we are aware that apparently conventional ideas are supported by a firm philosophical foundation. His use of the concept of 'seconde nature' is perhaps the most perceptive and systematic reconciliation of the contentious issues aroused by La Motte's criticism of versification, because it accounts for 'conventional' form and 'natural' expression in art by showing their mutual epistemological dependence.

---

[7] For a more detailed analysis of Condillac's theory of style, see Branca, '*L'Art d'écrire* de Condillac' (1980).

Condillac does not take sides in literary 'querelles', because he thinks that dogmatism is inappropriate to his rational approach:

Bien des écrivains regardent les régles comme les entraves du génie. D'autres les croient d'un grand secours; mais ils les choisissent si mal, et les multiplient si fort, qu'ils les rendent inutiles ou même nuisibles. Tous ont également tort: ceux-là de blâmer la méthode, parce qu'ils n'en connoissent pas de bonne; ceux-ci de la croire nécessaire lorsqu'ils n'en connoissent que de fort défectueuses. (Condillac, *Art d'écrire*, 1798: 339)

Condillac never wrote on the arts in particular, neither is the *Essai* expressly a text on aesthetics because he is not convinced that 'querelles littéraires' are a profitable exercise. All sides claim 'le naturel' for themselves, with no clear idea of what exactly it is. He prefers to avoid any partisan approach, and advises his tutee, the young Prince of Parma, to pay attention only to the rational principle of 'la liaison des idées': 'consultez donc uniquement le principe de la liaison des idées; et sans vous occuper de ce qui a été dit ou de ce qui ne l'a pas été, songez uniquement à ce qui peut se dire' (Condillac, *Art d'écrire*, 1798, 218). Nevertheless, the scope of his ideas is so wide that it tends to encompass a variety of contemporary approaches to literary aesthetics, and there are therefore some obvious parallels to be drawn with some of his more polemical contemporaries. Diderot discusses good composition in painting in terms of directing the 'attention' of the viewer along a 'ligne de liaison'. Jean-Jacques Rousseau is interested in figurative language, the tool which fashions conventional language from natural language, because it is essential to literary creativity. Buffon develops the principle of stylistic 'liaison des idées' as a way of revealing or displaying his natural history. Diderot and Beaumarchais's theory of the 'drame bourgeois' relies on the pursuit of 'intérêt' as a means of intimate communication of sentiment between stage and audience. Without wishing to overstate Condillac's role in the development of these ideas, his broad perspective seems emblematic of contemporary explorations of artistic expression and new ways to understand them.

3.4   Diderot and composition in painting

Condillac's theory of semiosis and the related concepts of 'la liaison des idées' and 'attention' provide a systematic account of composition in a way which resembles and enhances Diderot's idea of composition in painting. This is evident in the way Diderot discusses the merits of Doyen's *Le Miracle des ardents*, and why it is that a painting of a massacre manages to retain good taste rather than repulse the viewer. The reason is that the painter suggests a reading of his painting, he suggests a route that our eye should take, 'une ligne de liaison', which will balance offence with appreciation. Diderot generalizes the idea of 'une ligne de liaison' to all painting:

Il y a dans toute composition, un chemin, une ligne qui passe par les sommités des masses ou des groupes, traversant différents plans, s'enfonçant ici dans la profondeur du tableau, là s'avançant sur le devant. Si cette ligne que j'appellerai ligne de liaison, se plie, se replie, se tortille, se tourmente [. . .] la composition sera louche, obscure; l'oeil irrégulièrement promené, égaré dans un labyrinthe saisira difficilement la liaison. Si au contraire elle ne serpente pas assez; si elle parcourt un long espace sans trouver aucun objet qui la rompe, la composition sera rare et décousue. Si elle s'arrête, la composition laissera un vide, un trou. Si l'on sent ce défaut et qu'on remplisse le vide ou trou, d'un accessoire inutile, on remédiera à un défaut par un autre. (Diderot, *Salons*, 1983: Vol. III, 186)

Composition lacks order if the eye is led in all directions at once; like looking at someone who is cross-eyed, one does not know where to look.[8] On the contrary, the eye is bored by a symmetrically designed painting where the path is too obvious. If, on the other hand, the composition lacks subject material, then the 'ligne de liaison' will be broken, and the progress of the eye will be interrupted. Diderot develops these ideas in terminology which is reminiscent of Condillac's writing. He calls the ability to paint according to 'une ligne de liaison', 'un art de fixer l'œil de l'imagination à l'endroit où l'on veut' (Diderot, *Salons*, 1983: Vol. III, 185), which makes a great deal of sense in Condillac's 'attention' and wilful use of signs. Condillac uses

---

[8] For the analogy drawn by Dumarsais and Girard between equivocal language and 'le sens louche', see Chapter 2.

the example of a viewer analysing the composition of a painting to illustrate what he means by 'réfléchir': 'cette manière
d'appliquer de nous même notre attention tour à tour à divers
objets, [. . .] c'est ce qu'on appelle réfléchir'. In order to
explain his own experience as art critic, Diderot makes the same
analogy in reverse by comparing the painter's art to a language
(Diderot, *Salons*, 1983: Vol. III, 186). Viewing a painting and
'réfléchir' are analogous activities in the theories of Condillac
and Diderot, because both depend upon awakening sensations
and directing the 'attention' from one sensation to another.
In addition, language and painting both depend on a similar
manipulation of the 'attention' of another person. Diderot in
the quotation above describes how his eye is led by the artist
from one part of the composition to another, along a line of
interest which is created by the artist. This is a kind of communication between artist and viewer which depends on the
same duality of linear and holistic perception which Condillac
describes when he explains how impressionistic 'langage d'action' is gradually analysed into a sequential 'liaison des idées'.
Diderot too, in order to 'translate' the image into rational composition reads it in linear fashion. The linear reading of a painting, and the holistic composition of Condillac's model sentence
into a pyramidal structure of principal and accessory ideas, are
illustrations of the way in which Horace's axiom *ut pictura poesis*
is applied to the practice of art, because both painting and
writing abide by the same rules of composition, the same 'ligne
de liaison'.

3.5   Empathy and gesture in the 'drame bourgeois'

Condillac's interest in the psychology of communication has
significant parallels with the contemporary theatre of the
'drame bourgeois'. Whereas Condillac's concern was to show
how the origin of language lies in the ability to empathize with
another's sensate experience, the 'drame' seeks to encourage
a greater affinity between the audience and actors than is
arguably possible in the traditional genres of comedy or
tragedy. The process of intimate identification across a psychological divide relies in both cases on an idea of gestural lan-

guage and 'intérêt', except that the psychological divide in theatre is symbolically staged and all the more keenly felt because of the separation of audience from the actors on stage. It may be, in fact, that contemporary dramatists are increasingly aware of this divide, and more sensitive to the idea of intimate communication, since reform of theatre practice in 1759 finally removes members of the audience from the stage.[9] Like Condillac's two children in the desert who first learn language, therefore, actors and audience in the theatre become face to face across a necessary divide, and yet there is nonetheless a sharing of experience. In the 'drame', this empathy is achieved through a number of features which are discussed by Diderot and Beaumarchais. Firstly, there is the desire for greater realism and depiction of everyday life; secondly, there is the use of monologue and dramatic irony to increase the audience's awareness of events; and thirdly, there is the cultivation of a particular kind of emotionally charged dramatic language. Together, these features are designed to encourage a closer relationship between the audience and actors, and hopefully to provide the means for more effective moral instruction, which Diderot and Beaumarchais think is a primary concern of theatre.

Beaumarchais discusses the theory of the 'drame bourgeois', which he calls 'le genre honnête et sérieux', in the preface to *Eugénie*, entitled 'Essai sur le genre dramatique sérieux' (1767). He argues for a more realistic kind of drama which would better correspond to people's daily experience of life: 'la peinture touchante d'un malheur domestique, d'autant plus puissante sur nos cœurs qu'il semble nous menacer de plus près' (Beaumarchais, *Essai sur le genre dramatique sérieux*, 1988: 123). The problem with traditional tragedy or comedy is that they convey respectively feelings of 'admiration' or 'ridicule', neither of which are sentiments which encourage the audience to identify closely with the characters. Identification is important to the didactic role of theatre, because it is easier to teach good morals if the play relates as directly as possible to the life of the spectator. Beaumarchais calls this process of identification 'intérêt': 'qu'est-ce que la moralité? C'est le résultat fructueux et l'application personnelle des réflexions qu'un événement

---

[9] The Duc de Lauragais paid the Théâtre-Français an indemnity of 12,000 livres to remove spectators from the stage.

nous arrache. Qu'est-ce que l'intérêt? C'est le sentiment involontaire par lequel nous nous adaptons cet événement, sentiment qui nous met en la place de celui qui souffre, au milieu de sa situation' (Beaumarchais, *Essai*, 1988: 126). 'Intérêt' is a 'sentiment involontaire', like Rousseau's 'pitié' or Condillac's empathy, a feeling which is natural to man and allows him to see things from the point of view of another. The same 'rapport secret' is at work in theatre, and allows the spectator to learn from a play as he would from events in real life. Beaumarchais describes this 'rapport secret' as primarily a personal and intimate response, 'l'attendrissement', which makes each spectator feel closer to the action on stage than to those in the seats around him: 'il nous recueille, il nous isole de tout. Celui qui pleure au spectacle est seul; et plus il le sent, plus il pleure avec délices' (Beaumarchais, *Essai*, 1988: 127). Theatre becomes a personal and introspective experience: 'le tableau du malheur d'un honnête homme frappe au cœur, l'ouvre doucement, s'en empare, et le force bientôt à s'examiner soi-même' (p. 127).

The close empathy between spectator and actor is crucial to the 'drame', and is achieved in a number of ways. In the first place, the realistic depiction of day-to-day life is a constant reminder of reality, a check on any nascent feelings of 'admiration'. Landois's *Silvie* (1742), much admired by Diderot, has the following stage set: 'le Théatre represente l'interieur d'une chambre ou l'on ne voit que les murs; une table sur laquelle est une lumiere, un pot à eau & un pain: un habit d'homme & une mauvaise robbe de femme' (Landois, *Silvie*, 1742: sc. 1). There may also be an attempt to balance morally inspiring episodes with mundane matters, which sometimes leads from the sublime to the ridiculous. M. Félix, the eponymous character of Moissy's *Le Vertueux Mourant* (1770), mixes thoughts on immortality with supper. The nearer he feels to death, the happier he becomes: 'plus j'en approche, & plus mon ame se livre à une certaine joie qu'inspire la vertu [. . .]. Avant que la cloche funebre m'envoye enrichir la terre de ce qu'elle m'a prêté, la mort trouvera tous les liens qui ont pu m'attacher au monde, brisés par mes mains, son glaive n'a plus que le fil de mes jours à couper'. Mme Félix and a servant are at his bedside. Mme Félix replies: 'cette résignation m'annonce qu'il vous reste encore des forces qu'il faut aider par des secours.

Anselme, allez chercher un bouillon'. M. Félix moves with ease
from 'bouillon' to 'la lie de mes jours', with perhaps an analogy
between the two: 'vous scavé qu'il ne passe plus, un peu de gelée
me suffira; mais actuelement je n'ai besoin de rien, je sens que
mon être se dissoud, & s'écoule sous le poids de la vieillesse &
de la maladie, je ne fais plus qu'épuiser la lie de mes jours'
(Moissy, *Le Vertueux Mourant*, 1770: II, 1). The following act
opens with Anselme spoon feeding M. Félix 'un pot de gelée'.
M. Félix seems to be dying by sheer force of will, but verisimilitude is less important than moral edification. He is every-
man's hero with whom everyone can identify, as the 'bouillon'
reminds us.

A second important device which promotes 'intérêt' is the
use of dramatic irony and monologue. The spectator must be
party to all the thoughts and feelings which occur to the characters, in order to empathize as much as possible, regardless of
how predictable this renders the plot. Diderot claims, in fact,
to make complete predictability a stylistic objective, because
otherwise the element of surprise prevents the audience from
following closely the moral progress of the characters: 'j'entre-
prendrais un drame où le dénouement serait annoncé dès la
première scène, et où je ferais sortir l'intérêt le plus violent de
cette circonstance même' (Diderot, *Discours sur la poésie dramatique*, 1970: 448). Consequently, the plot of Diderot's plays is
more designed to promote 'intérêt' than suspense. In *Le Fils
naturel* (1757), for example, the characters supply a regular
report of the action from their respective points of view. Dorval
discovers in Act II, scene 1 that he is loved by both Rosalie and
Constance; he falls back into the ever-ready armchair and
explains in a long monologue the unhappiness of his situation.
In scene 7, he reads the letter from Rosalie, and explains the
irony of her words considering his feelings of guilt. These
monologues serve to keep the audience aware of the thoughts
of the characters, and thereby also to increase the effect of dramatic irony. When, for example, Constance thinks mistakenly
that a *billet doux* written to Rosalie is meant for her: 'pourquoi
m'avoir fait un mystère de votre penchant? [. . .] Vous ne me
répondez pas. (Dorval écoute la tête penchée et les bras
croisés)', the audience shares in Dorval's uneasiness, which
Constance cannot understand (Act II, sc. 3).

Beaumarchais, too, agrees that 'intérêt' is better sustained if the audience is kept informed of the feelings of the characters: 'une autre cause principale [. . .] de l'intérêt de ce Drame, est l'attention scrupuleuse que j'ai eue d'instruire le spectateur de l'état respectif et des desseins de tous les personnages. Jusqu'à présent les Auteurs avaient souvent pris autant de peines pour nous ménager des surprises passagères que j'en ai mis à faire précisément le contraire' (Beaumarchais, *Essai*, 1988: 137). Beaumarchais may also be revealing his roots in popular street theatre when he adds that 'intérêt' means audience participation as well as empathy. He would like the audience to cry out, to clap and voice their reactions (p. 137).

The third way of expressing 'intérêt' is through the quality of the language itself. The language of the 'drame' is not traditional verse, but a broken prose intended to reflect better the inexpressible torrent of emotions at moments of high passion. Diderot and Beaumarchais seem to suggest that speaking is inescapably a rational activity which sometimes conflicts with moments of high passion; a passionate language is almost a contradiction in terms, unless we mean a disjointed language with no necessary eloquence or logical exposition to make sense of the ineffable. Diderot thinks that the only way dramatic dialogue can do justice to these moments is to express its own inadequacy, that is, to be inarticulate, monosyllabic, and disjointed:

Qu'est-ce qui nous affecte dans le spectacle de l'homme animé de quelque grande passion? [. . .] Ce sont des cris, des mots inarticulés, des voix rompues, quelques monosyllabes qui s'echappent par intervalles, je ne sais quel murmure dans la gorge, entre les dents. La violence du sentiment coupant la respiration et portant le trouble dans l'esprit, les syllabes des mots se séparent, l'homme passe d'une idée à une autre; il commence une multitude de discours; il n'en finit aucun. [C'est] une suite de bruits faibles et confus, de sons expirants, d'accents étouffés. (Diderot, *Entretiens sur le Fils naturel*, 1970: 140)

Language inevitably imposes an artificial and incongruous structure on 'la violence du sentiment', which prevents the proper development of 'intérêt'. The problem is perhaps insurmountable, because language may be too blunt an instrument to define the complexity of 'sentiment'; perhaps 'sentiment' is 'un sujet trop fugitif' which slips through the semiotic net:

Je voudrais bien vous parler de l'accent propre à chaque passion. Mais cet accent se modifie en tant de manières; c'est un sujet si fugitif et si délicat, que je n'en connais aucun qui fasse mieux sentir l'indigence de toutes les langues qui existent et qui ont existé. On a une idée juste de la chose; elle est présente à la mémoire. Cherche-t-on l'expression? On ne la trouve point. On combine les mots de grave et d'aigu, de prompt et de lent, de doux et de fort; mais le réseau, toujours trop lâche, ne retient rien. (Diderot, *Entretiens*, 1970: 142)

The idea is in the mind, 'présente à la mémoire', but nevertheless inexpressible. Consequently, if there is an ideal, 'natural' language, then Beaumarchais thinks it must be: 'vif, pressé, coupé, tumultueux et vrai, [. . .] éloigné du compas de la césure et de l'affectation de la rime' (Beaumarchais, *Essai*, 1988: 133). In practice, the dialogue of the 'drame' employs rhetorical techniques like interrogation, and exclamation and suspended sentences, all of which allow the actor to raise and lower his intonation. In Landois's *Silvie*, for example, Des Francs is alone waiting to confront his unfaithful wife: 'ne frissonnes-tu pas de paroître devant moi? [. . .]. Je vais donc voir Silvie coupable, & de quel crime, grand Dieu! . . . Hé bien, en suis-je suffisamment convaincu? Me surprendrois-je encore à vouloir en douter?' (Landois, *Silvie*, 1742: sc. 4). The language tends to be effusive but oratorical. Gaiffe has shown that in fact the passionate monologue in the 'drame' is quite similar to the monologue of classical theatre, and comments that: 'plus d'un drame en vers et même en prose, s'habille d'oripeaux tragiques cousus bout à bout et trop facilement reconnaissables' (Gaiffe, *Le Drame au Dix-huitième siècle*, 1971: 496). Gaiffe's suspicions may be justified in practice, but there are nevertheless many assertive declarations of principle to the contrary. Landois, like Diderot and Beaumarchais, protests that 'le pompeux galimathias tragique' is 'un mauvais moyen pour exprimer ses sentimens' (Landois, *Silvie*, 1742: sc. 6). All are searching for a form of language which is 'énergique' without degenerating into 'cet Héroïque guindé', but none manage to break free as much as they would like.

Some authors see a renewal of metaphor as a way to revitalize language, with varied success. The *Journal de Trévoux* dislikes Saurin's imagery in *Beverley*, but excuses the excessive novelty on the basis that it is translated from the English:

L'Amour semait de fleurs ma couche nuptiale
Et l'Aurore avec moi réveillait les plaisirs.

(*Beverley*, II, 1; reviewed in *Le Journal de
Trévoux*, August 1768)

There are times, however, when novelty deteriorates into mixed
metaphor: 'mon cœur, nageant dans une douce flamme,
semblait m'echapper pour chercher le vôtre' (*Le Comte de
Bravemont*, quoted in Gaiffe, 1971: 517). On other occasions,
grandiloquence together with extended metaphor makes for
a dubious tone. In Moissy's *La Vraie Mère* (1771), M. Félibien
is convincing his brother-in-law that breast-feeding is natural:
'tiens-tu assez à la grossièreté de tes sens pour ne regarder ces
mammelles, respectable trésor de la nature, que comme un
relief de pur embellissement destiné à orner la poitrine des
femmes? [. . .] Ces sacrés réservoirs où la Nature a placé les pre-
mieres ressources de sa foible existence!' (Act II, sc. 1). The
choice of analogy is questionable, but energetically extended as
if it were more important stylistically to dazzle the audience with
exuberant imagery than rhetorically to convince them with a
more restrained and reasonable style. This dazzling effect is
what Beaumarchais would call 'un effet [. . .] une sensation
puissante et subite dans tous les spectateurs', and is designed
to cause an emotional impact, sustain 'intérêt', in other words
to cause the audience to empathize with the characters (Beaumarchais, *Essai*, 1988: 122). Mixing and extending metaphor is
therefore a useful way to compensate for the difficulty in language of expressing powerful, irrational emotions, and for this
reason is an important stylistic device in the 'drame'.

Another way to enrich dramatic expression is to use the visual
language of Diderot's 'pantomime' and 'tableau'. His interest
in stage direction and theatrical gesture has undoubtedly much
to do with his interest in the visual arts in particular and more
generally with his abiding assumption that there are transfer-
able attributes from one art form to another. But he also shares
Condillac's specific interest in early or natural forms of language. Diderot seems fascinated by a highly expressive language
with two channels, the visual and the oral, rather like Condillac's idea of a bilingual stage in language development when
'langage d'action' would have been used at the same time as

articulated language. In his 'drames', he tries to achieve the same simultaneity, 'combiner la pantomime avec le discours; entremêler une scène parlée avec une scène muette' (Diderot, *Entretiens sur le Fils naturel*, 1970: 153). Some scenes of his plays are, in fact, entirely visual interludes: at one point in *Le Fils naturel*, Rosalie is mute apart from intermittent sighs and tears in reply to Justine's equally wordless attempts to comfort her (Act II, sc. 1). This scene is a good example of the effectiveness of 'pantomime', because although Rosalie says nothing, her expressions of sadness and the attentions of Justine make her the centre of the dramatic moment. On other occasions Diderot does not entirely eliminate speech, but inserts precise stage directions into the dialogue, such as in the following example in which Clairville confronts Dorval with the truth regarding Constance and Rosalie: 'aussi, tournant sur eux des regards d'indignation et de mépris (Clairville regardant Dorval avec ces yeux, Dorval ne peut les soutenir. Il détourne la tête, et se couvre le visage avec ses mains), je leur fis entendre qu'on portait en soi le germe de bassesse' (Act III, sc. 1).

There is a close relation between dialogue and visual language in Diderot's 'drame' which means that it is perhaps unfair that Gaiffe should judge their passionate monologues without considering the contribution that 'pantomime' would have made to the expression. Diderot and others were sensitive to the inadequacy of language, and would doubtless have thought it misleading to read a 'drame' rather than see it performed. At every moment of a theatrical performance, gesture plays a complementary role to words: 'il faut écrire la pantomime toutes les fois qu'elle fait tableau; qu'elle donne de l'énergie ou de la clarté au discours; qu'elle lie le dialogue; qu'elle caractérise; qu'elle consiste dans un jeu délicat qui ne se devine pas; qu'elle tient lieu de réponse, et presque toujours au commencement des scenes' (Diderot, *Discours sur la poésie dramatique*, 1970: 491). As the curtain rises, therefore, the audience is met with a tableau, a silent, static opening, where the actors are composed like a painting, and attention is attracted along 'une ligne de liaison' from one area of the stage to another. When the action begins, pantomime accompanies dialogue to contribute both to the 'énergie' and the 'clarté', because gesture and movement convey and heighten the pathos. Without it, the broken language characteristic of the passionate monologue lacks coherence, because it is pantomime which provides the verisimilitude which language alone cannot. Consequently, it is a mistake to separate the two: 'pourquoi avons-nous séparé ce que la nature a joint? A tout moment, le geste ne répond-il pas au discours?' (Diderot, *Entretiens*, 1970: 139). Diderot says that the combined dramatic effect is 'terrible': 'c'est alors qu'on tremblerait d'aller au spectacle' (p. 152).

3.6   Rousseau and the figurative origins of language

Rousseau, in his characteristic dialectical fashion, turns Condillac's discussion of the figurative origins of language into an existential dilemma at the heart of linguistic man, and as a consequence he rejects all later notions of a rational 'liaison des idées' in favour of a suggestive aesthetic of metaphor. For both authors, learning language is a way of learning about the physical world, but for Rousseau, the result is to emphasize the existential difference between man and his environment.

Before language, man lives a radically subjective life because he is concerned only with his own sensory experience. In contrast, language allows an objective view of himself which at the same time introduces a radical alienation between what he is, and what he is seen to be. Metaphor is responsible for language and alienation because it is the instinctive 'poetic' reaction to new experience which allows man to compare himself to another, but also inevitably introduces a duality in his perception of reality: 'I am "like" another'. Rousseau's dialectic is that metaphor both destroys man's existential unity and creates language. He demonstrates by suggesting how the sign for 'man' would have been devised. When one man meets another, he has no abstract notion of 'man', only a subjective knowledge of himself, and hence cannot create a sign which denotes both himself and the other. Since man is instinctively afraid of new experience, and since he initially will see another as bigger and stronger than himself, the first sign he creates for another man will consequently mean 'fear, strange'; Rousseau suggests *géant*. Later he will see that the other man is, in fact, like himself, and he will no longer see him subjectively as *un géant*. As a result, he must invent another sign to mean 'like me'; hence the symbol for 'man'. Consequently, the first kind of language is figurative: 'comme les prémiers motifs qui firent parler l'homme furent des passions, ses prémiéres expressions furent des Tropes. Le langage figuré fut le premier à naître, le sens propre fut trouvé le dernier' (Rousseau, *Essai sur l'origine des langues,* 1995: Vol. V, 381). Although in contrast to Condillac, it is metaphorical, not analogical signs which are the first to be invented.

In the process of inventing the sign for 'man', one learns to objectivize, to distrust one's subjective perception of one's environment, because it turns out to be what Rousseau calls 'une illusion'. Consequently, the dual structure of metaphor is at the heart of language, and becomes the heart of linguistic man's vision of himself. In this vision, there is a figurative 'other', which is 'le géant', and an analogous 'other', which is 'l'homme'. Correspondingly, there is a figurative 'moi' and an analogous 'moi', and the individual is torn between language, which teaches him that the figurative is 'une illusion', and his senses which tell him otherwise. Essentially, Rousseau is suggesting that the role of language is communication, and that it is bound to encourage a less subjective vision of the physical world and of ourselves. Language is the first socializing step which will cause men to live according to how others see them, instead of living for themselves according to 'amour de soi'. However, at a later decadent stage of society, language can be abused to allow men to appear other than they really are. It persuades us to reject our own perceptions, which is hazardous if someone else is trying to impose his own subjective perception.

Rousseau does not abandon writing in despair of decadent language. Like Condillac, there is a streak of utopian thinking in much of Rousseau's work which is evident in the way he looks to the past to create a model for the future. In this case, he goes back to metaphor in order to create a contemplative style, like the subjective state of natural man, but in the medium of modern, sequential language. Metaphor is a way of slowing the narrative flow and focusing a disproportionate amount of the reader's attention on a few words. It manages this because it suggests more than it explains; the reader is required to reformulate 'reality' from what in rational terms is an insufficient number of elements. Rousseau's metaphors are innovative, partly in themselves, and partly in relation to contemporary practice. The caution is such in much eighteenth-century writing that 'analogy' is a better term for the kind of extended figure of speech which tries to paint in every detail rather than leave the reader to interpret. In order to show rationally that the analogy is not 'tirée de trop loin', there is often a lengthy explanation which destroys any momentary impact that the image could have had. There is nothing contemplative about these analogies; since the reader is passive, he is supplied with all the elements. Diderot, for example, lends Dorval the following analogy to express his emotional crisis:

DORVAL. Mais le malheur me suit, et se répand sur tout ce qui m'approche. Le ciel qui veut que je vive dans les ennuis, veut-il aussi que j'y plonge les autres? On était heureux ici, quand j'y vins.
CONSTANCE. Le ciel s'obscurcit quelquefois; et si nous sommes sous le nuage, un instant l'a formé, ce nuage, un instant le dissipera.

(Diderot, *Le Fils naturel*, IV, 3)

The effortless way in which Constance develops the conventional metonym 'le ciel' suggests a lucidity and rational control which does not encourage the spectator to share in Dorval's introspective doubt. The work of interpretation is done on the spectator's behalf.

Rousseau asks much more of his reader. There are certain moments in his writing when he divests himself of the pervasive rhetorical assumptions of contemporary writing, seeks not, therefore, to persuade his reader of the aptness of an image as Diderot does in the example above, but communicates instead an emotional charge which is moving without necessarily being explicable in rational terms. In practice, this means mixing metaphors, drawing unlikely analogies, prioritizing subjective impressions, using pleonasms, monologues, and memories, all with the purpose of describing the effect things and events have on personal sensibilities rather than describing the things and effects themselves. This procedure is sometimes called 'lyrical', and differs crucially in function from rhetoric in that it is not an argument; the writer seeks to share an emotional experience without necessarily wishing to persuade the reader of its rightness. The distinction is important because one can easily pay too much attention to the abundance of rhetorical devices in

Rousseau's style and forget that he often uses them for specifically non-rhetorical purposes. Rhetoric is such a powerful and prevalent concept of language, literature, and even the arts in general in the seventeenth and eighteenth centuries that any occasion when it is supplanted is significant.

Rousseau never says he is 'lyrical', perhaps because in the eighteenth century the word means mostly 'words with music', and is only just beginning to be used in the sense of 'personal expression of emotion'.[10] He does, however, describe his style in words which are perhaps meant to distinguish it as far as possible from rhetoric. In the second preface to *La Nouvelle Héloïse* he suggests that the theme of frustrated love is less distorted by his effusive style than it is by the affectations of 'les auteurs géomètres', because love is not a rational sentiment: 'voulez-vous que [les amants] sachent observer, juger, réfléchir? Ils ne savent rien de tout cela'. A little earlier he says that his figurative language is not designed to be eloquent: 'ces figures sont sans justesse et sans suite; son éloquence est dans son désordre' (Rousseau, *La Nouvelle Héloïse*, 1964: 16, 15). Elsewhere he makes a strong claim for clarity of expression over and above grammatical correctness: 'toutes les fois qu'à l'aide de dix solécismes je pourrai m'expliquer plus fortement ou plus clairement, je ne balancerai jamais' (Rousseau, *Lettre sur une nouvelle réfutation*, in Bruneau, 1954: 496).

There is an aesthetic of suggestion rather than rhetorical persuasion in some of Rousseau's style which differs notably from the use most of his contemporaries make of figurative language. There is a complex sequence of metaphors, for example, in the following lament by Saint-Preux when he has left Julie's side and arrived in Paris:

J'arrivai hier au soir à Paris, et celui qui ne pouvoit vivre séparé de toi par deux rues en est maintenant à plus de cent lieues. O Julie! plain-moi, plain ton malheureux ami. Quand mon sang en longs ruisseaux auroit tracé cette route immense, elle m'eut paru moins longue, et je n'aurois pas senti défaillir mon ame avec plus de langueur. Ah si du moins je connoissais le moment qui doit nous rejoindre ainsi que l'espace qui nous sépare, je compenserois l'éloignement des lieux par

---

[10] Michèle Aquien says that it is in the late eighteenth century that 'lyricism' comes to mean expression of personal sentiment rather than only 'words with music' (*Dictionnaire de poétique*, 1993: 'lyrisme').

le progrès du tems, je compterois dans chaque jour ôté de ma vie les pas qui m'auroient rapproché de toi! Mais cette carriere de douleurs est couverte des tenebres de l'avenir: Le terme qui doit la borner se dérobe à mes foibles yeux. (Rousseau, *La Nouvelle Heloïse*, 1964: 228)

Saint-Preux's recollection of how hard it was to be separated even by two streets occasions an extended metaphor on the theme of the journey. First, the road from the Alps to Paris symbolizes the spiritual trial of leaving Julie which saps his lifeblood: 'mon sang en ruisseau auroit tracé cette route immense'. Then it represents their time apart, the end of which he wishes were foreseeable like the end of a journey: 'je compterois dans chaque jour ôté de ma vie les pas qui m'auroient rapproché de toi!'. Their separation seems endless, however, and he next compares it to a horizon which is always obscured by darkness: 'cette carriere de douleurs est couverte des tenebres de l'avenir'. The last case is a mixed metaphor, because time is like a journey and its end is like a dark future. The whole passage is also a kind of syllepsis on the word 'route', because it has more than one metaphorical meaning: a spiritual trial, time passing, and the future.

Contemporary critics who urge caution with metaphor and syllepsis would probably regard this passage as confusing because it is so long and consists of so many variations on the theme of distance that it is no longer clear what is the precise nature of the comparison.[11] They would be right in the sense that not only does the tenor of the metaphor change from 'a spiritual trial' to 'time passing' to 'the future', but the vehicle which expresses it changes too, from 'cette route' to 'les pas' to 'cette carriere'. The last term is especially evocative, since in the preceding letters Julie exhorts Saint-Preux at length to make the most of his 'nouvelle carriere', meaning this time the new course of his life in Paris.

Rousseau's answers to the apparent confusion of this passage are given above: the geometric precision of rhetoric is inappropriate to a lover's outpourings of emotions, consequently their language is 'sans justesse' and 'dans le désordre'. The

---

[11] Almost any contemporary critic will urge caution with metaphor and syllepsis, but see, for example, Dumarsais's article in *Traité des tropes* (1730) 'La syllepse oratoire', or Voltaire, *Connaissance des beautés et des défauts de la poésie*, Moland 23, 1879: 356–7.

function of Saint-Preux's language, therefore, is not rhetorical: he is not trying to persuade anyone, not even himself. Its function is to reflect his growing distress and the way the journey has affected his personal sensibilities. The cumulative effect of the metaphors gives an impression of his growing awareness of the gravity of the situation, and the mounting panic as he fears there is no way out. The repetitive nature of extended metaphor suggests an overbearing fixation with an idea. The mental connections linking the metaphors into a sequence or 'variations on a theme' betokens a mind searching for resolution to what seems an intractable problem. These mental connections finally lead to a mixed metaphor, image heaped on image which renders their meaning equivocal and implies that Saint-Preux is abandoning himself more and more to obscurity.

There are many other occasions when the metaphors are more lyrical than rhetorical. Later in *La Nouvelle Héloïse*, Saint-Preux is beseeching Julie to be unfaithful to her husband: 'une nuit, une seule nuit a changé pour jamais toute mon ame. Ote-moi ce dangereux souvenir, et je suis vertueux. Mais cette nuit fatale regne au fond de mon cœur et va couvrir de son ombre le reste de ma vie' (Rousseau, *La Nouvelle Heloïse*, 1964: 337). 'Nuit' in the first instance means their first and only night of passion which brought them together. In the second instance, it means a repressive and abiding 'darkness' in his heart, so dark that he forever walks in its shadow. Rousseau's procedure here is similar to the first example: a literal sense of 'nuit' leads to a figurative sense, and finally to a mixed metaphor. In this case, it expresses Saint-Preux's realization that consummated love has not liberated him, but haunts him with the memory of what he can never attain again.

Water is a recurrent theme in Rousseau's metaphors, usually running water, but occasionally water which seems motionless. In Saint-Preux's more contemplative moments he retreats into his own thoughts so much that the outside world has come to a standstill. This happens twice during the 'promenade du lac' episode. The first occasion is when Saint-Preux decides that he and Julie ought to move further from the banks of the lake where they are fishing in their rowing boat, and venture out into the middle of the lake. He is overcome with the beauty of the scene and treats Julie to a florid description of the panorama, including the point where the powerful current of the Rhône flows into the glassy expanse of the lake: 'je lui montrois de loin les embouchures du Rhone dont l'impétueux cours s'arrête tout à coup au bout d'un quart de lieue, et semble craindre de souiller de ses eaux bourbeuses le cristal azuré du lac' (Rousseau, *La Nouvelle Heloïse*, 1964: 515). Their spell in the middle of the lake is an interlude before the storm breaks and they are obliged with great difficulty to return to the lakeside. The whole episode is also an interlude before Julie's husband returns from travels abroad, and consequently an opportunity for Saint-Preux to spend time in her company. He cherishes the moment, and one feels in this episode as a whole that he loses himself in the bliss of his good fortune. The 'crystal azuré du lac' is an expanse of tranquillity and purity which not even the most powerful intrusion from outside can penetrate very far.

The second metaphor of this kind is used a little later when the two lovers are walking on the banks of the lake: 'quelques ruisseaux filtroient à travers les rochers, et rouloient sur la verdure en filets de cristal' (518). There is a contemplative pause in Saint-Preux's mind after they have been walking in silence for some time and he becomes lost in his own thoughts. Running water turns to hard crystal.

These are a few examples of the lyrical metaphors used by Rousseau. They are, of course, only one kind of figurative language which Rousseau uses; there are many others, some of which are conventional or unremarkable.[12] They are nevertheless striking because there are few authors in the eighteenth century who make such wide use of them and integrate them so closely into the narrative and characterization. Saint-Preux would not be the same melancholy, impassioned, ardent lover of Julie if he were not able to pursue his metaphors in the way he does. The point about this literary style in relation to the theories of the origin of language of Rousseau and Condillac, is that it recovers some of the subjective communication by sentiment which they contend is characteristic of the first 'natural' languages. The channel of communication is empathy rather than rational exposition: just as natural language is a matter of

---

[12] Lecercle makes a detailed study of Rousseau's metaphors, lyrical and otherwise (*Rousseau et l'art du roman*, 1969, chapter VI).

sharing an emotion which is not analysable into its constituent 'ideas', so these metaphors lack coherence or consistency if we scrutinize them too closely. They work best, like the holistic signs of natural language, if we are receptive to the general impression or sensation that they suggest. If we are, we understand a certain kind of radical subjectivity, an emotional charge and a contemplative mood which might otherwise go unexpressed. The case of Rousseau's metaphor is also an instructive reminder that he is as much a utopian as a primitivist. Those, like Voltaire, who see only regression in some of Rousseau's ideas, such as the 'noble savage', need reminding that his ideal 'return to nature' is a renewal of an essential characteristic, not backsliding to uncivilized times.[13] He is utopian, because he looks to the past only to renew the future; in this case, he looks to the original metaphorical nature of language to renew modern literary language.

Rousseau's discussion of music in the *Essai sur l'origine des langues* seems to support the same aesthetic of emotional charge and suggestive communication. The role of the musician is not to represent directly, but to encourage the listener to feel the same sensations as he would feel in the presence of the object: 'l'art du musicien consiste à substituer à l'image insensible de l'objet celle des mouvemens que sa présence excite dans le cœur du contemplateur [. . .] Il ne représentera pas directement ces choses, mais il excitera dans l'ame les mêmes sentimens qu'on éprouve en les voyant' (Rousseau, *Essai sur l'origine des langues*, 1995: 422). The process is similar to the point in Condillac's theory, when it is possible for communicants to understand the cry 'ah!' in the hypothetical terms of what it 'would' be like to feel pain, even if no pain is felt at that moment. The important analogy between music and language is that both function with figurative 'signs' for our feelings: 'les sons dans la mélodie n'agissent pas seulement sur nous comme sons, mais comme signes de nos affections, de nos sentimens' (Rousseau, *Essai sur l'origine des langues*, 1995: 417). The feeling of aesthetic pleasure is fundamentally an object of sensation, it is an impressionistic event which cannot be explained by rational analysis. Consequently, he objects strongly

---

[13] Voltaire reads Rousseau's second discourse and writes to him: 'il prend envie de marcher à quatre pattes quand on lit votre ouvrage'. See Rousseau, Correspondance, Letter 317 (30 Aug. 1755).

to Castel's analogy between colour and music, because it suggests that aesthetic pleasure is structurally determined, that a universal theory of harmony is sufficient to explain the sensation of pleasure experienced by the listener/viewer. In chapter 16 of the *Essai sur l'origine des langues*, he singles out Castel's colour 'clavecin oculaire' as an example of the mathematician's approach to art. He says that it is possible to describe music very accurately according to systems of harmony, but the Pythagorean approach takes no account of the suggestive way in which it communicates. Castel's colour harpsichord implies that for every musical note there is an equivalent colour, as if there were a simple mathematical equation which derived from one into the other. The examples of Rousseau's metaphors, however, show that there is no 'geometric' formula to be found without destroying the emotional impact of the image; they remain at the level of suggestion. The mistake that Castel and others make is to think that art is quantifiable like physics, that the painter's use of colour can be defined as easily as the angles of light through a prism. Rousseau's development of the 'nuances' theme deserves quoting in full because he is one of the few to reject an accepted contemporary analogy:

A force de progrès on viendroit à l'expérience du prisme. Aussitôt quelque artiste célèbre établiroit là-dessus un beau sistême. Messieurs, leur diroit-il, pour bien philosopher il faut remonter aux causes physiques. Voilà la décomposition de la lumière, voilà toutes les couleurs primitives, voilà leurs raports, leurs proportions, voilà les vrais principes du plaisir que vous fait la peinture [. . .] L'analyse des couleurs, le calcul des réfractions du prisme vous donnent les seuls rapports exacts qui soient dans la nature, la règle de tous les rapports [. . .] Que dirions-nous du peintre assés dépourvu de sentiment et de goût pour raisoner de la sorte et borner stupidement au physique de son art le plaisir que nous fait la peinture? (Rousseau, *Essai sur l'origine des langues*, 1995: 413–14)[14]

Castel's mistake is to assume that there is only one 'nature', that prisms and paintings are governed by the same universal laws. From Rousseau's point of view, it might also be Condillac's mistake with regard to his concept of 'la liaison des idées', because it too applies a system of analysis to an impressionistic

---

[14] Thomas thinks that this passage is a parody of Rameau's theory of the 'corps sonore' (*Music and the Origins of Language*, 1995: 133).

event, it too analyses language into a sequence of nuances.
Condillac used the 'nuances' metaphor with specific reference
to figurative language to suggest that it is possible almost to
measure the angle of intersection between two ideas, and judge
objectively how well they compare, and how well they would
work in a figurative comparison.[15] Rousseau's idea of suggestive
metaphor has no such rational basis. His criticism of Castel, in
fact, implicates the whole Enlightenment enterprise of rationalizing the idea of beauty, of finding a balance between understanding and feeling, and of defining a 'science of sentiment'
which we have come to call aesthetics. Rousseau's belief is that
the rational component is unduly emphasized in these aesthetic
models, to the detriment of the element of 'feeling' which he
considers crucial, and without which there could be no
aesthetic event.

The ideas of Rousseau and Condillac are striking both for
their similarities and their differences. Both argue that figurative language plays a crucial role in the origin of language, both
share a 'poetic' view of language, but their paths subsequently
diverge. Condillac goes on to chart the intellectual progress of
language and intellect so that rational analysis and 'la liaison
des idées' are universal concepts which explain scientific as well
as artistic phenomena. Rousseau does not think that intellectual development is all of a piece, since at the outset there is
a divergence between two quite different perceptions of the
world, one through analogy and the other through metaphor.
It is perhaps characteristic of Rousseau that he should maintain
a tension at the heart of language and the nature of man,
whereas the resolution in 'la liaison des idées' of Condillac's
system represents an eighteenth-century aspiration to find universal principles to explain diverse phenomena.

3.7   Buffon's universal style

Perhaps the contemporary of Condillac's who makes the best
use of the idea of 'liaison des idées' in style is Buffon. The *Discours sur le style*, delivered to the Académie française in 1753,

---

[15] For Condillac's 'nuances' metaphor, see Chapter 1.

was republished throughout the eighteenth century, and more than a hundred times in the following century. His monumental *Histoire naturelle* was admired by Flaubert, Baudelaire, Barbey d'Aurevilly, and presumably generations of young children who read him as recently as the 20th century.[16] The phenomenal success of Buffon's work is in part due to the enormous care he took to refine his style; he is said, for example, to have rewritten *Les Epoques de la nature* (1788) sixteen times.[17] It is also because Buffon's work is a heady mix of Renaissance naturalism and eighteenth-century natural history, a mix of traditional 'style coupé' and universalist 'liaison des idées' that he is able to cross the divide between poetry and science. Rivarol was cynical of a hybrid genre which he said read like Bossuet writing pastoral poetry, but it is precisely the reconciliation of old and new, of scientific and poetic which is captivating.[18] Buffon always thought that scientific language could be beautiful, that precision and elegance could co-exist. His is a very traditional maxim of style, with important implications at a time when chemists and economists were inventing a technical jargon with no pretence to poetry.[19]

Buffon recommends a cultivated eloquence which would have all the power of free conversation without the disorder of 'enthousiasme'. Rhetorical talent is easy 'à tous ceux dont les passions sont fortes, les organes souples & l'imagination prompte', but real genius requires 'la culture de l'esprit' (Buffon, *Discours sur le style*, 1954: 500). Real genius involves rationally organizing our thoughts in order to express ideas and 'things' instead of becoming engrossed in the language itself. Buffon uses the 'nuances' metaphor to make his point: 'le ton, les gestes & le vain son des mots [. . .] comptent pour peu; il faut des choses, des pensées, des raisons; il faut savoir les présenter, les nuancer, les ordonner: il ne suffit pas de frapper l'oreille & d'occuper les yeux, il faut agir sur l'ame & toucher le cœur en parlant à l'esprit' (p. 500). Like Condillac, Buffon

---

[16] Bruneau, 'Buffon et la forme', 1954: 491. For a children's version of Buffon, see Rabier, *Le Buffon de Benjamin Rabier* (1917). The drawings are by Rabier, the text is Buffon's.

[17] Hérault de Séchelles, *Voyages à Montbard* (An VIII).

[18] Grente, *Dictionnaire des lettres françaises* (1995): 236.

[19] See Chapter 4 for discussion of these languages.

thinks that good style is best achieved by a logical relation of ideas: 'bien écrire, c'est former [. . .] une chaîne continue [. . .] d'idées' in which 'idées accessoires' are systematically related to 'idées particulières' (p. 502). Also like Condillac, Buffon believes that there is a way of imitating the workings of a rational mind in the logical progression of ideas in written style, and this belief is the reasoning behind his famous phrase: 'le style est l'homme même' (Buffon, *Discours sur le style*, 1954: 503). Good style is a reflection of human rationality, a matter of composing ideas into a chain of logically dependent phrases. The resulting composition is 'une dépendance harmonique des idées [. . .] une gradation soutenue', a natural flow which is a pleasure to read, but also the most instructive form of composition (p. 501).

If we compare Condillac's model sentence from Fléchier, which we discussed earlier, to the following opening sentence from Buffon's article 'Le Cheval', the similarities between 'la liaison des idées' and Buffon's 'style coupé' become obvious:

La plus noble conquête que l'homme ait jamais faite est celle de ce fier et fougueux animal qui partage avec lui les fatigues de la guerre et la gloire des combats; aussi intrépide que son maître, il l'aime, il le   3
cherche et s'anime de la même ardeur; il partage aussi ses plaisirs; à la chasse, aux tournois, à la course, il brille, il étincelle; mais docile autant que courageux, il ne se laisse point emporter à son feu, il sait   6
réprimer ses mouvements; non seulement il fléchit sous la main de celui qui le guide, mais il semble consulter ses désirs, et obéissant toujours aux impressions qu'il en reçoit, il se précipite, se modère, ou   9
s'arrête, et n'agit que pour y satisfaire; c'est une créature qui renonce à son être pour n'exister que par la volonté d'un autre, qui sait même la prévenir, qui par la promptitude et la précision de ses mouvements,   12
l'exprime et l'exécute; qui sent autant qu'on le désire, et ne rend qu'autant qu'on le veut; qui se livrant sans réserve ne se refuse à rien, sert de toutes ses forces, s'excède, et même meurt pour mieux obéir.   15
(Buffon, 'Le Cheval', 1975: 112)

The sentence is long, but 'coupé' into sometimes very short phrases, which in turn divide the meaning into manageable fragments. Although simple and clear, the stylistic imperative is to link phrases which could otherwise seem disjointed. Parataxis, or at the most an explicit co-ordinator like 'et', is more frequent than subordination: 'il l'aime, il le cherche et s'anime' (l. 3–4). Only the most nominal subordination is used, the relative 'qui', which is repeated to emphasize the explicit reference to the subject 'une créature' (l. 10–14). Parallel structures, often with alliteration, smooth the transition between phrases, and are preferred to dependent structures: 'la promptitude et la précision [. . .] l'exprime et l'exécute' (l. 12–13). The effect is to emphasize the sequence of ideas, their logical independence from each other, so that the final composed effect of the complete sentence seems like the result of a natural affinity. There seems a fortuitous concord which would be more imputable to the nature of the ideas than the writer's art of composition.

At the level of macro-structure, the rhythm of the sentence depends upon general statements which lead into detailed description, from 'idée générale' to 'idées accessoires'. The distinctive opening phrase, 'la plus noble conquête' is followed by an account of the horse's daring in war and peace; Buffon then operates a neat twist to move from daring to docility, 'mais docile autant que courageux' (l. 5–6), which leads to an account of the horse's obedience to man. Thus, the parallelism at a syntactic level is also evident in the balance of composition between the two complementary characteristics of the horse. The second general statement, 'c'est une créature . . .' (l. 10) is a conclusion which seems to arise inevitably from the preceding description, and leads to another litany of qualities, culminating in the final alliterative balance 'meurt pour mieux obéir'. The result is a sequence of ideas which seem to develop organically from a central proposition. The logical relations are less explicit and the reader feels less coerced and more beguiled into following a particular train of thought.

Buffon manages to captivate the reader, rather as the painter controls the viewer's attention in Diderot's description of the art of composition. We are led scrupulously, but insensibly from one element to the next, so that we feel we are participating in the composition of the work, and yet it is the artist who has imposed his perspective. This compositional exercise is meant, according to Condillac and Buffon, to be an imitative one, because the order on the page or canvas is supposed to reflect the mental pattern of ideas in the mind of the artist. For Buffon and Condillac, therefore, writing is a fairly direct product of our cognitive processes. When Buffon says famously, therefore, 'le style est l'homme même', he has a very elevated view of both style and man: the first we can gloss as 'literary aesthetics', with all the consequent assumptions of rationality that Baumgarten gave to the word 'aesthetics', and the second we can gloss as 'humanity' in the sense of a generic, universal class. In other words, aesthetics is what makes us human. It is unfortunate that Buffon's phrase has become very well-known for the wrong reasons: it is often interpreted, including by contemporaries like Mercier, to mean 'style is relative' or 'everyone has their own style', as if Buffon meant simply that writing is just one more characteristic of an individual, like a big nose or high voice.[20]

The key point about the theory and practice of Buffon's style is that it compares closely with Condillac's concept of 'la liaison des idées'. The additional feature in Buffon's writing, however, and one of the most recognizable characteristics of his *Histoire naturelle*, is a symbolism of the kind we normally associate with Renaissance naturalism. The combination of the two, 'liaison des idées' and this kind of symbolism makes for an interesting poetic adaptation of a rational theory. Part of the poetry of his *Histoire naturelle* lies in the affinity he sees, for example, between the upright posture of man and the horse, and their intrinsic nobility, or the marvellous sensibility to the symbolism of extended arms and outstretched spirit. Not all of the *Histoire naturelle* is like this, of course, but his technical observations are often prefaced with the kind of analogy we associate with Renaissance scholars like Giambattista della Porta.[21] Renaissance naturalism is the doctrine which considers that in nature there is a universal soul which links all beings by secret laws of similitude or dissimilitude, of sympathy and antipathy. The similarity of the viper's fang and the spines of the hawthorn mean that the hawthorn is a natural antidote for the venom of the viper. The essential aspect of naturalism which is of interest to Buffon is the belief that the physical world gives expression to the soul.

The combination of the clarity of 'style coupé' and this kind of symbolism is the source of much of Buffon's charm and poetic quality.[22] The following is from *De l'Homme, l'âge viril*: 'tout marque dans l'homme [. . .] sa supériorité sur tous les êtres vivans; il se soûtient droit & élevé, son attitude est celle du commandement, sa tête regarde le ciel & présente une face auguste sur laquelle est imprimé le caractère de sa dignité [. . .] Il ne touche à la terre que par ses extremités les plus éloignées, il ne la voit que de loin, & semble la dédaigner' (Buffon, 'De l'Homme', 1954: 298). The procedure is poetic; revelation through analogy, use of detail to evoke a global image, and of course, the symbolism of the body. It may seem odd that in a work of science Buffon should take such imaginative leaps, but his analogies are important to his theory of scientific writing. In contrast, Linnaeus, his contemporary rival in natural history, considered that the primary role of the scientist is to observe and to categorize. Buffon, however, thinks that style has a role in all kinds of writing, that one's aim is always to 'paint' and 'feel' a subject: 'voir, entendre, palper, sentir, ce sont autant de caractères que l'écrivain doit sentir et rendre par des traits énergiques' (Buffon, *Art d'écrire*, 1954: 510). In addition, his analogies appeal to the imagination, because they touch on universal themes. Pliny's much repeated remark, for example, that man is unique because he is so vulnerable at birth is interpreted allegorically by Buffon as an image of man born to suffer: '[l'enfant est] une image de misère & de douleur, [. . .] sa vie incertaine & chancelante [. . .] A peine a-t-il la force pour exister & pour annoncer par des gémissemens les souffrances qu'il éprouve, comme si la nature vouloit l'avertir qu'il est né pour souffrir' (Buffon, *Histoire naturelle de l'Homme*, 1954: 298). A little later, he describes the weakness of man's upper limbs as a symbol of the spirituality of man; as the eyes are the mirror of the soul, the arms are the servants of the will: 'sa main ne doit pas fouler la terre, & perdre par des frottemens réitérez la finesse du toucher dont elle est le principal organe: le bras & la main sont faits pour servir à des usages plus nobles pour exécuter les ordres de la volonté' (pp. 298–9). This kind of symbolism, appealing as it does to a common imagination of 'man born to suffer' or the 'spirituality of outstretched hands' is part of a broad vista, a 'tableau' of universal images.

[22] Ecouchard Le Brun later writes: 'Buffon, je l'avoûrai, j'aime assez peu les Vers; | Mais j'adore la Poésie', in 'Sur la différence des vers et de la poésie, à M. de Buffon' (1811): Vol. III, 416.

Buffon's style differs from Rousseau's in his novels or Diderot's in the 'drame'. Rousseau argues in the second preface to *La Nouvelle Héloïse* that he prefers the intimacy of a character 'portrait' to the universality of the 'tableau'. Diderot and Beaumarchais forgo Buffon's poetic vision of articulate man, and emphasize instead the inadequacy of language. It seems odd that a conversationalist like Diderot or a wit like Beaumarchais should doubt the possibilities of language in this way, and that a naturalist like Buffon should cultivate eloquence with such conviction, but their respective intentions are different. The language of the 'drame' is a cultivation of 'intérêt', which is an intimate empathy between actor and spectator, whereas Buffon's language relates at a more abstract level of universal ideas, like 'man born to suffer'. Buffon's reader is unlikely to 'se recueillir', to reach a heightened level of self-awareness as the 'drame' would encourage. Beaumarchais and Diderot are more interested in how language works in the intimate context of conversation and art than at the abstract level of universal ideas. Diderot in his role as art critic never forgets that the wandering eye which is led along the curve of interest in a painting is the eye of the viewer, of a physical person who is engaged in a meaningful dialogue with the painter. It seems, then, that Buffon, Diderot, and Rousseau have quite distinct ideas of literary aesthetics, and yet all their ideas are contained within the continuum that Condillac establishes between the original language of gesture and empathy, the metaphorical signs of the first institutional language, and the analytical composition of modern sequential language.

Conclusion

There is a notable contrast between the seductive continuity in Condillac's theory of representation and the variety of more selective ideas of his literary contemporaries. The widespread admiration with which contemporaries regard Condillac is doubtless derived in part from his apparent ability to devise a 'general theory' which encompasses a wide range of different concepts of language which might otherwise conflict. It is quite an intellectual feat to trace an evolutionary line from sensual perception, to empathy, to gestural language, to metaphor, to chains of thought, and finally to fully-fledged literary expression. All the more so since by the end of this process of development none of these modes of representation has been lost; they are all available to the modern literary writer. The only contemporary to come near Condillac is Diderot, but he never formulates his ideas in the same intellectually seductive terms of a general theory.

Implicit in this general theory is a very broad notion of how language imitates. At one extreme, language imitates the natural passions, it is a purely subjective manifestation of how an individual perceives the world through the senses. At the other extreme, language imitates the chain of thought in all rational thinking, and it is therefore as universal as the faculty of reason itself. Despite the gulf which separates them, language can do both on condition that the right literary devices are used; metaphor and gestural language in the first case, and a kind of 'style coupé' in the second.

Condillac is therefore singularly at ease with the idea of imitation in the midst of an intellectual environment fraught with anxieties on the subject. Diderot, for example, finds linguistic representation more of an irresolvable issue. Although he has answers to the question of how the apparently rational exercise of using language can be adapted to the representation of something quite subjective and indeterminate like 'sentiment', he has misgivings. In his terms, it may be that the semiotic 'filet' can not be made fine enough to capture something so elusive; or worse, it may be completely unsuited to the exercise. In which case, there is a problem at the heart of the theory of imitation if it is supposed to be as broad a concept as some would pretend.

Condillac's most important concepts in this context are 'first' and 'second' nature, because it is with these terms that he answers the question notoriously resistant to clarification in imitation: 'what is nature?'. Like Batteux whose answer to this question is 'la belle nature', Condillac suggests a qualifying adjective, but unlike Batteux, it is not a naming fallacy. 'Seconde nature' has real explanatory significance.

4

LINGUISTIC AND POETIC SOUND SYMBOLISM

The subject of this chapter is, in a way, a microcosm of the last. Condillac achieved an impressive continuity between quite different modes of linguistic representation, with the implicit idea that the most fundamental or 'natural' kinds are still accessible to the modern literary writer as a 'second' nature. There are a number of contemporaries who study in detail exactly how this can be achieved, in order to show that language is capable of a high level of naturalistic imitation, or, in their terms, that language can 'echo' nature.

Antoine Court de Gébelin and Charles de Brosses re-interpret the well-established idea of 'l'harmonie imitative' in poetry as a fundamental level of sound symbolism in language, present from the very origins of language itself. Olivet had already argued that French has an operable system of prosody, if not as systematic as Latin metrics, which the poet may use in order to convey sense through skilful marshalling of sound, or 'l'harmonie imitative'. He is supported to varying degrees by critics such as Louis Racine, Marmontel, and Batteux, but none draws out the implications for aesthetics in general quite so effectively as Gébelin and de Brosses. Both study etymology concurrently with the art of imitation, because according to their Cratyline theory of language, the origin of man's ability to speak lies in the essential desire to imitate his environment. Accordingly, they both devise a symbolic language which is at the same time the suggested origin and the underlying structure of modern language.

The correlation between their theories of etymology and contemporary literary controversy is clear on two counts. Firstly, the symbolic values they suggest for the sounds of language are similar to those conventionally understood in 'l'harmonie imitative'; for example, 'r' (an apical trill in the eighteenth century) symbolizes movement, roughness or unpleasantness.[1] Secondly,

---

[1] Seguin quotes Fouché, who says that the transition from apical to dorsal 'r' probably happened sometime in the mid-eighteenth century, and was at first

Gébelin in particular was read by Antoine de Piis and other poets, and is likely to a greater or lesser extent to have influenced their poetry. There is a curious circular relation between theorists who are prompted by literary controversy to investigate more fully the conventions of versification, and subsequent poets whose work is inspired by these new theories.

The ideas of Gébelin and de Brosses illustrate an acute contemporary sensitivity to the theory of imitation, and it is worth weighing this in the mind against the teleological temptation of some critics to regard them as prototypes of later concepts. It is inappropriate to claim, for example, that Gébelin is a precursor to nineteenth-century ideo-realism (Baldensperger, *Court de Gébelin et l'importance de son 'Monde primitif'*, 1940: 325), or that de Brosses is 'le point de départ [. . .] d'un courant de pensée dont l'aboutissement poétique [est] Baudelaire' (Genette, *Mimologiques*, 1976: 99), unless we also consider what de Brosses and Gébelin inherited from long-standing traditions of imitation in general and versification in particular. To this end, this chapter will relate the sound symbolism of de Brosses and Gébelin to the tradition of 'l'harmonie imitative', as defined by Louis Racine, Marmontel, and Batteux, and then show that their concept of 'étymologie' suggests a particular understanding of poetic language.

4.1   De Brosses's theory of phonomimetism

Charles de Brosses, Président de l'Académie des Lettres de Dijon, published his *Traité de la formation méchanique des langues et des principes physiques de l'étymologie* in 1765, claiming to have found a new way to study etymology and, at the same time, to describe accurately and systematically the sounds of modern language. He devised 'l'alphabet organique', which is partly a phonetic alphabet, and partly an application of Aristotelian principles of logical division.

There are seven primary characters: six 'lettres primitives' or consonants, 'b, k, d, j, l, s', corresponding to the six organs of articulation, 'les lèvres, la gorge, les dents, le palais, la langue, le nez'; and one 'son primitif', which is 'a', the most sonorous

confined to the lower classes and the bourgeoisie (Seguin, *La Langue française au XVIIIe siècle*, 1972: 42).

and open vowel. Each is an archetype for a range of realizations, so that 'b' stands for the set of labial sounds 'p, b, m, f, v, pl, bl [. . .]', and 'a' for the seven vowels of his schema, 'a, ai [è], e, i, o, ou, u' (see Figure 3; nasal vowels are represented by 'vowel + n'). He decides which sounds are archetypes according to the 'énergie' involved in articulation, so that the six derivative vowels are progressively closer realizations of 'a', and the six consonants are voiced or plosive, except for the peculiar inclusion of 's' (clearly /s/ from his examples). According to the same principle of 'énergie', he allots 'f' to the set of labials, and not the dentals, perhaps because it is the lips which visibly move.

It is easy from a modern perspective to quarrel with the distribution of sounds in de Brosses's 'alphabet organique', but he does not share the objectives of modern phonetics. To begin with, there is a noticeable reliance on Aristotelian principles of logical division in the way that de Brosses looks for generic types of sounds of which all others are simply different realizations. Secondly, as will become clear later, he is a product of a poetic tradition which encourages systematic analysis of subjective perception, and his 'alphabet organique' is therefore intended to further the understanding of how this kind of poetry works.

His main proposition is that the basic sounds of language are 'natural', in the sense that they are mechanically predetermined by the constitution of the vocal organs. Like Bernard Lamy and Gérauld de Cordemoy a century earlier, he is interested in the 'mechanics' of speech, or the articulatory phonetics, but with much more emphasis on the way sound is used to symbolize meaning.[2] De Brosses calls this the study of 'étymologie', by which he means a blend of phonetics, semiosis, and diachrony of language, that is, its material determinants, their use as signifiers, and the study of both in modern language. More simply, we might say that de Brosses studies the relation between sound and meaning.[3] The determining principle involved is 'imitation', and the wider aesthetic

---

[2] Gerauld de Cordemoy, *Discours physique de la parole* (1677); Bernard Lamy, *De l'Art de parler* (1675).

[3] Droixhe thinks that de Brosses's particular blend of interests is the beginning of the study of synchronic structure in language, and that: 'De Brosses symbolise exactement la naissance de la linguistique scientifique'. He concludes that his treatise is: 'une magnifique théorie onomatopéique qui n'a rien d'un système du glouglou' (Droixhe, 'L'Orientation structurale de la linguistique au XVIIIe siècle', 1971: 27–8).

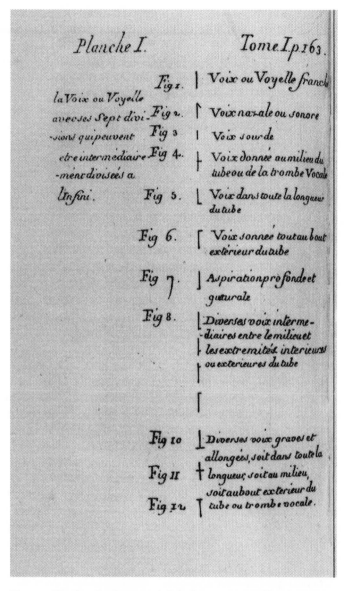

Fig. 3. Charles de Brosses, 'alphabet organique', in *Traité de la formation méchanique des langues et des principes physiques de l'étymologie* (1765; 1800: Vol. I, facing pp. 163 and 166).

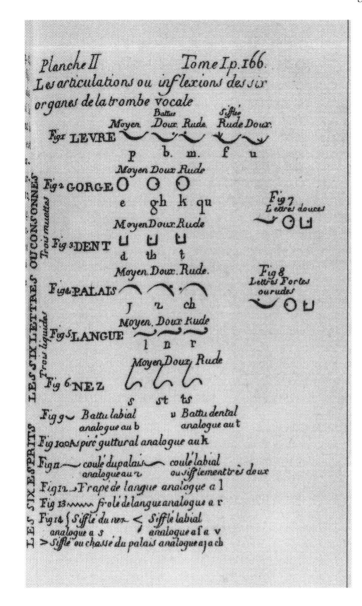

implications of his etymology become clearer as he develops his Cratyline theory of language.

De Brosses does not believe that language is a radically arbitrary system of sounds, but that it is a product of two things: firstly, man's primary intellectual impulse to imitate, and secondly, his primary perception, which is a kinaesthetic sense of one's own material existence. It seems inevitable to de Brosses that when man invents an articulated sign for an object in nature, or a personal emotion, he will draw a perceptual analogy between the signified and an articulation with analogous physical characteristics. The apical trill 'r', for example, feels abrasive, and is an appropriate sign to convey the meaning 'rough'. He says that words in modern French like 'rude, âcre, âpre, roc, rompre, râcler, irriter' are etymologically derived from this elementary principle (de Brosses, *Traité*, 1800: Vol. I, 242). De Brosses's originality, and the new way he devised to study etymology, is this principle of phonomimetism, that is to say, the analogy between the physical characteristics of an articulation and the meaning to be conveyed. The process seems as logical and inevitable to de Brosses as the way a painter chooses his colours:

Le choix [. . .] d'articulations [. . .] qu'on veut faire servir à la fabrique d'un mot [. . .] est physiquement déterminé par la nature et par la qualité de l'objet même, [. . .] tellement que l'homme qui sera dans le cas d'imposer le premier nom à une chose rude, emploiera une inflexion rude et non pas une inflexion douce; de même qu'entre les sept couleurs primitives, un peintre, qui veut peindre l'herbe, est obligé d'employer le vert et non pas le violet. (de Brosses, *Traité*, 1800: Vol. I, xii)

The seven 'primitive' colours are almost certainly Newton's, and the reference to the painter's application of colour seems a gesture towards the determining principle which the image of the spectrum seems to provide in painting.[4] De Brosses suggests that the seven characters of his 'alphabet organique' are the equivalent determining principle in language, and that sound in language reflects nature in the same way as colour in painting. The imitative impulse is the same in either case, and is an essential intellectual characteristic of man: 'c'est une vérité

---

[4] See Chapter 1.

de fait assez connue, que l'homme est, par sa nature, porté à l'imitation: on le remarque de la manière la plus frappante dans la formation des mots [...] L'homme n'hésite, ne réfléchit, ni ne compare, il imite avec sa voix le bruit qui a frappé son oreille, et le son qui résulte est le nom qu'il donne à la chose' (de Brosses, *Traité*, 1800: Vol. I, 229–30). Man's first impulse is not to compare or to think, as Condillac suggested, but to imitate. The linguistic example he gives here is onomatopoeia, but there are a total of six linguistic devices which convey meaning through sound: 'les interjections, les mots enfantins, le nom des organes même de la voix, le nom des choses extérieures qui peuvent produire quelque bruit à l'oreille (méthode la meilleure de toutes pour les faire promptement reconnaître), la structure machinale de certains organes les approprie naturellement à nommer certaines classes de choses du même genre' (de Brosses, *Traité*, 1800: Vol. I, 261). Interjections reveal 'une relation vraiment physique et de conformité entre certains sentimens de l'ame et certaines parties de l'instrument vocal'. 'La douleur' is guttural, '[elle] frappe sur les basses cordes: elle est traînée, aspirée et profondément gutturale, *heu! hélas!*', while 'la douleur douce, la tristesse' is more nasal, 'la voix devient nazale, parce que la plainte, qui de sa nature approche du chant, emploie le plus sonore des deux tuyaux' (de Brosses, *Traité*, 1800: Vol. I, 204). 'La voix du dégout et de l'aversion' is labial, not only because of the articulatory feeling of the 'f, v, p' sounds, but also because the lips project forward in a visual image of repulsion: '*fi! vœ! pouah!* celle-ci se sert aussi de la lettre labiale la plus extérieure de toutes, parce qu'il y a ici tout à-la-fois sentiment et action; sentiment qui répugne, et mouvement qui repousse: ainsi, dans le son il y a tout à-la-fois voix et figure: voix qui exprime, et figure qui rejette par le mouvement extérieur des lèvres allongées' (de Brosses, *Traité*, 1800: Vol. I, 205).

The second kind of imitative sounds are baby words like 'papa' and 'mama', which use the gestural value of labials to indicate a first consciousness of exterior things (labials, then, seem to have two 'meanings' according to context). The third kind of sound is related directly to the six consonants of the 'alphabet organique', because the names for the vocal organs, and associated functions, are derived from the sound they produce: 'l'homme forme volontiers les noms qu'il donne à chaque organe de sa parole sur le caractère ou l'inflexion propre à cet organe: comme gorge, langue, dent, bouche ou babine'. In this way, the sound 'g' means all that is associated with 'la gorge' (or in English 'gullet'), producing the words 'gargouiller, garchis, glougloux, glotte, glouton' or by association with the idea of depth, 'gouffre' (de Brosses, *Traité*, 1800: Vol. I, 227). The fourth device is onomatopoeia in words such as 'sonore', which uses repeated open vowels; 'tambour' which uses open vowels and two percussive consonants 't, b'; or 'trictrac', a game of dice (p. 229).

It is not uncommon to find discussion of onomatopoeia in other contemporary texts on language, but de Brosses's examples are particularly interesting because they exploit the synaesthetic potential of his principle of phonomimetism. He suggests that there is transfer of meaning between the senses, so that 'r' suggests roughness, but also bitter taste in 'âpre, âcre, aigre'; or that the sound 'fl' of 'flairer' suggests the delicate, elusive quality of a smell (de Brosses, *Traité*, 1800: Vol. I, 234). One reason why contemporary writers use metaphor so cautiously is that they do not take for granted the synaesthetic implications of figuratively transferred meaning. Literary commentaries often draw attention to the pertinence or otherwise of specific analogies, as if the comparison can never safely be assumed without corroboration. De Brosses's etymology tests the idea of transferred meaning, and provides just the kind of corroborative thinking that would have encouraged poets to exploit the symbolic potential of language. His study is certainly a linguistic exercise, but also in a way an original kind of stylistic commentary, a critique of literary language.

The fifth device is the key phonomimetic ability to reflect the nature of the object with the physical characteristics of an articulation, so that the abrasive feeling of the 'r' sound is appropriate to the meaning of 'râcler'; 'st' expresses 'fermeté, fixité' in French 'stabilité', Italian 'stare', or English 'stone', because: 'les dents étant le plus immobile des six organes de la voix [. . .] le *T* a été machinalement employé pour désigner la fixité' (de Brosses, *Traité*, 1800: Vol. I, 238). The sixth and last kind of sound is not mentioned in the quotation above, because it is supplementary to the first. 'Les accens [. . .] une espèce de

chant, joint à la parole' are the natural and oratorical intonations expressing a 'sentiment intérieur', or symptom of inner
feeling, which is as universal and immediately recognizable as
facial expression.

These six devices rely on a perceived organic conformity,
'une convenance' between sound and meaning, which is man's
primitive way of relating his exterior and interior world. As language develops, it may become a more or less conventional
system of signs, but its origin is motivated by an imitative relation between signifier and signified. De Brosses's principles of
etymology seek to reveal that the imitative relation between
sound and meaning is still discernible in modern language.

According to these principles of sound symbolism, de Brosses
dissects modern French, to expose a sub-lexical level of
meaning which sometimes supports conventional meaning,
and sometimes demonstrates how the original symbolic language has been obscured by a complex series of figurative
associations and semantic extensions. Latin 'scrupulus', for
example, is derived as follows: the guttural sound 'C' suggests
'le creux, la cavité naturelle'; 'S' is an augmentative, 'un signe
qui marque encore plus, qui ajoute à la peinture de la cavité
l'idée d'action qui la produit'; 'R' suggests abrasive movement;
together, the root 'SCR' supports the accepted meaning of
'scrupulus', which is 'un petit éclat de pierre, ou un gravier
détaché d'un bloc en le creusant et l'excavant avec force' (de
Brosses, *Traité*, 1800: Vol. II, 478, 251). Modern French
'scrupule' is a metaphorical extension of the original meaning,
because to have a small but troubling moral matter on one's
mind is like feeling a stone in one's shoe. In another example,
de Brosses describes how far this process of metaphorical extension can go, until there appears no relation between sound and
meaning at all. The 'ST' of 'stellae' suggests their 'fixité'. By
association with the starry sky, the lizard 'stellio' derives its
name from its patterned skin. Through the analogy between
the lizard's skin and the poison it produces, 'stellion' comes to
mean a certain kind of fraudulent legal contract, and de Brosses
concludes: 'ainsi l'opération de l'esprit [pervertit] l'opération
de la nature' (de Brosses, *Traité*, 1800: Vol. II, 310).

In this quotation, and in his etymology in general, 'nature' is
a determining principle, an underlying design to language

which guards against the caprice of convention. It provides reassurance to a literary culture which mistrusts metaphorical use of language, because it appears that even the most erratic semantics is ultimately imitative of 'nature'. It is remarkable, however, that he should think it necessary to go to these lengths in order to justify linguistic imitation, and one can only assume that the contemporary debate required a systematic treatment such as his. His explanations sometimes become very involved, so that individual words can become a kind of semiotic puzzle in which their meaning is pieced together from the internal relation of sounds. The combination, for example, of 'rudesse R' and 'cavité C', contributes to the meaning of 'scabROsus'; 'R' and 'échappement F' reflect the meaning of 'FRustra' (de Brosses, *Traité*, 1800: Vol. I, 242); 'AC doit être considéré en lui même comme désignant dans le sens propre ou figuré, tout ce qui est pointu, perçant, pénétrant, allant en avant', in such words as 'âcre, aiguille, acide, agacer, aigle, ancre, angle' (de Brosses, *Traité*, 1800: Vol. II, 300–3). Natural symbolism is present everywhere we look in language, it is an unconscious but universal 'mother tongue': 'une langue primitive, organique, physique et nécéssaire, commune à tout le genre humain, qu'aucun peuple au monde ne connaît ni ne pratique dans sa premiere simplicité; que tous les hommes parlent néanmoins, et qui fait le premier fond du langage de tous les pays' (de Brosses, *Traité*, 1800: Vol. I, pp. xiv–xv). He presents sound symbolism as an unspoken but undeniable determinant of language. De Brosses's theory of 'étymologie' is devised to evaluate this phenemonon. It is 'un glossomètre' to measure how far the capricious evolution of language has strayed from the universal language of sentiment, '[pour] voir d'un coup-d'œil [...] la manière dont ils nuancent leurs changemens' (de Brosses, *Traité*, 1800: Vol. I, 178). The 'nuances' metaphor arises again in order to suggest that it is, in fact, possible to make sense of a phenomenon which looks indeterminate.

One cannot ignore in the contemporary context the influential ideas of John Locke and so many other language theorists who denied any imitative motivation between signified and signifier beyond trivial onomatopoeia. Locke consequently posits a radically arbitrary sound–meaning relation: 'we may

conceive how *words* [. . .] come to be made use of by men, as
the *signs of their ideas*: not by any natural connexion, that there
is between particular articulate sounds and certain *ideas*, for
then there would be but one language amongst all men; but by
a voluntary imposition, whereby such a word is made arbitrar-
ily the mark of such an *idea*' (Locke, *An Essay Concerning Human
Understanding*, 1977: 207). While eighteenth-century thinkers
do not ignore him, they do take him to task in certain ways.
Condillac, for example, argues that Locke made a crucial error
in leaving his study of language until Book III, since in Condillac's opinion he should have made it the first concern of his
inquiry into knowledge. Condillac seeks to rectify this error in
his *Essai sur l'origine des connoissances humaines* (1746) by discussing language in Book I.

In the case of Locke's radically arbitrary linguistic sign, some
thinkers reconsider it in the light of its implications for literature and the arts. In the first place, it appears to deny the
expressive potential of poetic language in ways we will discuss
shortly. More fundamentally, it fits uneasily with the idea that
the practice of great authors can somehow contribute to what
critics call 'nature' in art. It may well be partly for these aesthetic reasons that neither de Brosses nor Condillac are able to
accept Locke's radical arbitrariness without modification. De
Brosses modifies it, ironically, by applying Locke's own theory
of Sensualism to the letter; in other words, by deriving language
directly from the senses. He quotes Locke at length, and comments: 'je ne doute point que si nous pouvions conduire tous
les mots jusqu'à leur source, nous ne trouvassions que dans
toutes les langues les mots qu'on emploie pour signifier des
choses qui ne tombent pas sous les sens, ont tiré leur première
origine d'idées sensibles' (de Brosses, *Traité*, 1800: Vol. II, 87).
He goes on to say that even abstract, metaphysical words are in
the end derived from 'une analogie radicale' with a physical
sensation. If this is so, then the challenge is to demonstrate
exactly how abstract language is related to the sensations. Locke
says merely that signs for ideas are imposed 'voluntarily', but
does not explain this sense of volition. De Brosses suggests that
the volition responsible is a desire to imitate, and that it per-
sists in modern language, even if at times it is hard to trace.

4.2   Court de Gébelin's theory of phonomimetism

Gébelin has read de Brosses and bases his own schema of sound symbolism on similar principles of imitation and phonomimetism. He is perhaps spurred by the unfulfilled ambitions which de Brosses declares in his treatise:

Il serait à propos de faire un ouvrage qu'on va regarder d'abord comme immense, et qui ne l'est point du tout. Ce serait de dresser par racines une nomenclature universelle de tous les mots des langues d'Europe et d'Orient [...] en telle sorte que l'acception idéale, ou la figure matérielle des mots s'altèrant légérement d'un chaînon au suivant [...], et que l'on passe par des nuances insensibles d'une idée, d'une figure ou d'un son à d'autres très-differens, sans être choqué du contraste. (de Brosses, *Traité*, 1800: Vol. II, 456–7)

Gébelin's etymological dictionary lives up to de Brosses's expectations, because it is 'immense' in the sense that it embraces all the 'nuances' of language, but also very systematic, because it reduces them to a small set of symbolic roots. Gébelin's etymological dictionary of French is one volume in a nine-volume encyclopaedia, *Monde primitif, analysé et comparé avec le monde moderne* (1773–84). The other eight volumes are an exhaustive inquiry into the primitive origins of modern culture, ranging from the history of allegory, of French, Latin and Greek, of grammar, of language, of the calendar, heraldry, money, games, and much more. It had a successful publishing record, and subscribers included Diderot, Batteux, de Brosses, d'Holbach, Turgot, Naigeon, Montesquieu, Senancour, Vigny, and also Benjamin Franklin who sent Gébelin information on American Indian languages in 1781.[5] Contemporary critical reaction is mixed. *L'Année littéraire* in 1776 thinks that *Monde primitif* is 'si rempli d'érudition', while the *Journal des savants* remarks that Gébelin 'exagère le symbolisme'.[6] The ambivalence arises from different interpretations of his intellectual zeal, the confident elaboration of de Brosses's phonomimetism which leads Genette to regard him as 'l'image même du mimologiste

---

[5] See Baldensperger, 'Court de Gébelin' (1940): 316, 329. See also my footnote on Gébelin in Chapter 1.8.

[6] *L'Année littéraire* (1776): Vol. VIII, 270; *Journal des savants* (Nov.–Dec. 1773). Quoted from Baldersperger, 'Court de Gébelin', 1940: 328.

heureux' (Genette, *Mimologiques*, 1976: 120). His ideas on sound symbolism make exhilarating reading, his enthusiasm is contagious, because he does not regard the sound–meaning relation as problematic. On the contrary, it is a methodological model for the primitivist history of his *Monde primitif.*

Most of Gébelin's ideas on sound symbolism are contained in Volume I, which is a general introduction to the other nine volumes, Volume III, concerning the origin of language, and Volume V, which is an etymology of French as de Brosses intended. There are also interesting remarks in Volume II on universal grammar, and Volume VI, which is an etymology of Latin. Like de Brosses, he believes that imitation is the determining factor in language. In the introduction to Volume III he sets out his essential faith in this principle:

Ici, comme dans nos premiers Volumes, nous sommes partis d'un seul principe, l'IMITATION; & ce principe est le même qui nous a mis en état de remplir notre but. L'homme a eu un modèle pour parler, *la Nature & les Idees*; il en eut un pour écrire, les objets même de ses idées & de ses discours. Ainsi nous avançons dans notre carriere avec le même flambeau, le principe de l'Imitation. [. . .] il nous devoile [. . .] l'Origine de la Parole & celle de l'Ecriture, qui sembloient ensevelies pour jamais dans la nuit des tems. (Gébelin, *Monde primitif,* 1775: Vol. III, p. ii)

He assumes that 'Nature' is a 'modèle' which is copied according to the principles of 'imitation', and that the obscure origins of language become clearer when we understand its imitative principles. Like de Brosses, he is only interested in the physical realization of speech in as much as it illustrates the art of representation: 'il ne suffisoit pas d'avoir exposé la Physique de la parole; il falloit sur-tout rendre raison des moyens par lesquels l'homme avoit apperçu qu'il pouvoit peindre ses idées par le secours de l'Instrument Vocal' (Gébelin, *Monde primitif,* Vol. II: p. v). It is not the instrument itself which interests him, but the way it is used to express meaning. He assumes also that 'l'arbitraire ne mène à rien' (Gébelin, *Monde primitif,* Vol. III: 289), that there is a necessary 'convenance' between sound and meaning, and that 'les touches', or linguistic articulations, are selected by the speaker as the painter selects his colours: 'ces touches complettoient entre elles toutes les qualités des objets que nous avions à rendre, comme le Peintre rend la Nature entière, parce qu'il trouve dans ses couleurs élémentaires, tout ce qu'il faut pour rendre toutes celles que lui offre la Nature' (Gébelin, *Monde primitif*, Vol. I: 10). The analogy, which he shares with de Brosses, requires a good deal of justification, of course, because a painter only reproduces one perception of nature, which is vision, so that the imitative relation between colour in nature and colour in painting is correspondingly less problematic. We know that language, on the other hand, does not represent vision directly, nor indeed touch, taste or smell. At best, it can use onomatopoeia to reproduce sound. The idea of phonomimetism, however, is to go beyond these limitations, and to allow language to find synaesthetic correlations, to reproduce our experience of nature in all its sensory dimensions. Language would combine the sense of vision in painting, sound in music, touch in sculpture, as well as smell and taste.

It seems an ambitious project to claim that all the senses can be expressed in language, but this is precisely Gébelin's objective. The synaesthetic principles on which phonomimetism is based are closely related to a key tenet of neoclassical aesthetics, that is that the arts (and different senses) are better explained by their similarities than their differences. The principle held to be common to all the arts (and to all the senses) is imitation of nature, so that poetry and painting, for example, are thought to partake fundamentally in the same process—hence the Horatian axiom *ut pictura poesis*. The idea of synaesthesia is an inevitable by-product of this aesthetic, because it is a way to make sense of the principle that our perception of nature can be readily 'translated' from one sense to another, from vision in painting, for example, to sound in music. Given Gébelin's comparison of painting and speech, perhaps one should interpret his linguistic theories as a further example of what Cassirer thinks is one of the most extraordinary aspects of Enlightenment philosophy: that most studies of psychology and epistemology, and we should say also aesthetics, are based on an interest in synaesthesia, which is often discussed in terms of 'the Molyneux question'.[7] One way of reading Gébelin's work,

---

[7] Cassirer, *The Philosophy of Enlightenment* (1951): 108.

therefore, is as an investigation into the philosophical basis of art and imitation.

By way of contrast with what we are assuming is an aesthetic implication to Gébelin's synaesthesia, Lessing's new semiotic theory of art specifically rejects synaesthesia. In *Laoköon* (1766), he comments that: 'colours are not [musical] tones and [. . .] eyes are not ears' (Lessing, *Laoköon*, 1966: 54). He thinks that it is futile to look for a transcendent principle of imitation in which all the arts would participate because, in fact, the arts are better understood according to the ways in which the same meaning is communicated in different ways. His principal example is Laocöon, who is fully robed and wearing a priest's head-dress in Virgil's poem, because 'with the poet a dress is no dress; it conceals nothing; our imagination sees through it, [we imagine] his suffering in every part of his body'. In contrast, the sculpture of Laocöon is almost naked, because the expression of pain can only be communicated by the contracted abdominal muscles, which would be hidden beneath the priest's robes (Lessing, *Laoköon*, 1966: 28).

In view of Lessing's concern for synaesthesia in art, Gébelin's frequent analogies between sound symbolism and art, and Cassirer's assumption that synaesthesia tends to be an unavoidable issue in a great deal of Enlightenment philosophy, it is reasonable to speculate on the aesthetic implications of Gébelin's theories—in particular because contemporary poets, as we will see later, do not miss the poetic possibilities of his ideas. If there are indeed aesthetic implications in Gébelin's ideas, then they are surely intended to support the traditional aesthetic encapsulated in Horace's axiom *ut pictura poesis*, in which case they are an incredibly elaborate justification of a traditional aesthetic which may be becoming more controversial.

The sound symbolism which Gébelin proposes is very detailed, but does not differ in principle from that put forward by de Brosses. Accordingly, his ideas and supporting arguments need only a brief summary. He distinguishes first between vowels ('sons'), which are 'le souffle' of language, and represent sensation, and consonants ('intonations') which represent ideas. In 'l'alphabet naturel' there are seven vowels which constitute 'la langue des Sensations' and have the following symbolic values:

A: the most sonorous of the 'octave' of vowels, is a symbol 'des passions fortes, de l'étonnement, de l'admiration, de la surprise' (Vol. I: 24), 'l'image naturelle de toute idée de superiorité, de priorité, de domination: & par conséquent le nom de la propriété' (Vol. I: 25).

Hê /E/: 'extrêmement ouvert & aspiré, désigna la sensation de la vie & tout ce qui contribue à la vie, la terre, par exemple' (Vol. III: 290); 'la vie, la nourriture, la terre nourrice' (Vol. III: 324).

E /e/: 'fut consacré à l'existence, au sentiment que l'on en a, & tout ce qui y est relatif' (Vol. III: 290). 'Est' is a grammatical auxiliary which allows a vital flow in syntax (Vol. II: 171–2).

I: 'fut relatif à la main & tout ce qui concerne le sens du toucher, & les soins, les secours qui en sont l'effet' (Vol. III: 290).

O: 'désigne la sensation de la vue, l'œil, & tous ses effets' (Vol. III: 290); 'O' is for light, fire, sun, and vision (Vol. III: 313–14).

U /y/: 'l'action d'humer, le gout & l'odorat' (Vol. III: 290); 'tout ce qui se hume, l'eau, les liquides, les parfums' (Vol. III: 324).

OU: 'l'ouie, l'oreille & tous leurs effets' (Vol. III: 290); 'le vent' (Vol. III: 321); 'l'air' (Vol. III: 324).

These seven vowels are subdivided further into a total of twenty-eight sounds, according to whether they are aspirated, nasal or 'plus lente' (i.e. 'a' rather than 'â'). He distinguishes next between seven natural consonants, divided according to place of articulation and divided further still according to whether they are pronounced 'fort' or 'foible'. In total there are fourteen:[8]

labial (p, b, v, m): 'douceur; pour prononcer des choses flatteuses; les noms de la bouche ou de ses effets, du boire, du manger, de la parole, &c.; bouche, bec, museau, manger, mordre, parole' (Vol. III: 334–7).

---

[8] *Monde primitif* is partly modelled on Kircher's *Oedipus Aegyptiacus* (1652–4). Kircher also devises a hieroglyphic alphabet of twenty-one characters. Devismes later presents enharmonic scales of twenty-one notes, one for each letter of the alphabet (*Pasilogie, ou de la musique considérée comme langue universelle*, 1806).

dental (t, d): 'elles sont l'antipode des labiales, étant les plus éclatantes, les plus sonores, les plus bruyantes' because the firmness of the teeth produces harder sound than the soft lips (Vol. III: 334); symbolizes 'les objets étendus, vastes, dominans' and the associated idea of perfection (Vol. III: 340).

nasal (n): 'ne peut se prononcer qu'en faisant sortir l'air avec force par les narines, en le repoussant hors de l'instrument vocal; elle sera donc une consonne sourde & repoussante' (Vol. III: 334).

lingual (l, r): opposite qualities, because 'l' is a gentle articulation, 'très-douce & très-coulante', 'r' is a harsh articulation, 'rude & roulante' (Vol. III: 334). Both symbolize movement, but 'l' for 'ce qui se meut avec douceur, qui produit des sensations douces & légères' (Vol. III: 346), and 'r' for 'mouvements rudes & fors; qui vont par sauts, par secousses' (Vol. III: 341).

guttural (c, g): depth, 'tous les objets creux', because sound is produced from the back of the mouth.

'sifflante & chuintante' (s, 'sh', z): 'spiritus, soufle' (Vol. III: 349).

These are the 'mots radicaux et primitifs', which can be composed to form what Gébelin calls 'un tableau de la parole'. In words, for example, such as 'rester, station, statue, stupide', the fixed 't' obstructs the flowing 's', to suggest constrained movement (Gébelin, *Monde primitif*, Vol. III: 353–4). In each word, there is a 'liaison' between the letters which, when skilfully traced, reveals a semantic image. Gébelin thinks that the word-image is a device which helps slow, sequential language keep up with the faster, impressionistic nature of thinking: 'rien de plus rapide que l'idée: il faudroit donc que son imitation par la parole fût aussi rapide, ce qui est impossible [. . .] La parole est un dévelopement des idées: or tout dévelopement éxige nécessairement une durée plus considérable [. . .] Que fait donc celui qui parle, & qu'impatientent tous ces délais? [. . .] Il ne l'indique [l'idée] que par le geste' (Gébelin, *Monde primitif*, Vol. I: 17). Sequential language is unsatisfactory in itself, a pale imitation of nature. Ideally, the imitation would be as close as possible, 'tel le modèle, telle la copie' (Gébelin, *Monde primitif*, Vol. III: 283). The grounds for Gébelin's faith in the ability of language to imitate nature so closely are that phonomimetism is a kind of genius which we all have, a sixth sense which allows us to reproduce synaesthetically our perception of the outside world in the sounds of language. What is so seductive about his idea of sound symbolism is that 'nature' is perfectly reproduced in a universally comprehensible manner through the application of subjective faculties of sensory perception. There is a concurrence of the objective and subjective, and consequent parallels with certain theories of imitation in art in general, and poetic language in particular. The shared principles are especially clear, as we shall see, in the poetic convention of 'l'harmonie imitative', a similarity which makes Gébelin's sound symbolism look like a technical adaptation of traditional poetics.

4.3   Sound symbolism in poetry

One of the issues arising from La Motte's 'querelle' is the relevance of Latin metrics to French poetry. Olivet claimed that the use of long and short syllables as a principle of versification was not completely beyond French, but that rhyme is a necessary supplementary device which compensates for its prosodic shortcomings. La Motte disputed the suitability of prosody or rhyme in French poetry, because unlike in Latin or Greek, they are not obvious extensions of any intrinsic aspect of the language. The distinction between long and short syllables has virtually no semantic value in French, and its formal use in poetry has more to do with reverence for Latin and Greek poetry than any natural quality of the French language. As a consequence of these different views, prosody becomes a locus for discussion regarding the merits of form in poetry.

After La Motte and Olivet, the same issues arise in discussion of 'l'harmonie imitative'. Poetry is the art of harmony; partly 'l'harmonie mécanique', or the mastery of verse, and partly 'l'harmonie imitative', or the management of sound to reflect meaning.[9] In practice, 'l'harmonie mécanique' and 'imitative'

---

[9] Louis Racine: 'l'harmonie du discours consiste donc en deux choses: dans l'arrangement des mots, ce qui j'appellerai *l'Harmonie Mechanique*, & dans le rapport de cet arrangement avec les pensées, ce qui j'appellerai *l'Harmonie Imitative*' (*Réflexions sur la poésie*, 1750: Vol. V, 148–9).

may conflict so that, for example, alliteration is usually considered cacophonous, but may be appropriate to express a specific meaning. As a general rule, in fact, 'l'harmonie imitative' might be defined as latitude in the formal conventions of versification for a specific expressive purpose. Charles Batteux defines 'l'harmonie imitative' as 'l'accord des sons avec les choses signifiées' (Batteux, 'Harmonie' in *Principes de la littérature*, 1753; 1802: 134). Jean-François Marmontel describes it as poetic management of language, 'toute l'économie du discours', for which the first requirement is sensitivity to the physical and acoustic possibilities of language: 'c'est par l'analyse des élémens physiques d'une langue qu'on peut voir à quel point elle est susceptible d'harmonie'. Thus, 'le son de l'*a* est le plus éclatant de tous, et la voix, comme pour complaire à l'oreille, le choisit naturellement [. . .] dans les cris de surprise, de douleur et de joie'. He cites Virgil:

> [Tum casia atque aliis intexens suavibus herbis]
> Mollia luteolâ pingit vaccinia calthâ

The couplet is from *Ecloga* II, l. 50, where a young boy is surprised by a nymph, who intertwines him in sweet herbs.[10] In a modern commentary on Catullus, C. J. Fordyse makes a similar remark on the following verse from *Carmen* 64: 'aequoreae monstrum Nereides admirantes' (l. 15). At the marriage of Peleus and Thetis, even the sea creatures rise from the depths to admire the passing cortège of ships. Fordyse comments that Catullus conveys 'the sense of wonderment [. . .] the lingering looks of surprise' in the long, open vowels of 'Nereides admirantes' (*Catullus*, 1990: 280n., 278n.).[11]

There is no doubt that the highly complex metrics of Latin and Greek poetry uses these kinds of devices all the time; the difficulty arises when Marmontel makes the same claim for French. He suggests the following inventory of acoustic qualities: 'le son de l'*o* est plein, mais grave [. . .] l'*é* plus faible et moins volumineux [. . .] l'*i* est plus grêle, plus délicat que l'*é*

---

[10] Rushton Fairclough translates as follows: 'then, twining them with cassia and other sweet herbs, I sets off the delicate hyacinth with the golden marigold'. The sense of 'intexens' is reflected in the following so-called 'golden line' (adjective 1, adjective 2, verb, noun 1, noun 2), and in the intertwining 'a' sounds (Coleman, *Eclogues*, 1977: 102).

[11] He suggests other similar devices in *Carmen* 64: 91, 98, 67, 274; and also in Virgil, who he says is more sparing of this device (*Catullus*, 1990: 278n.).

[. . .] l'ou est plus grave, mais moins faible que l'*u* [. . .] l'*e* muet ou féminin est à peine un son' (Marmontel, 'Harmonie du style', in *Elémens de littérature*, 1819: 8–9). A verse from Boileau's *Lutrin* is regularly cited in this context (and in Chapter 2 above) as an example of suggestive prosody: 'Soupire, étend les bras, ferme l'œil, & s'endort' (Chant II, verse 164); 'soupire' has the vocalic quality of a sigh, with first a short /u/, then a long /i/, followed by 'une muette', which is the inevitable vocalic sound following the /r/. The action of extending the arms is at first abrupt, and then slow and continuous, like the short /en/ of 'étend', and the long /e/ and /a/ of 'les bras'. Sleep overtakes us quickly with the three short syllables in 'ferme l'œil', and deeply in the two final long syllables of 's'endort' (Olivet, *Prosodie*, 1737: 326).

The consonants are also said to suggest particular meanings. Louis Racine quotes his father's *Andromaque* to demonstrate the figurative quality of the 's' sound in, 'Pour qui sont ces serpens qui sifflent sur vos têtes?' He comments that 'on fait entendre les serpens sur la tête des Eumenides, en multipliant la consonne qui imite le sifflement'. The 'r' sound is 'la lettre canine', a barbed sound which he thinks can nevertheless be used sparingly to suggest 'rudesse':

Quand l'imitation demande de la rudesse dans les sons, nos bons poètes scavent apeller les consonnes à leur secours, & dire, pour depeindre un monstre,

> Indomptable taureau, dragon impetueux
> Sa croupe se recourbe en replis tortueux
> (L. Racine, *Réflexions sur la poësie*, 1750: Vol. V, 127)

The couplet is from his father's *Phèdre*. In the first line, there is a heavy, brutal quality in the four-word rhythm, the chiasmus, and in the alliteration of 'p's and 't's. The seven words of the second line are more sinuous, more devious in the tortuous repetition of 'sa-se', or 're-re', like monstrous coils, with also a scaly harshness from the 'r' and 'c' sounds. The same kind of suggestive sound is used by Catullus in one of his most famous love poems:

> Odi et amo, quare id faciam, fortasse requiris.
> nescio, sed fieri sentio et excrucior
> (*Carmen* 85)

The lover is caught in the tension between love and hate, he is rent asunder by opposing forces. John Ferguson comments that ' "excrucior" must be seen as balancing "odi-et-amo"', because the smooth beginning of the poem contrasts markedly with the harsh 'c, r' sounds at the end (*Catullus*, 1985: 279). Marmontel cites another example of suggestive sounds from Fénelon's *Télémaque*: 'on fit couler des flots d'huile douce et luisante sur tous les membres de mon corps', and detects 'l'harmonie imitative', with important implications for the status of poetic prose. He comments on the letter 'l': '[elle] semble communiquer sa mollesse aux syllabes dures qu'elle sépare [. . .] L'l, si j'ose dire, est elle-même comme une huile onctueuse, qui, répandue dans le style, en adoucit le frottement' (Marmontel, 'Harmonie imitative', 1819: 16). Prose, therefore, can use the same devices as poetry and to the same expressive effect.

Marmontel's assumption that 'l'harmonie imitative' is as appropriate to prose as it is to verse is supported by other critics who regard sound symbolism as a characteristic of all expressive language, and an intrinsic way in which we use language to reflect certain ideas. Batteux says of these devices, 'ses sons imitatifs sont fondus dans toutes les langues: ils en sont comme la base fondamentale. C'est le principe qui a engendré les mots descriptifs'. His reference to 'la base fondamentale' may be an allusion to Rameau's musical theory of the 'bass fondamentale', thus inferring that sound symbolism is an underlying natural structure which determines the rest of language.[12] Whether or not the reference is to Rameau, he goes on to draw other analogies between musical imitation and 'l'harmonie imitative'. Batteux thinks that music imitates sound most easily, but can also imitate movement, and even colour, because: 'l'imagination a trouvé des rapports analogiques avec le grave, l'aigu, la durée, la lenteur, la vîtesse, la douceur', and he suggests that in music, 'le bleu est doux, le rouge est vif, le vert est gai' (Batteux, *Principes de la littérature*, 1753; 1802: 136).

These authors think that the way to understand 'l'harmonie imitative' is to assume that synaesthesia is an active principle of language. As a consequence, there is nothing in nature which theoretically is beyond representation in art. In other words, it

---

[12] For Rameau's musicology, see Thomas, *Music and the Origins of Language* (1995): 74–5; or my Chapter 1.3.

is possible to reduce our entire sensory experience of the world
to the visual art of painting, the aural art of music, or the tactile
art of sculpture. However, even if these thinkers look to synaesthesia to understand the suggestive quality of sound in language, and indeed to understand imitation in general, the
problem is that it does little to clarify the precise character of
the imitative representation. The relation between copy and
model, between art and nature is still elusive, if not more elusive
than before. Marmontel recognizes as much, and thinks that if
synaesthesia is an agent of 'l'harmonie imitative', then perhaps
one ought to accept a certain vagueness about the copy;
perhaps by 'imitation' we should not imply a 'reflection', an
'echo', but 'une image idéale'. Marmontel's ideas of 'l'echo'
and 'l'image' are worth quoting at length, because they focus
on the crucial issue which relates 'l'harmonie imitative' to
general theories of imitation in the arts:

[L'harmonie imitative] peint, non pas le bruit ou le mouvement, mais
le caractère idéal ou sensible de son objet [. . .] Alors le style n'est pas
l'echo, mais l'image de la nature [. . .] Cette sorte d'analogie suppose
un rapport naturel, et une étroite correspondance du sens de la vue
avec celui de l'ouïe, et de l'un et de l'autre avec le sens intime, qui est
l'organe des passions. Ce qui est doux à la vue nous est rappelé par
des sons doux à l'oreille, et ce qui est riant pour l'ame nous est peint
par des couleurs douces aux yeux [. . .] Mais cette ressemblance est
vague et par-là peut être plus au gré de l'ame qu'une imitation fidèle:
car elle lui laisse plus de liberté de se peindre à elle-même ce que l'expression lui rappelle. (Marmontel, 'Analogie du style', 1819: 206–7)

Imitation in 'l'harmonie imitative' is more a question of suggestion, 'rappeler', than it is duplication of nature. Hearing
'suggests' sight, which appeals to 'le sens intime', which 'suggests' colour. Although the resemblance between the model in
nature and the artist's copy is consequently only 'vague', it is
nevertheless more aesthetically pleasing than 'une imitation
fidèle'. If, on the contrary, 'l'harmonie imitative' were simply a
matter of onomatopoeia, it might be a more faithful representation of nature, but it would nevertheless be less aesthetically
pleasing. A greater pleasure derives from the fact that synaesthesia leaves latitude for subjective selection, for idealization
according to the particular genius of the poet.

This interpretation of 'l'harmonie imitative' by Marmontel is
indicative of why the practice of 'l'harmonie imitative' is one of

the best illustrations of what neoclassical artists and critics mean by 'idealizing art', and indicative also of their perception of the relation between copy and model. This is to say that poetic language has its conventional, lexical meaning, but there is also the ingenious sensitivity of the poet, who helps us 'see' the coils and scales of the monster by a skilful assembly of 's, c, r' sounds. Language can 'display' the sensibilities of the poet, as well as communicate conventional meaning. The poetic practice of 'l'harmonie imitative' is clearly not confined to the eighteenth century, and yet it is taken less for granted by critics like Marmontel, and elaborated in quite unparalleled ways by thinkers like Gébelin. For these reasons, it is of special interest in contemporary aesthetics.

The paradox of 'l'harmonie imitative' is that the more it is discussed, the more didactic it can appear; to be 'in touch' with nature is to do as the critics say. Louis Racine composes an 'Ode sur l'harmonie' with this paradoxical intention of suggesting the natural origins of poetry, but at the same time supporting the authority of the 'anciens'. The poem follows the concurrent progress of civilization and poetry, from barbarity to social and poetic harmony, quoting from a host of respected 'anciens', and placing modern poets like Jean-Baptiste Rousseau in the same tradition. His ode is designed to provide the art of poetry with a founding myth, but also to persuade modern poets to respect its greatest practitioners. He translates verse from the Latin and Greek, ostensibly as homage to Homer, Virgil, and Horace, but also to demonstrate that the beauty of Classical metrics can be faithfully rendered into French 'harmonie imitative'. He pays tribute to Homer's *Iliade* in the following manner:

> Par quel art le Chantre d'Achille
> Me rend-il tant de bruits divers?
> Il fait partir la fléche agile,
> Et par ses sons sifflent les airs.
> Des vents me peint-il le ravage?
> Du vaisseau que brise leur rage,
> Eclate le gémissement;
> Et de l'onde qui se courrouce
> Contre un rocher qui la repousse,
> Retentit le mugissement.
>   (L. Racine, *Ode sur l'harmonie*,
>   1750: Vol. IV, 176–81)

An arrow is about to be loosed. The soft palatals in the rhyme 'Achille-agile', repeated in 'fléche agile' are a prelude to actual release, when the arrow flies through the air with 's' and 'f' sounds. A ship is to be broken on the rocks. The violence of the wind is at first only *in potentia*; the soft 'v' of 'vents, vaisseau' is balanced by the menacing severity of 'r' in 'ravage, rage'. Then the violent 'r' of 'rocher, repousse, retentit' breaks the ship with a crash of 'c's in the *enjambement* 'courrouce | Contre'. Racine devotes another stanza to Horace:

> Qu'avec plaisir je me délasse
> Sous ces arbres délicieux,
> Que la main d'Horace entrelasse
> Par des nœuds qui charment mes yeux!
> Leurs branches se cherchent, s'unissent
> S'embrassent & m'ensevelissent
> Dans l'ombre que sont leurs amours;
> Tandis que l'onde fugitive
> D'un ruisseau que son lit captive,
> Murmure de ses longs détours.

The poet yawns in the indolent shade of his tree with a series of open vowels in the first three lines, particularly 'a'. Perhaps he falls asleep with repeated 's' alliteration and internal rhyme, 'Horace-entrelasse', 'nœuds-yeux', but he is captivated by the interwoven branches above him, meeting and missing like the 's' and 'ch' sounds of line five, until the tangle is resolved in the following line into a simple alliterative series of 's' sounds. He devotes other stanzas to Malherbe, Corneille, Jean Racine, La Fontaine, Boileau, and Jean-Baptiste Rousseau, whom he quotes directly. Jean Racine suggests the sound of thunder breaking and rumbling:

> Frappé du bruit de son tonnerre,
> Je crois sentir trembler la Terre
> *Sur ses antiques fondemens.*

In the last line, the vowels rise, 'u, e, i', to a sharp and jarring 'q', after which the thunder rumbles into open, nasal vowels. Interesting though Louis Racine's French examples are, the stakes are higher in his translations from Latin and Greek, because he intends to prove that French has a poetic language of its own as expressive as the poetry of the Classical languages:

> Quelle humeur triste & dédaigneuse
> Nous dégoute de notre bien?
> Notre Langue est riche & pompeuse
> Pour quiconque la connoit bien

In this ode, there is often a streak of patriotic defence of French poetry against the weight of Latinate history, or at least a desire for creative autonomy. Louis Racine's ode is an answer to the question he poses in his article on 'l'harmonie imitative': 'pouvons nous nous vanter [. . .] d'avoir une véritable harmonie, nous qui ne parlons qu'un jargon formé de la corruption de la Langue latine dans les siécles de la barbarie?' (L. Racine, *Réflexions sur la poësie*, 1750: Vol. V, 125). His answer is a recurrent plea to modern poets not to reject French versification out of hand, but to exploit those poetic devices which it has to offer. The problem is that the device available, 'l'harmonie imitative', is largely modelled on Latin poetry, which has the advantage of systematic long and short syllables and highly complex but almost universally accepted metrics. Since the French language does not have these features, Olivet's *Prosodie* was sure to attract the censure of 'modernes' like La Motte, who could see only too clearly that whatever the nature of French poetic language, it did not in principle have much in common with Latin conventions. It seemed as a result that French versification was being practised in a theoretical vacuum, because the Classical tradition is rejected without there being much idea of what there is to replace it. There are perhaps two solutions: either what was required was a confident, systematic treatment of 'l'harmonie imitative', such as Gébelin could provide, which would have the effect of making verse seem firmly supported by an intrinsic sound symbolism in the French language; or on the contrary, what was needed was precisely a way of coming to terms with the less systematic nature of French verse, that is, a kind of aesthetic which Marmontel calls 'l'imitation vague'.

4.4   Diderot's hieroglyph

It is in the sense of 'l'imitation vague' that Diderot discusses the idea of the literary 'hieroglyph'. It is essentially a fresh

interpretation of an old idea, with a novel aesthetic of suggestion which does not need Gébelin's elaborate, systematic
approach. Diderot is interested in 'l'harmonie imitative'
because, like Marmontel, he believes that 'l'imitation vague' has
interesting implications for imitation in general. The title of
Lettre sur les sourds et muets (1751) is not often quoted in full,
but is the best synopsis of a complex work: 'Lettre sur les sourds
et les muets à l'usage de ceux qui entendent et qui parlent. Où
l'on traite de l'origine des inversions, de l'harmonie du style,
du sublime de situation, de quelques avantages de la langue
française sur la plupart des langues anciennes et modernes, et,
par occasion, de l'expression particulière aux beaux-arts'. He
intends to write about deaf mutes for those who are neither deaf
nor mute, because in so doing, we understand that language is
essentially a system of signs, no different in principle to the sign
language of the deaf and dumb. This assumption provides a
more objective perspective on recurrent debates concerning
the philosophical and stylistic value of literary devices such as
inversions and harmony, because the most constructive question, if language is a system of signs, is firstly, what is the sense
conveyed, and secondly, how is it conveyed? Diderot's title also
implies rather provocatively that the only objective standpoint
from which to judge the relative merits of these issues is that of
the deaf mute; the message to the inveterate 'querelleurs' is to
'shut up'. At the end of the title, as if incidentally and 'par occasion', Diderot says that he will also inquire into 'l'expression
particulière aux beaux-arts', the common language or mechanism according to which all the arts reproduce nature. This is
perhaps the major interest of the *Lettre*, but in characteristically
elusive fashion, Diderot leaves it to the end of his title, almost
as a subtext. The common language and transcendent principle of the arts turns out to be 'l'harmonie du style', which is
what we have been calling 'l'harmonie imitative'.

The examples he gives of 'l'harmonie imitative' are not original, but are sometimes the very same passages which we have
quoted above. His innovation, however, is to describe them as
'hieroglyphic', with the implication that they cannot in the final
analysis be deciphered and rendered into ordinary language.
Egyptian hieroglyphs in the eighteenth century are the subject
of some controversy, because it is unclear whether they are a

system of linguistic signs, a priest's cabala, or meaningless ornament.[13] Diderot uses the term to suggest an elusive, enigmatic
literary aesthetic which he explains using the example of Louis
Castel's 'clavecin oculaire'. In the *Lettre*, Castel performs his
colour music to Diderot's fictitious deaf mute, who assumes that
Castel is also a deaf mute, and that his display of coloured filters
is a sign language. There are no words to this music, however,
and Diderot specifically calls the pieces 'des sonates de
couleurs' (Diderot, *Lettre sur les sourds et muets*, 1965: 50). In a
way, Diderot is suggesting that Fontenelle's apocryphal exclamation 'sonate, que me veux-tu?' applies to language and the
arts in general, because they all have in common an unresolv-
able 'hieroglyphic' aspect to the way they express meaning. The
model he proposes for this aesthetic is 'l'harmonie imitative'.
He demonstrates with a quotation from Voltaire's *La Henriade*:

> Et des fleuves français les eaux ensanglantées
> Ne portaient que des morts aux mers épouvantées

Diderot says that the meaning of this couplet is expressed on
two levels, that 'les choses sont dites et représentées tout à
la fois'. The first is conventional, syntagmatic meaning, 'un
enchaînement de termes', the second is impressionistic, para-
digmatic meaning, 'un tissu d'hiéroglyphes entassés les uns sur
les autres [. . .] Je pourrais dire en ce sens que toute poésie est
emblématique'. The emblems he finds are those we have seen
before. The open, sonorous vowel /o/ of 'portaient' suggests
the meaning 'gonflé', it is obstructed and closed by the following 't', and there is a relative fall with the following close vowel
/e/: 'Mais qui est-ce qui voit dans la première syllabe de *portaient*, les eaux gonflées de cadavres, et le cours des fleuves
comme suspendu par cette digue? Qui est-ce qui voit la masse
des eaux et des cadavres s'affaisser et descendre vers les mers à
la seconde syllabe du meme mot?' (Diderot, *Lettre sur les sourds
et muets*, 1965: 70). He phrases his interpretation of 'l'harmonie
imitative' as a question, because unlike Olivet, Marmontel, and
others, he wonders how accessible this kind of language is: 'il y
a mille fois plus de gens en état d'entendre un géometre qu'un
poëte' (p. 78). The emblematic quality of poetic language is

---

[13] Jean-François Champollion's first decipherment dates from his 'Lettre à
Dacier', 17 Sept. 1822.

elusive, intuitive, and like the mysteries of Egyptian hieroglyphs, perhaps beyond all but the most sensitive readers: 'Partout ou l'hiéroglyphe accidentel aura lieu, soit dans un vers, soit sur un obélisque, comme il est ici l'ouvrage de l'imagination, & là celui du mystere, il exigera pour être entendu ou une imagination ou une sagacité peu communes' (p. 81). It is unclear in Diderot's time whether the wisdom exists to understand Egyptian hieroglyphs, and he suggests that poetic language is just as mysterious. Perhaps only those who write hieroglyphic and poetic language understand the signs they use.

Diderot's interpretation of 'l'harmonie imitative' is typical of his ability to grasp the fundamental issues at stake in contemporary debate. He understands that although it is generally acknowledged that poetry speaks with two quite different voices, the word and the hieroglyph, one wonders exactly how far removed one is from the other; one wonders whether, in fact, we need two theories of art, one imitative and one an aesthetic of 'suggestion'. These are the questions which Diderot poses and which he thinks Batteux evades in *Les Beaux-Arts réduits à un même principe* (1746). Batteux has failed to reduce the aesthetic experience to a single principle, despite the declared objective in his title; he merely labels it 'belle nature', repeats the ill-defined conventional wisdom, and does nothing to advance our understanding of what constitutes the transcendent aesthetic principle of art. Diderot, on the other hand, discusses 'l'harmonie imitative' because it demonstrates a sub-lexical aesthetic of suggestion, 'l'emblème fugitif', which escapes linear language, and which it may be possible to extend to the arts in general.[14] His aim is to define the elusive presence common to all the arts:

rassembler les beautés communes de la poësie, de la peinture & de la musique; en montrer les analogies; expliquer comment le poëte, le peintre et le musicien rendent la même image; saisir les emblèmes fugitifs de leur expression; examiner s'il n'y aurait pas quelque similitude entre ces emblèmes, &c., c'est ce qui reste à faire, & ce que

---

[14] It is interesting that Diderot's idea of linear language as impressionistic is precisely the opposite of his idea that composition in painting depends on 'une liaison des idées'. 'Prosody' seems to mean two different things: understanding a painting is like reading a well-constructed sentence, but understanding poetry is like contemplating a 'tableau'. See Chapter 3.

je vous conseille d'ajouter à vos *Beaux-Arts réduits à un même principe*.
(Diderot, *Lettre sur les sourds et muets*, 1965: 81)

Diderot thinks that it is possible to clarify the idea of 'nature' in
art by thinking about the practice of 'l'harmonie imitative'.
'Nature' can be an intellectualization of material nature, according to the artist's ability to select what is most appropriate to his
work. In the case of poetry this can be achieved through the
device of 'l'harmonie imitative', and Diderot thinks that if we
look for the equivalent 'emblème fugitif' in music and painting,
it may be possible, by comparing our findings, to reveal what
they have in common, that is to say, to reveal the particular kind
of nature which art in general represents. Diderot does not
attempt to answer this question in the *Lettre*, his objective is more
to point out that 'nature' is problematic, and that the imitation
of 'nature' involves an elusive element of genius which is
perhaps beyond rational explication. At his time of writing, he
and Marmontel are alone in this interpretation of 'l'harmonie
imitative' as a 'hieroglyphic' or 'vague' imitation, quite unlike
the systematic rigour of Gébelin or de Brosses. Joseph de
Maimieux later agrees with Diderot and Marmontel, and thinks
that literature is like 'les tables isiaques', incomprehensible, mystical symbols of the Egyptian priests that we are free to interpret
as we will, as long as we all finally exclaim 'Ah, que c'est beau!'
(Maimieux, *Eloge philosophique de l'impertinence*, 1788: 135; see
my Chapter 5). Maimieux abandons the search for 'nature'
precisely because it is too closely associated with a systematic,
rational approach to art which seems to stifle the subject,
'hieroglyphic' component of expression.

4.5   The perfect language

It seems appropriate to interpret the sound symbolism of
Gébelin and de Brosses in the context of the poetic tradition
of 'l'harmonie imitative'. They share an interest in the physical
production of speech as it relates to the spiritual, semantic value
we attach to it, and the same aesthetic implications are mani-
fest in each. The continuity of thought is based on an abiding
interest in language as a model of representation, a view of

language as an almost instinctive way in which thought is made corporeal, and by extension an indication as to how the artist may intellectualize material nature. Gébelin and de Brosses are not the first to suggest that sound functions almost as a language in itself. Olivet hoped that his *Prosodie* (1736) would encourage others to understand that 'l'harmonie imitative' is a kind of language within language: 'puisse-t-il quelque jour donner lieu d'approfondir un Art, qui feroit naître de nouvelles beautez, & comme une nouvelle Langue, dans celle que nous croyons savoir' (*Olivet*, 1767: 17). Marmontel himself has a utopian vision, 'un beau songe, un modèle imaginaire', of 'l'harmonie imitative' refined to the point where it imitates nature perfectly, and becomes a kind of universal poetic and philosophical language:

[Une langue] composée ensemble et de concert par un métaphysicien comme Locke, un poète comme Racine, et un grammairien comme du Marsais. Alors on voit éclore une langue à la fois philosophique et poétique, ou l'analogie des termes avec les choses est sensible et constante, non-seulement dans les couleurs primitives, mais dans les nuances les plus délicates; de manière que les synonymes en sont gradués du rapide au lent, du fort au faible, du grave au léger, etc [. . .] On goûterait le plaisir de parler un langage qui n'aurait eu ni le peuple pour inventeur, ni l'usage pour arbitre [. . .] Voilà un beau songe, me dira-t-on: je l'avoue; mais ce songe m'a semblé propre à donner l'idée de ce que j'entends par l'harmonie d'une langue; et tout l'art du style harmonieux consiste à rapprocher, autant qu'il est possible, de ce modèle imaginaire, la langue dans laquelle on écrit. (Marmontel, 'Harmonie du style', 1763; 1819: 33–4)

Marmontel is not so much dissatisfied with the inadequacy of traditional verse, like La Motte who regarded much of the formal requirements of poetry as 'unnatural'. Rather he is fascinated and tantalized by the gap in artistic imitation between model and copy, between 'nature' and 'l'harmonie imitative'. To those like La Motte, who are dissatisfied with traditional versification, he proposes to advance the practice of imitative verse according to the wisdom of Locke's philosophy and Dumarsais's grammar. It would be a language of refined synonymy, capable of reflecting the complexity of nature, the tiniest nuances between the primary colours of nature. Most importantly in the context of the 'querelle', it would be a language derived neither from convention nor invention, but an enigmatic blend of the two.

Gébelin and de Brosses are the kind of grammarian philosophers of whom Marmontel seems to be thinking in the above quotation, and who fulfil the aesthetic potential of 'l'harmonie imitative', bringing to fruition the latent possibilities of traditional poetics and providing a model of imitation. Gébelin himself is aware that his language scheme is rooted in poetic tradition. In Volume III of *Monde primitif*, concerning the origin of language, there is a chapter with the following title: 'Les rapports des mots avec la nature sont la source de l'énergie du Discours, le fondement de la Poésie, de l'Eloquence de l'Harmonie' (p. 277), in which he says that linguistic imitation is the source of creativity, but has been obscured by 'ce grand cheval de bataille qu'on appelle USAGE' (Gébelin, *Monde primitif*, Vol. III: 278). His intention is to legitimize 'usage' and the observance of convention, by demonstrating it to be an indirect fidelity to nature, the practice of well-founded rules, so that the artist's respect for tradition is also sensitivity to nature: 'ceux donc qui marchent sur les traces des grands hommes qui les précèderent & qui croyent en les imitant, n'imitent que des modèles humains, suivent réellement un modèle très-supérieur à ceux-là, [...] la Nature, ce grand ordre harmonique qui compose l'Univers' (pp. 279–80). The argument is well-rehearsed throughout 'la querelle des anciens et des modernes'; there is a canon of artists who are worthy of imitation in themselves, because of their refined sensitivity to nature. Gébelin, de Brosses, and indeed all the linguistic theorists of this study, however, do not fit easily into the simple binary paradigm of 'anciens' and 'modernes', because the polemic does not lead them to take sides, but instead encourages them to call into question the underlying assumptions of the debate. They provide what they think is lacking in these debates, which is a common standard of judgement by which to understand the controversial idea of 'nature'. Gébelin wonders how the work of any writer can be measured against 'nature' without a measure of what we mean: 'comment juger les Anciens eux-mêmes, si l'on n'a pas une régle à laquelle on puisse comparer leur travail?' (Gébelin, *Monde primitif*, Vol. III: 278). His language scheme is designed as such a measure, a demonstration of how far it is possible to find nature reflected in conventional language. It is a confidence-building exercise at a time when Latinate metrics and French neoclassical traditions are increasingly being called into question; Olivet's criticism of La Motte's prose poems includes a feeling of urgency: 'il étoit temps, & plus que temps, de réveiller le souvenir de la prosodie, & de l'harmonie' (Olivet, *Prosodie*, 1767: 5). Like Gabriel Girard who earlier compiled a dictionary of synonyms as a kind of 'nuancier' of acceptable semantic subtlety, Gébelin's language scheme is a systematic study of sound symbolism designed as a poetic guide to 'l'harmonie imitative'. The fear of a theoretical vacuum left by a rejection of tradition makes this kind of exercise especially valuable.

The intentions of *Monde primitif* are clearly mixed, because it is also an antiquarian study with wide historical and conceptual concerns. The poetic implications, however, were noticed by a number of poets, most notably Antoine de Piis, who was a great admirer of Gébelin and who uses his sound symbolism in a long, didactic poem, *L'Harmonie imitative de la langue française* (1785). It represents the consummation of Marmontel's 'beau songe', the combined efforts of the philosopher, the grammarian, and now the poet to find a perfectly imitative language. It may also be an indication of Piis's practice in his less didactic poetry, and perhaps also the practice of other contemporary poets.

4.6   De Piis and sound symbolism in poetry

Piis's poem takes the form of four 'chants', with accompanying notes.[15] In his comments on Chant I, he quotes Marmontel (without naming him) to disagree with his suggestion that French is only capable of 'une ressemblance vague'. As evidence, he refers by name to Gébelin, 'dont les erreurs ne doivent pas faire oublier l'immense érudition', who he thinks has demonstrated beyond doubt the underlying system of sound symbolism in language (Piis, *L'Harmonie imitative*, 1785: 72, 73). Piis subsequently quotes Olivet, to maintain that, even

---

[15] All of Chant I, and parts of Chant IV are included in Roudaut, *Poètes et grammairiens au XVIIIe siècle* (1971). Part of Chant I is in Delon, *Anthologie de la poésie française du XVIIIe siècle* (1997).

if prosody is less important in French than Latin and Greek, it
is still the *sine qua non* of poetry (p. 73). As evidence, he quotes
from Boileau, Jean Racine, Voltaire, la Fontaine, and Delille,
and concludes 'le Français peut dire aux Grecs et aux Latins:
anch io son pittore' (pp. 79–80). He also mentions the English
poet Thompson (p. 84), and part of Chant II is in the melan-
cholic style of Edward Young (p. 32). His intention, therefore,
seems to be to adapt 'l'harmonie imitative' to contemporary
tastes without losing the support of tradition. Much of Chant I
consists of a description of the symbolic values of each of the
letters of the alphabet. In the following description of the
sound 'a', the resemblance to Gébelin's symbolism is striking:

> A l'instant qu'on l'appelle, arrivant plein d'audace,
> Au haut de l'alphabet, l'*A* s'arroge sa place,
> Alerte, agile, actif, avide d'apparat,
> Tantôt d'un accent grave acceptant des entraves,
> Il a dans son pas lent l'allure des esclaves,
> A s'adonner au mal quand il est résolu,
> Avide, atroce, affreux, arrogant, absolu,
> Il attroupe, il aveugle, il avilit, il arme,
> Il assiège, il affame, il attaque, il alarme,
> Il arrête, il accable, il assomme, il abat,
> . . . .
> A l'aspect du Très-haut sitôt qu'Adam parla
> Ce fut apparemment l'*A* qu'il articula.
> (Piis, *L'Harmonie imitative*, 1785: Chant I, 21).[16]

'A' is a maximally open sound, a sign of domination, awe, and
associated meanings. The remainder of his poem is an exercise
in descriptive poetry and sound symbolism, a series of vignettes
of storms, church organs, iron and stone masons at work, of a
charming description of the moment a bottle of champagne is
uncorked or a Bordeaux is poured:

> Si pour me ranimer je gagne mes Pénates
> Oh! de quel bruit plus doux, cher Bacchus, tu me flattes?
> Rompant son fil d'archal, le Champagne élancé
> Cherche en l'air à se rejoindre à son bouchon chassé;
> En coulant du goulot d'une oblongue bouteille,

---

[16] Piis published a modified edition of *L'Harmonie imitative* in *Œuvres choisies*
(1810), in which there are a number of alterations, noted by Roudaut, *Poètes et
grammariens* (1971): 198.

Le Bordeaux plus couvert charme aussi mon oreille,
Et ses flots, l'un de l'autre, au passage jaloux
Comblent mon gobelet en doublant leurs gloux-gloux.
(Piis, *L'Harmonie imitative*, 1785: Chant III, 42)

The sounds 'r' and 'l' suggest two kinds of movement; first the brusque uncorking of 'rompant', then the light ebullience of 'élancé'. In line four, the 's' and 'ch' sounds effervesce alternately; there is 'la sensation de la vie, le sentiment de l'existence' in the alliterative 'e' sounds, and wonderment in the 'a' sounds. A Bordeaux wine pours more audibly with the 'ou' sound for 'l'ouïe & tous ces effets', and more specifically with the hollow 'c, g' sounds to suggest the flowing out from within the bottle.

Piis accounts for the natural sound symbolism of language in a curious allegory, which cleverly portrays language as both a direct reflection, or 'echo' of nature, and also a reflection of man's consciousness. When Adam first speaks in the Garden of Eden, his voice echoes, and he is intrigued by this aural shadow which eludes him. His search for the source of the echo eventually leads him to sleep, and when he awakens he finds himself in the company of Eve, the realization of the 'shadow' that his own language has suggested to him. The allegory reminds us of Rousseau's story of how language arises concurrently with the speaker's consciousness and awareness of others.[17] It also makes a case for an Adamic language of onomatopoeia and of phonomimetism, of reflection of nature and reflection of consciousness. He describes Adam's first experience of language and nature as follows:

Peins-toi le premier soir du premier jour du monde
Ou le globe, plongé dans une paix profonde,
Sous les rayons de l'astre, émule du soleil
S'argente aux yeux d'Adam qui résiste au sommeil;
. . . .
Il écoute, étonné, la nature muette.
Tourmenté malgré lui d'un souci curieux,
Il lève en soupirant ses deux mains vers les cieux;
'O mon maître, dit il, quel est donc ce silence?'
Silence! dit l'echo, qui prend alors naissance.

---

[17] See Chapter 3; and Derrida, *De la Grammatologie* (1967): 393.

Que fait le premier homme à ce bruit étranger?
(On ignorait encor la peur et le danger)
Il visite avec soin la forêt toute entière,
'Ah! pauvre Adam, dit-il, c'est à toi de te taire;
'Quel autre que ton Dieu peut répondre à ta voix?'
Ta voix! reprend l'echo renouvellant ses droits.
Adam s'occupe encor d'une recherche vaine,
Mais le sommeil surprend sa paupière incertaine,
Eve doit au matin s'offrir à ses desirs,
Et l'echo plus discret taira leurs doux soupirs.
(Piis, *L'Harmonie imitative*, 1785: Chant III, 47–8)

Adam's loneliness in nature, his desire for a companion is not in the first instance answered by God or by Eve, but by his own voice. The first sin is curiosity about his own voice, a desire for self-knowledge masquerading as an unknown presence in the forest. Alienation from God occurs when Adam becomes rhetorically independent, when he reaches a reflexive state of consciousness which allows himself to pursue a conversation with himself: ' "Quel autre que ton Dieu peut répondre à ta voix?" | Ta voix!' Eve is the incarnation of reflexive consciousness, her creation permanently excludes the voice of God.[18]

Piis's allegory is similar to Rousseau's story of the moral and linguistic awakening of consciousness. It shares also the principles underlying the phonomimetism of de Brosses and Gébelin, that language is derived from an inherent desire to imitate or 'echo' nature, and also a kind of kinaesthesia or self-awareness. Presumably, we are to imagine Adam toying with the idea that nature echoes his own voice, that by listening to the echo he is listening to himself and to nature at the same time, and that he amplifies this relation into a language which is in part imitative of nature, and in part an expression of his own consciousness. This tension between the model and imitative copy is similar to the tension we find in the language schemes of Gébelin and de

---

[18] Compare this to the Greek myth of the nymph Echo who is punished by the gods for her misdemeanours by being deprived of the gift of speech and condemned to repeat only the last syllable of words spoken in her presence. Later, she falls in love with Narcissus, but is spurned by him because she cannot declare her love. She hides in a solitary cavern and dies of a broken heart. All that is left of her is the echo of her voice (*Larousse Encyclopedia of Mythology*, 1990: 162). Sarasin writes a poem on the same theme, 'L'Echo' (*Anthologie de la littérature française du XVIIe siècle*, 1993: 255).

Brosses, and similar also to the tension within the concept of 'nature' in the theory of imitation. Like Georges Lote's characterization of the eighteenth-century as a whole, Piis's Adam is 'hanté du désir de peindre au moyen des sons' (Lote, *L'Histoire du vers*, 1992: Vol. VII, 223).[19] Piis thinks that a poet ought to be capable of describing a storm as expressively as Gluck in the opening scenes of his *Iphigénie*,[20] or animals as realistically as Oudry's *trompe l'œil* paintings (Piis, *L'Harmonie imitative*, 1785: 97, 99). One is led to wonder whether Piis's enthusiasm for Gébelin's sound symbolism goes beyond his didactic poem, whether *L'Harmonie imitative de la langue française* is only a demonstration of his poetics elsewhere, and to what extent his approach is shared by contemporary poets. It is worth looking at a less didactic poem by Piis, in order to judge the extent of the practical application of Gébelin's sound symbolism.

The following is one of many 'poèmes anacréontiques' written by Piis:

> LE PRINTEMS
> est la saison de l'amour;
> Ode anacréontique.

> Saison aux autres préférable,
> Saison où l'homme est tourmenté,
> Du besoin le plus agréable,
> Du besoin de la volupté:
> Viens par ton baume salutaire,   5
> Ranimer en moi le desir,
> Et que sous l'ombre du mystere,
> Je connoisse encor le plaisir.

> En été, Vénus presque nue,
> Néglige un peu trop se[s] attraits,   10
> Et par la chaleur abattue,
> Dort sur les gerbes de Cérès:
> Elle est trop folâtre en automne,
> Lorsqu'au milieu de son pressoir,
> Bacchus pour divertir Pomone,   15
> L'enyvre du matin au soir.

---

[19] Georges Lote, in one of the best studies on 'l'harmonie imitative', dislikes Piis: 'on voit à quelles puérilités aboutissent les classifications du XVIIIe siècle', but thinks that his *L'Harmonie imitative* illustrates a poetic tendency, that it is 'un véritable livre d'exercices où se condensent les idées de l'époque' (*L'Histoire du vers*, 1992: Vol. VII, 223, 235).   [20] *Iphigénie en Tauride*, first performed in 1779.

En hiver sa robe effarouche
L'amant qui veut faire un larcin;
Le baiser qui part de sa bouche,
Peut se refroidir en chemin.   20
Mais au printems elle est si belle,
Son teint si frais, son œil si doux! . . . .
Le monde est un temple pour elle,
La nature est à ses genoux.

Par les frimats, le nom d'Hélène   25
Dans mon cœur sembloit effacé,
Et le zéphir qu'Avril ramene,
En y soufflant l'a retracé.

Quand sur le globe de la terre,
L'amour croît avec le gazon,   30
Tête-à-tête avec ma bergere,
Je sens décroître ma raison.
(Piis, *Recueil de poésies fugitives*,
1781: 228)

The poem is unremarkable in form or subject. It is a plea to
Cérès, the divinity of fertility, to inspire the slumbering amorous
desires of the barren season of winter, the soporific season of
summer, and the drunken season of autumn; a man's fancy
turns to his 'bergere' in the burgeoning days of spring. The
approach is orthodox, but not without ambiguity. The last two
lines of the first stanza leave us wondering what is the double
obscurity of 'l'ombre du mystere', why should springtime bring
mystery as well as sunlight and shadow, and what could be the
'plaisir' which the poet wants to 'connaître'? The answer comes
in the last two lines of the poem; the idea seems to be to lose
his 'raison' in a 'tête-à-tête' with his 'bergere'. One almost
feels the 'points de suspension' at the very end of the poem;
now that spring has come and reason has succumbed to love,
presumably the poet can end his supplication and get on
with the matter in hand. If this is the direction of the poem, it
is not entirely evident from the reassuring atmosphere of
personified 'Amour' and 'Saison', the staid Classical references
and generally unremarkable temper. An analysis according to
Gébelin's sound symbolism, however, supports a more libertine
interpretation.

    'E' or 'Hê' is for existence, life, respiration, and abundance.

The first stanza is a tribute to the life-giving force of spring, and there is a concentration of 'e' sounds in the rhyming words. In the last stanza, too, there is strong 'e' assonance in all but one of the rhyming words, and the last two lines are particularly remarkable. In the penultimate line, the rapid alternation of 'e' and 'a' sounds between the ideas of life and domination contribute to a breathless feeling, until the rhythm slows in the last line to open, nasal vowels, when reason has succumbed to love, and the object of the poet's seduction is won. The rebirth of spring, the rise of love and fall of reason is captured in the rhythmic and vocalic fall we hear in these last two lines. The 'e' sound is used with different implications in the first and last stanza. In the first, it is the sensual and spiritual sense of 'desir', 'mystere', 'tourmenté', while the emphasis shifts in the last stanza to the less abstract 'Hélène', 'terre', 'bergere'. The process of seduction has moved on from the ethereal 'besoin le plus agréable' to the earthly 'L'amour croît avec le gazon'. The poet's use of the 'e' sound suggests a process of seduction in which the object of his desire is led astray by the spiritual effusion of stanza one, to find herself all the more caught up in his coarse aspirations revealed by the end of the poem.

'A' is for domination, subjugation, possession, and 'le cri des passions fortes'. It is the most sonorous of the vowels, the most easily perceived, and hence the sound with the most impact on the sense and the greatest seductive power. In the course of the poem, the progress towards subjugation and pleasure is reflected in an incremental use of 'a' sounds; five in stanza one, seven in two, eight in three, and a crescendo of fifteen in the final stanza. The progress begins with the poet's description of love in summer, beaten down by the heat. The delicate alliteration of 'e' and 'u' in line 9 contrasts with the staccato rhythm of line 11: 'En été, Vénus presque nue/par la chaleur abattue'. By the end of the third stanza, however, spring has returned, and love is supreme: 'La nature est à ses genoux'. The rise and fall quality of the whole poem is captured neatly in these two contrasting lines: the prospects held out in the first stanza are abruptly withdrawn in the following two stanzas, to return with the spring in the last stanza; the 'bergere' is beguiled by the lyrical ebullience of the opening stanza, only to feel the poet's fervour fall in stanzas two and three, leaving her all the more impatient and desirous of the rekindling of love in the last stanza. The seduction is complete when the ethereal love of stanza one is rendered corporeal by the end of the poem as 'L'amour croît avec le gazon' (l. 30). The sense we get in the crescendo of 'a' sounds is a gradual enveloping of the 'bergere' in sensuality and 'volupté', a carnal desire concealed beneath an ethereal hedonism. The vowel sounds become more and more open as the poem progresses, until the 'bergere' is in danger of being swallowed whole in her eagerness to embrace nature.

'O' is for light, the eyes, and all that is circular. In contrast to the crescendo of 'a' sounds, the use of 'o' diminishes markedly from thirteen and twelve in the first two stanzas, to five and five in the last. There is a disparity between the slow rebirth of the spring, and the darkening intentions of the poet. The light of spring itself does not come, rather a natural love is born as the fertility sign 'e' returns in stanza four. The opening light and vision of springtime is replaced in the last stanza with the nascent inner light of the lovers as they gaze earnestly into each others eyes, 'tête-à-tête'. The circle of experience has drawn tighter since the first stanza, the poet has sharpened his focus on 'le nom d'Hélène, mon cœur', and all is captured within the double circularity of 'le globe de la terre'. The promised burgeoning of a new spring has not been honoured; instead, the vision of love is a shrunken, introspective world, where only the two lovers matter. The grand scheme of things is not after all so important as the intimate feelings of the lovers. Why worry, the poet seems to ask, what the world outside may do or say, when one's desires are so easily satisfied so close to home?

The labials 'p, b, v, m' are soft and reassuring, and associated with food and the mouth. The first stanza repeats them in key words which constitute a narrative in themselves, 'homme, tourmenté, besoin, baume, ombre, mystere, plaisir', and in an alliterative *enjambement* 'volupté | Viens'. Desire and the rites of spring are couched in soothing, flattering tones. In line 19 they are used in conjunction with the suggestive lip-rounding of the vowels, to portray the lover's kiss; if we scan this line as 'le baisEr qui pArt de sa bOUche', the alliterative labials 'b, p, b' and the gradual projection of the lips 'e–a–ou' suggest the moment of the kiss.

'R' is for abrasive movement, harshness and hostility. The soft labials of the kiss in line 19 are frozen in the midst of winter, eroded by the alliterative 'r's in lines 17 and 20: 'En hiver sa robe effarouche [. . .] Peut se refroidir en chemin.' If love is to be rekindled from the depths of frosty winter and sleepy summer, the awakening of desire is likely to be less benign and gentle than suggested by the soothing labials of the first stanza. In their midst, the alliterative *enjambement* 'salutaire, | Ranimer' (ll. 5–6) is an indication of the violence of sentiment when dormant desire is aroused. It is the barbed sound concealed by the soothing qualities of the labials.

Gébelin's sound symbolism suggests a subtext to Piis's poem, a shadow cast by the text, 'l'ombre du mystère', which is partly cryptic and partly meaning in sharp, figurative profile. My intention with this perhaps playful over-reading is not to propose this interpretation exclusive of any other, but to imagine the sensibilities of an enlightened contemporary reader, who would have been accustomed to the practice of 'l'harmonie imitative', who would have appreciated the poetry of Gébelin's etymology, and who would have been aware of the polemical nature of traditional French verse. Georges Lote comments on eighteenth-century poetry that 'la seule grande nouveauté qu'on puisse signaler, c'est l'importance que prend l'harmonie imitative', which is not to say that it cannot be traced back to the Renaissance, and ultimately to Classical metrics, but that a sensitive reading of eighteenth-century poetry calls for a keen awareness of its place in contemporary poetic minds (Lote, *Histoire du vers*, 1992: 249).

Increasing interest in 'l'harmonie imitative' may have been particularly relevant to the fashion for descriptive, pastoral poetry. Piis, for example, claims to have written *L'Harmonie imitative* on the banks of the river Garonne, far from the sterile intellectual circles of the city: 'Je compose en plein air, sans livre et sans tablettes' (Piis, *L'Harmonie imitative*, 1785: 31). Jacques Delille, also, is acutely aware of the importance of 'l'harmonie imitative' in his translation of Virgil's *Georgics* (1769) and in his own composition, *Les Jardins* (1782).[21] Jean-Antoine Roucher

---

[21] André Spire emphasizes the particularly suggestive sounds in a didactic piece by Delille: 'Peins-moi *l*égèrement *l'*amant *l*éger de *Fl*or, | Qu'un doux *r*uisseau mu*rmur*e un ve*rs* plus doux enco*re*, | Entend-on de la me*r* les ondes bouillonner?

frequently mentions Gébelin in the notes to *Les Mois* (1779), and his verse may owe something to Gébelin's sound symbolism.[22] A charming love poem by Evariste de Parny uses 's, ch, v, ou' sounds to suggest the ghostly but reassuring presence of a spurned lover who longs to remain the familiar of his erstwhile mistress:

> Souvent du zéphyr le plus doux
> Je prendrai l'haleine insensible;
> Tous mes soupirs seront pour vous:
> Ils feront vaciller la plume
> Sur vos cheveux noués sans art,
> Et disperseront au hasard
> La faible odeur qui les parfume.
>   .   .   .   .   .   .
> Et si souvent d'un joli sein
> Le nœud trop serré se denoue;
> Si le sofa plus mollement
> Cède au poids de votre paresse,
> Donnez un souris seulement
> A tous ces soins de ma tendresse.
>   (Parny, 'Le Revenant', in *Les Poésies érotiques*, 1778)

André Chénier's last poem before the scaffold is the poet's struggle to reconcile the futility of verse in the face of death. He is to lose his life, as inevitably as the last rays of sunlight cast the final shadows on the sundial; his inescapable desire to write poetry is a measured cadence leading inevitably to death. And yet it is also beauty's ultimate defiance of ugly tyranny. His poem suggests this tension in the use of harsh 'c, r' sounds and sharp, defiant 'e' sounds amid the prison gloom of dark, nasal vowels:

> Avant que de ses deux moitiés
> Ce vers que je commence ait atteint la dernière,
>   Peut-être en ces murs effrayés

| Le ve*r*s, comme un to*rr*ent, en *r*oulant doit *t*onner. | Qu'Ajax *s*oulève un *r*oc et le lance avec *p*eine | Chaque syllabe est lour*d*e et chaque mot se t*r*aîne. | Mais vois d'un pied *l*éger, Camille e*ffl*eurer *l*'eau; | Le *v*ers *v*ole et la *s*uit, aussi prompte que l'oiseau' (Spire, *Plaisir poétique et plaisir musculaire*, 1986: 315).

[22] Roucher, *Les Mois* (1779): Vol. I, 34. Jean and Janine Dagen suggest in their *Anthologie de la littérature du dix-huitième siècle* that Roucher probably practised Gébelin's symbolism (1994: 779). Delon makes the same suggestion (*Anthologie de la poésie française du XVIIIe siècle*, 1997: 490).

> Le messager de mort, noir recruteur des ombres,
> Escorté d'infâmes soldats,
> Ebranlent de mon nom ces longs corridors sombres,
> Où seul dans la foule à grands pas
> J'erre, aiguisant ces dards persécuteurs du crime,
> Du juste trop faibles soutiens,
> Sur mes lèvres soudain va suspendre la rime;
> (Chénier, Ode IX, in *Œuvres*, 1950: 193)[23]

This kind of euphony is familiar to readers of Verlaine, Baudelaire, or Rimbaud. A century after Gébelin, René Ghil attempts to present this kind of poetic language in theoretical terms as 'l'instrumentation des lettres, la musique verbale'. It is interesting to note that some of his evidence for linguistic symbolism, for 'une poésie scientifique [. . .] un système phonétique rationnel' is drawn from eighteenth-century scientists, like Ferrein, who defined the role of the larynx in the production of speech sounds, and Kratzenstein, who modelled the vocal tract with different shaped brass tubes, to demonstrate the articulation of vowel sounds. Ghil also chooses to illustrate his 'wagnérisme', or 'synthèse des arts', with the example of Castel's colour harpsichord.[24] Some authors have suggested also that Rimbaud and Baudelaire profited from reading de Brosses and Gébelin.[25] All these writers are presumably interested in the work of Gébelin and de Brosses because it has some relevance to poetry and writing in general. But if this is the case, one wonders why it is called 'étymologie'? The term seems curiously misleading, if what they were writing was in fact an 'art poétique' of sorts. The answer to this question is interesting in itself, but significant, also, in the light it casts on the general nature of the 'querelle'. In the minds of the 'anciens', 'tradition' is not the dictatorship of the present by the past, it is inspiring, dynamic, and creative; it is part of the present. The ideas of synchronicity and diachronicity are not mutually exclusive. In contrast, the rejection by the 'modernes' of tradition,

---

[23] Guitton thinks that Chénier explores sound symbolism in another poem, 'Le Jeune Malade', and that it is one example of 'la linguistique sensualiste, [. . .] cette science des accents et des timbres' in contemporary poetry (Guitton, 'Les Tentatives de libérations du vers français dans la poésie de 1760 à la révolution', 1969).
[24] Ferrein, 'De la formation de la voix de l'homme' (1741): 409–32; Kratzenstein, 'Sur la naissance de la formation des voyelles' (1780): 358–81. See Ghil, *Traité du verbe* (1888): 20–4.   [25] Roudaut, *Poètes et grammairiens* (1971): 10.

of paradigms of artistic creation drawn from the masters, is based on the assumption that the creative autonomy of the artist is paramount, that his struggle is to free himself from influence, that the highest art is necessarily a departure from the past. It would be wrong, therefore, to understand the 'querelle' merely as a polemic for and against past masters. Something quite radical must have happened to the very notion of 'tradition' which means it can not be seen in dynamic terms by the 'modernes' as it is by the 'anciens'. In order to understand why, it will help to define 'étymologie' as it relates to the neoclassical idea of 'tradition' and a certain conception of poetic language.

4.7 'Etymologie' as a theory of poetry

Since Saussure, the problem we face in interpreting 'étymologie' is to reconcile sound symbolism with the arbitrariness of language. He thinks that there is no aprioristic reason why certain sounds should be predestined to signify certain ideas, with the minor exception of onomatopoeia, which he thinks is a much smaller element of vocabulary than we think. The meaning of the phonetic sequence in French /s ö r/, for example, could equally be expressed by a different sequence of sounds, and the diversity of languages seems irrefutable evidence of their essential arbitrariness (Saussure, *Cours*, 1967: 1124). Consequently, any resemblance between sound and sense is a secondary signifying process, an a posteriori perception, a reverse transcription which has nothing to do with the fundamental way in which language signifies. In Saussure's terms, 'meaning' is defined exclusively as an aprioristic process, that is, the way in which a particular sequence of sounds comes in the first instance to represent a particular idea. In contrast, poetic language marshals sound to reflect meaning with devices such as assonance, consonance, rhyme, metre etc, which cannot be said to be part of the 'meaning' of language in the strict Saussurian sense. It is clear that they are intentional, a posteriori, and unsystematic.

The distinction between poetic and 'normal' language is less clear, however, when we read Saussure's study of anagrams in

Latin verse. In this case, he is perplexed by the systematic way in which the theme or title of certain Latin poems, particularly from Virgil and Lucretius, is repeated in phonetic anagrams throughout the text, with no external evidence to prove that this was an intention of the poet. There did indeed seem to be a way in which the sound was marshalled to convey the sense of the poem. Saussure writes:

Est-ce encore par hasard que les syllabes d'*Ulixes* semblent cherchées dans une suite de mots comme
/Urbium simul/Undique pepulit lux umbras resides
   U--------UL-U---------ULI--X------S----ES
(Starobinski, *Les Mots sous les mots*, 1971: 150)

The anagrams are often names of mythological heroes or gods, usually occurring at key junctures in the poem. Saussure never published his results, but he fills over a hundred notebooks without ever finding evidence from Latin authors or modern commentaries that these anagrams were intentional. He was evidently perplexed and fascinated by a compositional device which appeared to convey a major part of the meaning, and a phenomenon which, if truly unintentional, would contradict his theory of arbitrary language. If anagrams can be said to be 'meaningful', then so can assonance, consonance, metre, rhyme, and poetic language in general.

There may be no answer to Saussure's question about intentionality, perhaps because it is wrongly posed. Anagrams may well have been a compositional device of Latin poetry, but if they are like other devices in the highly intricate metrics of Classical poetry, they will have been learnt and practised assiduously at school as part of the drill of writing verse, they will have been repeated and exercised by poets until they required no conscious effort, they will have become, in fact, a kind of 'second nature', quite unlike the conscious process that Saussure assumed. New compositional devices, or those borrowed by innovative poets from Greek to Latin, would effortlessly, naturally be integrated with existing verse forms in a culture which understood the dynamic force of inherited convention, of tradition. Rather like the dancer in the recurrent eighteenth-century metaphor, the formal steps are learnt so well that the movement looks natural. Surely the only way to understand 'dance' is as a way of harnessing the natural ability of the body to move for a specific representational purpose. In Hogarth's terms, the body becomes 'legible' through the application of particular 'codes', and we call the resulting aesthetic pleasure 'grace'. Hogarth prefers to talk of 'grace' rather than 'beauty', precisely because it is a better suggestion of the way nature coincides with artifice to produce meaning.[26] Condillac makes the same point as Hogarth when he argues that all forms of representation, language, or art, are 'second' nature. In order to understand how dance 'signifies' we need to take both an aprioristic view of 'natural' movement, and also an a posteriori view of codified movement. Saussure adopts exclusively an aprioristic view, and his theory is consequently not adapted to explaining poetic language. If we agree with him that there is no reason why certain sounds should be predestined to signify certain ideas, it seems probable that once adopted, these sounds may be perceived, marshalled, codified to reflect meaning. Saussure thinks this is not what we ought to call 'meaning', but it is possible to show how the two are complementary. Even Saussure agrees, with most eighteenth-century thinkers on language, that it is not possible for a language to be wholly arbitrary. The phonetic sequence /s ö r/ means nothing if only one speaker uses it; it is only convention which breathes linguistic life into an inert, meaningless sequence of sounds. Convention is animated by volition; a community must wilfully designate certain sounds for certain meanings. One is entitled to wonder whether convention is only important in the primary semiotic process, or whether it is not a constant vitalizing force. We would have to agree with Saussure that what is truly remarkable in semiosis is the fact that it occurs at all, that there can be any verbal representation of an idea or object, and this must mean that the arbitrariness of language is an important theory. Nevertheless, if convention and volition are such key factors, it seems odd to confine them to only one stage in language; perhaps we should not disregard wilful semiosis at a later stage, that is to say in language as it is practised, no matter how subjective and unsystematic it appears. Poetry is wilful language. It takes an a posteriori view of words, it maps sound onto established

---

[26] Hogarth, *The Analysis of Beauty* (1997): chapter XVII, 'Of Action'.

meaning. It is fluid and unsystematic in the sense that not all members of a speech community will necessarily understand the sense of a sound, and yet neither is it completely subjective. It uses what Roman Jackobson calls 'elective affinities', that is, it is a vehicle for collective volition which is at the heart of language itself (Jackobson, *The Sound Shape of Language*, 1979: 179). He suggests that with time and practice, there are recognizable ways in which sound conveys the sense of language, or in the words of Sully-Prudhomme, 'l'accoutumance prête au mot la physionomie de ce qu'il désigne' (Sully-Prudhomme, *Testament poétique*, 1901: 125). Gombrich agrees when he compares painting and poetry, and says of sounds symbolism: 'just as there is no innocent eye, there is no innocent ear' (Gombrich, *Art and Illusion*, 1996: 307).

J. H. Prynne demonstrates this brilliantly in an essay entitled 'Stars, Tigers and the Shape of Words' (1993), in which he discusses the implications of Saussure's arbitrariness for poetic language, with particular reference to Jane Taylor's nursery rhyme 'The Star', and William Blake's 'The Tiger'. He interprets 'The Star' as reassurance to a child at bedtime: 'The vast scale and remoteness of phenomena are potentially frightening, as also the imminent loneliness at bed-time; but each word reduces this scale to the friendly and protective charm of little things' (Prynne, 'Stars, Tigers', 1993: 10). Accordingly, the child is encouraged to look for little, reassuring things by a process of 'auditory noticing' (Prynne, 'Stars, Tigers', 1993: 9). In the first line, 'Twinkle, twinkle, little star', the suffix '-le' is repeated three times, encouraging us to associate 'twinkle' with 'little', as if 'twinkle' were a 'little twink'. Historically, it is a convention of English word formation to add '-le' to words or stems, to give a diminutive or frequentative meaning, and 'twink' is attested as a variant of 'blink, wink'. The small child knows nothing of this, but the 'hypnotic influences of jingle and klang-effects' have made 'accumulated potential significations stored in the history of [. . .] usage' accessible to the child's intuition (Prynne, 'Stars, Tigers', 1993: 10, 16). If 'twink' was originally an arbitrary sequence of sounds, then 'twinkle' is partly motivated through association with 'little'. Prynne calls poetry a 'memory theatre', because it is a place where the historically motivated sense of 'twinkle' can be re-enacted by re-association with the word 'little' (Prynne, 'Stars, Tigers', 1993: 18). This process of a posteriori codification of sounds is allowed to become prominent in poetry, which means that poetic language is not in principle any different to 'normal' language. Prynne concludes by contrasting Saussure's view of language as a psychological, logical system with a different view of language as partly a product of usage, a socio-historical artefact: 'We may if we wish leave arbitrariness in more or less full control of the central citadel of linguistic theory, but out in the larger semantic fields and forests its writ does not successfully prohibit a wider and more hybrid repertory of contrarious procedures' (Prynne, 'Stars, Tigers', 1993: 35). He too recognizes that there are two perspectives on language and meaning, that the importance we ascribe to sound in conveying meaning depends on taking an a posteriori view of language as performance. His is a poet's reaction to sound and sense, but there are also linguists who agree with him.

After publication of Saussure's *Cours* in 1916, Otto Jespersen was one of the first to disagree with Saussure's strong arbitrary theory, because it takes no account of performance. In a famous study he investigates the persistent association of the sound /i/ with the meaning 'small', and finds widespread agreement in a number of different languages (Jespersen, *Language, its Nature, Development and Origin*, 1922: 402). He gives examples in English: 'little, tiny/teeny, kid, slim, imp, pigmy, midge, bit, tip, slit', and diminutives such as 'Bobby, baby, auntie, birdie'. Roman Jakobson gives evidence to show how language uses 'antiphony', or vowel opposition in pairs of words with opposite meanings: 'gleam' and 'gloom', 'here' and 'there', or in French 'petit' and 'grand'. He does not find it surprising that sound in language is formulated to reflect such contrasts as light and dark, light and heavy, or big and small, because these contrasts belong to 'the elementary structures required by perceptual differentiation' (Jackobson, *The Sound Shape of Language*, 1979: 433).[27] In other words, language is adapted to reflect our perception of the world; even if the sound of language is arbitrary in the first

---

[27] Compare *Gulliver's Travels* for antiphony of front and back vowels; Gulliver visits first a land of small people, the Lilliputians, where his adopted name is Grildrig, and then a land of giant people, called Brobdingnagians. Jespersen calls this phenomenon 'sound gesture', and recounts the wartime story, when, in time of drought, a sign was put up in a Norwegian public toilet using two interesting neologisms: 'don't pull the string for *bimmelim*, only for *bummelum*' (Jakobson, *The Sound Shape of Language*, 1979: 184, 182; my italics). Everyone understood what he meant.

instance, the tendency within a speech community is to look for sound patterns, distinctive distributions, and order. If we adopt Saussure's exclusively aprioristic approach, we would not regard this phenomenon as an essential factor in signification. If, on the other hand, we regard language as a socio-historic artefact, so that we adopt an a posteriori view, we would have to regard sound as an integral part of meaning in language. From this perspective, poetic language becomes 'natural', in that it harnesses the perceived patterns in language by turning them into tools of composition. It can also be the testing ground for new devices, a forum for electing new affinities between sound and sense.

There is, then, a tenable argument that language is as much poetic as it is arbitrary, on condition that we do not adopt Saussure's exclusive aprioristic approach. Gébelin and de Brosses do not adopt his aprioristic approach, which means that from a modern point of view, it is easy to mistake their 'étymologie' for either unsystematic linguistics or rationalistic poetics. They suggest that the force of convention which first breathed linguistic life into inert sequences of sounds is still active in the way we write and understand poetry; sound is constantly, wilfully marshalled and re-marshalled to convey sense. It is for this reason that their language schemes are as much an 'art poétique' as they are a history of word formation. De Brosses, for example, suggested a historically accurate origin for the word 'scrupule', which showed also how the sounds 's, c, r' are suggestive of the meaning. From this point of view, past and present complement each other in a way which helps us understand the 'querelle des anciens et des modernes' as quite a profound difference in the way 'tradition' is interpreted. When the 'anciens' appeal to tradition and convention as integral to creativity, they do not share Saussure's fundamental distinction between the synchronic and diachronic. They would not have been perplexed as he was to find anagrams in Latin poetry, because they would have assumed more easily that conventional means of signification can be learnt, internalized, and become what Condillac calls a 'second' nature, so that they are difficult to distinguish from the 'natural' or arbitrary meaning of language. The two natures are different, yet complementary. Hogarth's 'grace' is a similar conflation of aprioristic and a posteriori perspectives, because the aesthetic experience of 'beauty' depends on a codification of the natural body to make it 'legible'. If the aesthetic experience necessarily depends on codifying nature, it seems inappropriate for the 'modernes' to reject convention *per se*. Perhaps this is not their point, perhaps they perceive convention to have become so institutionalized, so ossified that it has lost its dynamic force, that it is no longer 'elective affinities', but permanently 'elected affinities'. The creative forum, where both past and present had a voice, has been replaced by a dictatorship of the past over the present.

The place of 'étymologie' in this debate is as a restatement of values, a technical demonstration of wilful language spanning the potential divide between past and present. It is an illustration of the aesthetic threshold which Münch observes in the eighteenth century, because the most salient feature of these elaborate language schemes is their effort to amass evidence for a phenomenon which had previously been taken for granted. Such are their efforts that modern critics like Genette interpret Gébelin and de Brosses as initiators of a tradition of poetic language which culminates in the symbolist poetry of Baudelaire or Rimbaud, whereas in fact, they are restating the traditional theory of 'l'harmonie imitative' in unparalleled detail. In the wider context of the 'querelle', their reasons for choosing 'l'harmonie imitative' in particular may be based on an abiding interest in language as a model of representation, a view of language as an almost instinctive way in which thought is made corporeal, and by extension an indication as to how the artist may intellectualize material nature.[28]

Conclusion

Perhaps it is best to return to the Greek sense of the word 'étymologie' which de Brosses and Gébelin prefer, that is, the study of 'true meaning', which implies no necessary hiatus between

---

[28] It is interesting to see how persistent is the recourse among poets to articulation as a way of understanding sound symbolism. See e.g. André Spire, *Plaisir poétique et plaisir musculaire* (1986); John Ciardi, who describes the relation between sound and sense in poetry as 'muscular enactment' (*How does a Poem Mean?*, 1960: 764); or the title of Donald Davie's book on diction in poetry, *Articulate Energy* (1992). Lote calls the device of 'l'harmonie imitative' 'le phonétisme esthétique' (*Histoire du vers*, 1992: Vol. II, 229).

tradition and innovation, diachrony and synchrony.[29] The transcendent principle which permits this reconciliation is imitation, and so it is that an elaborate, ostensibly linguistic study engages with the essential issue at stake in the aesthetic debates of the eighteenth century, and in particular with the debates surrounding the importance of prosody and 'l'harmonie imitative' in French verse. 'Etymologie' is more misleading now than it perhaps was in the eighteenth century, because at the time it seems to make effortless assumptions that there is indeed an 'echo' between sound and sense. The original echo that Adam hears in Piis's allegory is still audible to the most sensitive poets, it can still be marshalled and re-marshalled in language which is inherently wilful and poetic. Georges Lote thinks that these abortive attempts to revitalize poetry ultimately prove to be futile, that 'la période postclassique [. . .] n'a guère que des intentions'.[30] And yet what noble intentions to explore the elusive blend of nature and convention which produces art, to try to understand exactly what it is that Adam hears on that first night in Eden, when he perceives an aural image of himself in the echoing forest. To borrow Olivet's words on prosody, there are 'ressorts cachez' in art, and perhaps in man's essential imitative nature, which Gébelin and de Brosses mean to reveal, and they do so with quite unparalleled sensitivity to the sound of language. There is some justification in Lote's observation of the postclassical period, as long as we do not from this notion leap to the conclusion that it is also an unpoetic period. An era which spent so much time in reflective mood as to the very nature of the poetic exercise could only have done so on the basis of a heightened sensitivity to poetry; like the lover who says not only 'I love you', but 'I love you because'. The poets and thinkers of this chapter seem to listen to an echo of themselves reading poetry, to take a reflexive view of themselves, in order to understand the enigmatic way in which art reflects nature.

[29] For other interpretations of the word and concept of 'etymology', see Zumthor, 'Etymologie (essai d'histoire sémantique)' (1958).

[30] Lote, *Histoire du vers*, 1992: Vol. VII, 4, 9.

5

THE DISSOLUTION OF LANGUAGE

For much of the eighteenth century, language is an appealing locus for aesthetic debate because it seems as much a rational, universal system of signs as it is a mode of personal expression. As such, it combines the 'science' and the 'sentiment' of aesthetics well. The situation changes completely towards the end of the century when the most striking feature of debate is the breakdown of this consensus. Language as 'science' and as 'sentiment' become radically separate. On the one hand, the influential linguistic theory of 'idéologie' takes no account of literary expression, and on the other, the literary principle of 'impertinence' does not advocate any rationalization of the creative process.

'Idéologie' is the study of thought as a system of signs, largely inspired by selective interpretations of Condillac and Locke, and with such little interest in the expressive part of language that it is about as close to 'le degré zéro de la rhétorique' as one could hope to get.[1] In contrast, 'impertinence' is exclusively interested in the expressive part of language on the basis that the force of literary inspiration is too powerful and subjective to be tamed by literary rules and conventions. 'Impertinent' writers reject the putative clarity of classical grammarians in order to embrace poetic obscurity, much as Victor Hugo declares in a later poem:

> j'ai dit à l'ombre: 'Sois!'
> Et l'ombre fut.
> · · · · · · · · ·
> Oui, si Beauzée est dieu, c'est vrai, je suis athée.
> (Hugo, 'Réponse à un acte d'accusation',
> in *Les Contemplations*, 1834; 1972: 641)

In the latter part of the eighteenth century, the mutual incompatibility of 'idéologie' and 'impertinence' mean that the language debate is polarized in a new way, and as a result

---

[1] The expression is Ricoeur's in *La Métaphore vive* (1975): 180.

technical discussions of language look more technical and austere, and literary principles look less rational and objective. Linguists and literary writers do not speak the same language any more.

Part of the reason for the divergence is that linguistic writers after the Revolution are no longer interested in the question of the origin of language, which seemed to previous eighteenth-century thinkers to lead inevitably to fundamental issues of semiotics, representation, and aesthetics. Instead, they are concerned with the synchronic issues involved in devising an efficient, universal language scheme for clear, philosophical, and sometimes propagandist communication. It would no doubt have seemed naïve and short-sighted to thinkers like Condillac to treat language in this way, as a system of weights and measures for thought, as if ideas could be retrieved from words like Swift's 'Sun-Beams out of Cucumbers' (Swift, *Gulliver's Travels*, 1971: 178). Condillac and his contemporaries always thought that a philosophy of language had to take account of abstract concepts like aesthetic pleasure which are not quantifiable like mathematical symbols. They struggled to clarify something obscure in language called 'beautiful style', and they took pleasure in making a game of the inherent slipperiness of the exercise, with synonyms or 'calembours'. They would doubtless have thought that universal languages with unambiguous signs were deeply unrealistic, and also no fun at all. These different perspectives on language are remarkable when we consider that until the Revolution, the eighteenth century in France only produced one aprioristic universal language scheme, which is Faiguet's in his article 'Langue nouvelle' for the *Encyclopédie*. In the decade after the Revolution at least seven were generated, of which I shall consider three in this chapter.[2]

The divorce of literary and what we shall broadly call 'scientific' language, is most vividly expressed by Lancelin, who is worth quoting at length since his judgement testifies to a fundamental change in the way that writing is perceived, a change that we have inherited in modern times and that we largely take for granted. Of specialized scientific language, he says:

[2] I shall discuss Delormel, Maimieux, and Sicard, but not Condorcet, Bertin, Hourwitz, or Blanc (see bibliography).

Cette langue n'est point faite pour flatter l'oreille et remuer l'imagination par des compositions brillantes, originales, mais pour décrire
soigneusement tous les objets, et analyser avec précision les idées
de tous genres, [elle] auroit une marche sévère, méthodique et uni-
forme, qui la rendroit peu propre aux productions poétiques et
littéraires: mais ce serait là, selon moi, un assez petit inconvénient;
le géomètre, le physicien, le chimiste, enfin l'analyste, [. . .] doit avoir
une langue toute différente de celle d'un poëte, du romancier, de
l'orateur; il n'a pas besoin, comme ceux-ci, de peindre ou d'émouvoir
les passions: ministre de la raison, il doit se borner à offrir clairement
à l'esprit les choses telles qu'elles sont, à exposer froidemen les faits
et les vérités premières [. . .] Le monde fabuleux et chimérique est le
domaine de l'imagination et de la poésie; l'univers réel est celui de
l'intelligence pure, des expériences et de l'analyse [. . .] Je crois même
qu'il est nécessaire d'élever un mur de séparation entre le pays des
fictions et des chimères, et le domaine de la nature ou de la réalité
[. . .] Ainsi donc, il faut avoir deux langues, l'une pour exprimer
l'ensemble des faits et des vérités, l'autre pour peindre tous les pro-
duits de l'imagination. (Lancelin, *Introduction à l'analyse des sciences*,
1801: Vol. I, 315–16)

No one before the Revolution distinguished so clearly and confidently between scientific and poetic language, and those who
tried were not able to draw on the enormous support that contemporary linguistic discussion lent to Lancelin's view. He does
not speak in a vacuum, since he is drawing the inevitable implications from the new study of 'idéologie' and the profusion of
universal language schemes in the last decade of the eighteenth
century. This chapter will essentially be an interpretation of
what Lancelin and his contemporaries understood to be the
difference between 'l'analyste', and 'un poëte', between
'exposer froidemen' and 'émouvoir'.

5.1   The linguistic philosophy of 'idéologie'

'L'analyste' is the 'idéologiste', the proponent of a new science
of ideas, founded largely, but selectively, on the semiotics of
Condillac and Locke. It is a heuristic theory which is as much
mathematical as linguistic, and which seeks to reduce thinking
to propositional analysis and logic. 'Idéologie' means 'the study
of ideas', how they relate to each other, how they are combined

to form new ideas and extend the field of knowledge, on the understanding that the only means to carry out these intellectual operations is to manipulate signs. It will be important to remember in the following discussion that 'idéologie' depends on a semiotic theory which is primarily mathematic, and which, therefore, has important consequences for the theory of language.

Destutt de Tracy, Maine de Biran, Degérando, and others referred to themselves as 'idéologistes', and it is only after Bonaparte's *coup d'état* of the 18 brumaire that Royalists refer to them pejoratively as 'idéologues', in order 'to denigrate liberal-republicans and other critics from the left, especially those who appealed to general principles such as liberty or the rights of man' (Head, 'The origin of "idéologue" and "idéologie"', 1980: 257).[3] Maine de Biran calls 'idéologie' 'la science des sciences', because it is the general theory of scientific method and intellectual progress. The 'idéologiste' studies general methodology, he occupies a theoretical vantage point over the other sciences in order better to understand how each finds a path to intellectual progress. Maine de Biran describes 'idéologie' as intellectual cartography, essential if thinkers are not to lose their way in the rapidly expanding field of intellectual endeavour:

L'idéologie plane, pour ainsi dire, sur toutes les sciences, car les sciences ne se composent que de nos idées et de leurs divers rapports. Ces idées forment comme un pays immense et infiniment varié, partagé en une multitude de districts, coupé par un plus grand nombre de routes de communication. Pendant que les savants voyageurs se dispersent dans ces districts, vont et viennent dans ces routes, l'idéologiste, placé sur une éminence et comme immobile, observe leurs directions, en tient note, en dresse la *carte:* de là, il arrive que souvent il connaît mieux les chemins que les voyageurs eux-mêmes, qu'il peut leur fournir d'utiles indications et en quelque sorte les *orienter.* (Maine de Biran, 'Note sur les rapports de l'idéologie et des mathématiques', 1988: 8–9; his emphasis)

The world of ideas is so extensive, and there are so many different potential routes towards intellectual progress, that there

---

[3] Head says that the first recorded use of 'idéologue' as a pejorative term is in a Royalist newspaper of 12 Jan. 1800, when Cabanis and Volney are identified with the bloody Revolution and doctrinaire theorizing; Chateaubriand makes the same use of the term in *Le Génie du christianisme* (1802).

needs to be a co-ordinated approach to intellectual progress. If not, there is a danger that individual thinkers will find their own idiosyncratic routes, and there will be no mutual understanding of each other's discoveries. A contemporary example is the advantage of a systematic nomenclature in chemistry. Before Lavoisier, the same compound could be given a different name, depending on the particular chemical reaction used to produce it. Lavoisier thought that there are only a finite number of chemical elements in the world, so that the most logical naming procedure would be based on the simple elements which made up the compound. 'Iron oxide' means the same thing to all chemists; they speak the same language, but crucially, it is a new, specialized language.[4]

The ambition of 'idéologie' is to provide a new intellectual language that would be universally understandable. Its grammar and vocabulary would be designed to reflect heuristically the clear patterns of thought necessary to all scientific discovery. The language of 'idéologie' would 'decompose' the act of thinking into its elementary components. The problem both with science and language is that progress towards more complex understanding and more abstract words sometimes means that first principles are forgotten. Abstract words and theories are susceptible to misunderstanding, because we forget the simple ideas that compose them. These simple ideas are the origin of thought and language, the beginning of all intellectual journeys. It is important not to lose sight of these 'origins', since they help to make sense of where the intellectual traveller is heading. 'Idéologie' is the study of ideas from their conception to their advancement, and also the clarification of signs for ideas which may otherwise obscure what they mean to represent, and risk hindering intellectual progress.

Maine de Biran demonstrates with an example from algebra to show, firstly, how a proposition may be misleading and, secondly, the tremendous advance in thinking that is possible when abstract concepts are properly understood. He cites the apparent paradox when it is said that 'minus multiplied by minus is plus' (Maine de Biran, 'Note sur les rapports de

---

[4] See Andersen, *Between the Library and the Laboratory: The Language of Chemistry in Eighteenth-century France* (1984): 116.

l'idéologie et des mathématiques', 1988: 13–14).[5] The paradox is that 'minus' is the operation of subtraction; it cannot itself be operated on. The paradox is due to conventional abuse, or abbreviation of notation, which means that '−1' is actually the abbreviation for the operation 'o − 1'; in other words, the symbol '−' actually means the operation 'subtract', but has come also to mean the property of being negative. In the phrase 'two minus seven', 'minus' is being used as an operator, a kind of verb, whereas the formula '−17' is a kind of noun phrase, in which 'minus' is an adjective. The apparent paradox is due only to using the same symbol for these related but different concepts.

Maine de Biran goes on to say that this kind of terminological confusion has unfortunate consequences for our conception of number. We imagine that '−1' has the same kind of existence as '+1'. In fact, the negative numbers have no a priori existence, but are constructed from the positive numbers. The value '−1' only makes sense as the solution to the operation '1 minus 2'. In other words, the negative numbers are a conceptual projection backwards from 'o'; '−1' means 'the same distance from zero as "+1", but in the opposite direction'. Thus, negative numbers are invented, but nonetheless necessary in order to give a solution to the operation '1 minus 2'. There is no mystery about the existence of negative numbers, as long as we understand what we mean by 'existence'. However, the ambivalent sense of the '−' sign does not help us to understand that positive and negative numbers have different kinds of existence. The first stage in understanding negative numbers, therefore, is to clarify language.

One concept of number may be inadequate to solve all problems; that is, there may be problems which can only be solved by inventing new numbers. For example, we next create the fractions, or rational numbers, such as $\frac{7}{5}$, so that the operation

---

[5] Maine de Biran actually says in the text: '− multiplié par − donne +, et − divisé par − donne −', which is clearly not true. Every schoolboy knows, and a mathematician of Maine de Biran's standing would certainly know, that a minus divided by a minus gives a plus. It is evident from the rest of the passage that Maine de Biran is a good mathematician, and it seems impossible that he should make this error. One can only speculate that it arises from a slip of the pen in Maine de Biran's manuscript, or a printing error in Tisserand's first edition of the work in 1920, subsequently repeated in the 1988 edition to which I refer.

of division always has a result. However, even this is not enough to describe values which clearly exist as lengths in geometry. For example, the circumference of every circle is always the same proportion of its diameter, and geometrically this value, written 'π' clearly exists. However, it is not equal to any fraction; we can make closer and closer approximations to it, '$\frac{3}{1}, \frac{31}{11}, \frac{314}{100}, \frac{3141}{1000} \ldots$', but we never obtain the exact value. We now have two notions of number; the rational numbers arising from arithmetic, which Maine de Biran calls 'quantité discrète', and the so-called 'real' numbers, arising from geometry, which he calls 'quantité continue'. Confusing the two leads in Maine de Biran's words to 'une multitude d'obscurités, de mésentendus et de disputes' (Maine de Biran, 'Note sur les rapports de l'idéologie et des mathématiques', 1988: 14). Using the rational numbers, one could argue that 'π' does not exist; using the real numbers, one must conclude that it does; each is right within its concept of number.

The question arises, will the process of inventing new numbers ever end? To solve general quadratic equations (such as $x^2 = -2$), the real numbers are insufficient, and so-called 'imaginary' numbers must be invented. This stock of numbers, which Maine de Biran calls 'des racines qu'on appelle *imaginaires*' is now called the 'complex numbers' (Gauss introduced the term in 1831). One of the Holy Grails of eighteenth-century mathematics was to find a convincing proof of the fact that no further numbers need be invented in order to solve the entire family of equations which naturally arise.[6] Maine de Biran says that, by continuing to think clearly about what it means for numbers to exist, the 'idéologiste' will be led to the Grail.

The important point to remember about this mathematical example is that it demonstrates the value of questioning signs,

---

[6] That is, equations including higher powers of x than x^2, e.g. $x^4 - 13x^3 + 5 = 0$. This had been suspected since the seventeenth century, and proofs were attempted by D'Alembert in 1746, Euler in 1749, Lagrange in 1772, and Laplace in 1795. It is now called the Fundamental Theorem of Algebra, and the first viable proof was given by Gauss in 1799, but did not find immediate favour in France. The solution was finally accepted when Argand's 1814 proof was presented in Cauchy's textbook of 1820, *Cours d'Analyse*. For more detail, see van der Waerden, *A History of Algebra* (1985). My thanks to Dr Graham Nelson for help with the mathematical interpretation of 'idéologie'.

and 'decomposing' our ideas, in order better to understand abstract concepts. The intellectual journey which began with a clarification of the ambiguous meaning of the sign '−' led subsequently to a better understanding of the abstract concept of negative numbers. They are more abstract than the real numbers, because they have no a priori existence, but they nonetheless 'exist', because they can be demonstrated to be logical extensions of the real numbers. On the assumption that abstract concepts can exist in their own way, other kinds of numbers are conceivable, like the rationals and ultimately the complex. This procedure is both a method of discovery, and a prescription for terminological precision. If everyone were able to 'decompose' an idea in this way, words would become sufficiently clear to avoid disagreement arising solely from terminological confusion or abuse.

This model of clear thinking and unambiguous signs is not based primarily on natural language, since it is not possible to regard it in quite the same way as we have just seen. Linguistic signs cannot be decomposed, like the mathematical concept of number, into universally accepted ideas, because they are in the end unquantifiable and too subjective. Destutt de Tracy chooses mathematics as his semiotic model because he thinks it is the clearest example of the process of abstraction which leads to complex ideas. The invention of the sign '2' is a convenient generalization from the operation '1 + 1', and by analogy we can then go on to invent more complex signs still, such as '3', meaning '1 + 1 + 1', and so on, until we have an unambiguous scale of values which allows us to compose and decompose as simple or complex a numerical sign as we like (Destutt de Tracy, *Elemens d'idéologie*, 1825: Vol. I, 239–40). Words, however, cannot be measured according to such a scale of semantic values, and hence the same clarity is not possible in natural language. Destutt de Tracy prefers numbers as a model of thought, because

De tous les rapports existans entre nos idées, les rapports de quantité sont les plus exactement appréciables, étant toujours composés de la même valeur, celle de l'unité répétée plus ou moins de fois. Il n'est donc pas aussi aisé de faire voir l'effet des mots sur la combinaison des rapports de nos idées, qui ne sont pas des rapports de quantité, c'est à dire qu'il n'est pas possible de marquer avec autant de précision le point où l'esprit s'arrêterait faute d'un mot, et celui jusqu'où il va au moyen de tel mot ou de tel autre. (Destutt de Tracy, *Elemens d'idéologie*, 1825: Vol. I, 245–6)

The semantic dividing line between words is always indeterminate; he seems to suggest that their meanings overlap to produce phenomena like synonymy, metaphor or even puns, so that it seems that the more we manipulate linguistic signs, the more we dally with meaning and obscure sense. Natural language, then, is an inappropriate model of thought, and in a six-page footnote Destutt de Tracy stresses how different it is from algebra. He says that words are a conceptual artifice, a contrived form of reasoning which is incapable of the same clarity. There are fixed proportions in algebra which make a taxonomy of thought much more workable: 'la langue algebrique ne s'applique qu'à des idées de quantité, c'est à dire à des idées d'une seule espèce, qui ont entre elles des rapports très-fixes et très-précis; ils sont toujours composés de l'unité ou de ses multiples [. . .] Par ce moyen, il n'y a jamais ni incertitude, ni obscurité, ni variations dans la valeur des elemens du discours de cette langue' (Destutt de Tracy, *Elemens d'idéologie*, 1825: Vol. I, 249 n.). Decomposition into 'des idées d'une seule espèce' is not possible in natural language in the same way as in algebra, because syntactic operations do not produce quantifiable results in the same way as 'multiplication' or 'division' in mathematics: 'les modifications que nous leur [les mots] faisons éprouver dans [le] discours, soit en joignant un adjectif à un substantif, soit en donnant un attribut à un sujet, sont bien plus variées et bien moins mesurables que celles que font éprouver aux caractères algebriques les signes *multiplié par*, ou *divisé par* [. . .] C'est là une différence immense' (p. 250 n.).

The immense difference means that something has to be done about the language of science. If science is to continue to be explained in natural language, then the role of 'idéologie' is to clarify the semiotics and make it at least more consistent than it otherwise is. There are many ambiguous signs in language like '−' in algebra which would benefit from systematic clarification. Perhaps, however, the solution is to invent a completely new, universal language of ideas, which would owe nothing to natural language, and would instead be devised purely according to the heuristic principles of 'idéologie'. Inevitably, such a language would resemble algebra more than it would natural language, and would by implication finally abandon the assumption made by all the linguists that we have seen so far in this study. Girard, Dumarsais, Condillac, Gébelin, and others believed that it was possible to resolve the nebulous appearance of language so that there was no need for a professional intellectual language. In contrast, the 'idéologistes' accept that there should, in fact, be two languages; one for Lancelin's 'analyste', and one for his 'poëte'. The idea of a professional intellectual language is not new; it is a recurrent theme, at least since Locke, of discussions regarding the deceptive nature of language. The distinctive aspect of the last decade of the eighteenth century, however, is that the theory was put into practice with remarkable vigour. Many attempts were made to devise a heuristically perfect language which would facilitate intellectual progress in all the sciences, even the 'metaphysical' sciences of politics, linguistics, and morality. The period stands in marked contrast to the rest of the eighteenth century, which largely adopts Locke's resignation to the ambiguity of words, and also his scepticism that it is ever possible to resolve them in a new, a priori language.

5.2   Universal language schemes: Locke, Delormel, and Maimieux

Locke entertains the idea of a specialized philosophical language which would avoid the equivocation of natural language, but has little hope that it can ever be achieved. It arises as an implied solution to his conception of the deceptive nature of language, but he thinks that it is not worth pursuing. Words, according to Locke, are always composites: 'the *ideas* they stand for are very complex, and made up of a great number of *ideas* put together' (Locke, *Essay*, 1977: 248). Moral words are especially complex, and are seldom sufficiently 'decomposed' by speakers to avoid misunderstanding. Words like 'murder' mean different things to different people, depending on the particular complex composition of the concept in their own minds. The solution to this ambiguity is presumably to make explicit the composition of simple ideas which contribute to the meaning of abstract words like 'murder'. Locke thinks that it is unrealistic and 'ridiculous' to attempt to do this in common language, since there is no way of imposing language by decree on the common population. It would, however, be desirable to clarify language for philosophers: 'though the market and exchange must be left to their own ways of talking and gossipings not be robbed of their ancient privilege [...] methinks those *who* pretend *seriously* to *search after* or maintain *truth*, should think themselves obliged to study how they might deliver themselves without obscurity, doubtfulness, or equivocation' (Locke, *Essay*, 1977: 257). Just as 'merchants and lovers, cooks and tailors have words wherewithal to dispatch their ordinary affairs', philosophers too need a professional language (p. 259). He considers the possibility of a dictionary of abstract ideas, each idea decomposed so as to render it unambiguous; a kind of 'natural history' of language that would clarify the equivocal sense of moral words like 'murder' (p. 265). In practice, however, such a dictionary would be an enormous collaborative project between the greatest thinkers of the time, and almost certainly an impracticable proposition; yet the technique of decomposing ideas remains philosophically essential. It leads Locke to the following statement, which 'idéologistes' would in principle agree with: 'I am so bold to think that *morality is capable of demonstration*, as well as mathematics' (Locke, *Essay*, 1977: 260).

The 'idéologistes' are more optimistic than Locke that a dictionary of ideas is possible; Lancelin speaks for them all when he exclaims: 'il faut écrire un dictionnaire!' (Lancelin, *Introduction à l'analyse des sciences*, 1801: Vol. I, 319). There is a prevailing atmosphere of optimism in their work, that man after the Revolution is capable of controlling his own destiny, including his own language. A contemporary article in *Le Spectateur du Nord* says of the eighteenth century: 'le siècle du Magnétisme animal, des Ballons, de la Liberté et de l'Egalité est fait pour produire des choses extraordinaires', of which it says that a new language would be one.[7] The Montgolfier brothers flew the first hot-air balloon in 1783, Frantz Mesmer and Jacques-François Puységur were discovering hypnotism, which they called

---

[7] *Le Spectateur du Nord* (6 Apr. 1798), in Knowlson, *Universal Language Schemes*, 1975): 163 n.

'animal magnetism' in the 1780s and 1790s, and the Revolution seemed to provide the greatest opportunity in history for man to cast himself in a new social, political, and perhaps spiritual mould.[8] Small wonder, perhaps, that in these circumstances there was intense interest in inventing a new language for a new age.[9]

The first stage in the invention of these languages is to arrive at a system of nomenclature which is perceived as adequate to express all the objects of mind and world. The nomenclaturist approach is similar in some ways to the projects of John Wilkins, Georges Dalgarno, or Comenius a century earlier, except that post-Revolutionary language 'projectors' appeal only to 'common sense', rather than to any ontological reality for their classifications. They are not designed along Realist lines to explain first causes, but are intended instead for the practical purpose of communicating as logically and clearly as possible. Contemporaries sometimes consider them in the same light as the administrative division of France into 'départements', or the decimalization of weights and measures.[10] The perceived advantages were always very practical: more effective pedagogy and propaganda, increased trade and better understanding between nations.

Jean Delormel explains to the Convention nationale in 1795, that his project for a universal language serves two purposes. Firstly, it will facilitate the Republican ideal, which is to 'rapprocher les hommes et les peuples par le doux lien de la fraternité' (Delormel, *Projet d'une langue universelle*, 1795: 2). His

---

[8] For Mesmer, Puységur, and hypnotism, see Zweig, *La Guérison par l'esprit* (1991): ch. I; for Mesmer, see Darnton, *La Fin des Lumières: Le mesmerisme et la Révolution* (1984). See also Delille's poetic interest in mesmerism, in *L'Imagination* (1785–94); 1832: Chant II, pp. 65–6.

[9] Condorcet, however, invents a universal language from a feeling of foreboding rather than optimism. The end of human civilization may be perilously near, and it is vital that human knowledge be recorded in some universal form, understandable by later civilizations, and stored in a secure place. His algebraic language has never been published as he originally intended, as part of the 'Dixième époque' of his *Esquisse d'un tableau historique des progrès de l'esprit humain* (written in prison before he was guillotined in 1794). Granger has published it separately ('Langue universelle et formalisation des sciences. Un fragment inédit de Condorcet', 1954).

[10] See e.g., Lancelin, *Introduction à l'analyse des sciences* (1801): Vol. I, 312. Revolutionaries even decimalized time; the Northumberland Astronomical Observatory at Cambridge University has a Revolutionary clock which divides the day into ten 'hours'.

second reason is that it is against Revolutionary principles to inherit language from tradition: 'le peuple français se renouvelle, il est temps de quitter cette imitation servile et routinière qui nous avoisine encore de la barbarie, et de créer une langue absolument neuve' (Delormel, *Projet*, 1795: 12). The comment is an extraordinary rejection of any dependence on the past, of any residual links with tradition. Language is perhaps a good example in the Revolutionary mind of a socio-historic institution with its roots in barely civilized times, dependent for its evolution on contingent cultural circumstances (a dominant group imposes its idiom), and which has traditionally been defined in terms of past usage. From this point of view, it is more a reactionary than a progressive influence. Gébelin's primitivist ideas would be unimaginable in this context. His idea was that there is a dynamic between past and present which is inherent in language, and without which poetry is unthinkable. He seems aware of the tendency of the 'modernes' to devalue the role of tradition, and he produces an elaborate demonstration of how the tension between convention and innovation is, in fact, very creative. The tension is gone in the minds of people like Delormel who have very different imperatives to Gébelin. The only dynamism they understand is a new beginning.

Delormel begins by decimalizing the alphabet, in order partly to reform spelling, so that there are ten vowels and twenty consonants. His next priority is to establish a workable nomenclature of words. Every word would begin with 'une lettre appelée *figurative* ou *indicative*', which would indicate to which category it belongs: 'grammaire, art de parler, état des choses, utiles, agréables, morale, sensations, affections [. . .]'. The next letter would indicate to which sub-category it belongs, and the last letter of the word, or 'indicative finale' would indicate tense (Delormel, *Projet*, 1795: 20–2). Like many contemporary language projectors, Delormel is keen to make his nomenclature as easy to remember as possible. To this end, he proposes a system of diacritics which would act as modifiers, thus reducing the total stock of words from 30,000, he thinks, in a normal dictionary, to only 10,000 (Delormel, *Projet*, 1795: 10). To illustrate his principles, he provides a small dictionary of the first category in his nomenclature, 'Grammaire', on pages 35–47 (Figure 4).

DICTIONNAIRE

DE LA

LANGUE UNIVERSELLE.

PREMIÈRE CLASSE.

GRAMMAIRE.

AD NOMS. (1)

PREMIÈRE SÉRIE OU FORMATION.

PREMIER MODE.		SECOND MODE.		TROISIÈME MODE.	
A,	moi.	*va,*	de moi.	*ma,*	à moi.
E,	toi.	*ve,*	de toi.	*me,*	à toi.
I,	lui.	*vi,*	de lui.	*mi,*	à lui.
U,	un.	*vu,*	d'un.	*mu,*	à un.
ei,	elle.	*vei,*	d'elle.	*mei,*	à elle.
eu,	une.	*veu,*	d'une.	*meu,*	à une.
ou,	du.	*vou,*	de.	*mou,*	à du.
au,	qui.	*vau,*	de qui.	*mau,*	à qui.
az,	nous.	*vaz,*	de nous.	*maz,*	à nous.
ez,	vous.	*vez,*	de vous.	*mez,*	à vous.
iz,	eux.	*viz,*	d'eux.	*miz,*	à eux.
uz, des *masc.*		*vuz,* de *masc.*		*muz,*	à des.
eiz,	elles.	*veiz,*	d'elles.	*meiz,*	à elles.
euz, des *fém.*		*veuz,* de *fém.*		*meuz,*	à des.
ouz,	des.	*vouz,*	de	*mouz,*	à des.

(1) Ils se divisent en adnoms de la première, de la
seconde et de la troisième personne, et adnom commun
aux trois personnes, et tout-à-la fois relatif et interrogatif.

C 2

Fig. 4. Jean Delormel, first and last page from the category 'Grammaire' in his nomenclature, in *Projet d'une langue universelle, présenté à la Convention nationale* (1795: pp. 35, 47).

(47)

A

Akvau, modificateur.
Ajvau, conjonction.
Apvau, interjection.
Amvau, conducteur.
Avé, déclinaison, conjug.
Alvé, -- de nom.
Advé, -- de verbe.
Avei, genre.
Alvei, masculin.
Advei, féminin.
Azvei, neutre.
Aveu, nombre.
Alveu, singu ier.
Alzeveu, duel.
Adveu, pluriel.
Avou, mode.
Alvou, cas ou mode des noms.
Alavou, nominatif.
Alevou, génitif.
Alivou, datif.
Alovou, vocatif.
Aluvou, accusatif.
Alauvou, ablatif.
Advou, mode des verbes.
Adavou, indicatif.
Adevou, impératif.
Adivou, subjonctif.
Adouvavou, optatif.
Adovou, infinitif.
Aduvou, participe.
Adauvou, gérondif.
Adévou, supin.
Afa, temps.
Aleifa, prétérit.
Alleifa, -- défini.
Alleifak, indéfini.
Aleinafa, imparfait ou pré-
  térit simultané.
Aleileifa, prétérit antér. ou
  plusque-parfait.
Anafa, présent.
Agleifa, futur.
Agleileifa, futur antérieur.

A

Afe, personne, *terme de
  grammaire.*
Alfe, première.
Adfe, seconde.
Azfe, troisième.
Afi, syntaxe.
Aro, sujet.
Aru, accord.
Afau, régime.
Afé, phrase.
Alfi, incidente.
Aiafé, parenthèse.
Azefé, période à 2 membr.
Azifé, -- à 3 membres.
Azofé, -- à 4 membres.
Aefei, figure.
Afei, fig. de gram., de mot :
  catachrèse, méthoni-
  mie, métalepse.
Alfei, crase, contraction.
Adfei, inversion.
Azfei, hypallage.
Arfei, onomatopée.
Agfei, métaphore.
Agafei, antiphrase.
Agefei, euphémisme.
Asfei, synecdoche.
Asafei, antonomase.
Asefei, syllepse.
Asifei, communication dans
  les paroles.
Asofei, exagération.
Asolfei, litote.
Asodfei, hyperbole.
Afeu, point, ponctuation.
Azefeu, deux points.
Alfeu, point et virgule.
Adfeu, trait d'union, ex.
  dit-il.
Arou, traduction.
Alfou, thême.
Adfou, version.
Ama, langue.

His project is most interesting, however, for what it self-consciously leaves out. After the administrative rigour of a decimalized alphabet and a catalogue of ideas, one wonders what ordinance there will be for literary language. And yet there is none. He intends only to establish some logical ground rules for a new language, and leave the further development to 'les hommes de goût, à l'usage': '[les accens] donnent de l'ame aux discours, et il apartient à l'usage de les fixer [. . .] Qu'il me suffise donc de fixer le mécanisme du langage, la passion donnera l'accent [. . .] J'abandonne [. . .] à l'essort du génie, et à l'usage, dirigé par les hommes de goût, le soin de tirer des idées primitives [. . .] et dans leurs sens propres, et dans leurs sens figurés [. . .] En un mot, c'est ici où finit mon travail' (Delormel, *Projet*, 1795: 29–30). It seems contradictory that he should propose a semantically unambiguous language, but disregard metaphor, intonation, and morphological derivation ('des idées primitives'?). 'L'ame du discours' is less important to him than 'le mécanisme du langage', whereas all the rationalizing tendencies earlier in the eighteenth century were intended to cope with both. Olivet and Dumarsais made special studies of prosody and metaphor on the assumption that they are as rationally determinable as any other part of language. In contrast, Delormel is content to draw a veil over the nebulous aspects of linguistic expression, what Umberto Eco calls a 'cloak', so that he reduces language to an unambiguous process of coding and decoding.[11] Nomenclature seems to disguise the more nebulous aspects of language, all those elements which cannot be accounted for by a simple process of 'identification' according to latitude and longitude in a two-dimensional map of language. The meaning of words is determined simply by plotting their position on an administrative map of language.

Delormel's project was not adopted by the Convention nationale, but others were much more successful. Joseph de Maimieux's *Pasigraphie* (1797) was a universal character set, a mute representation of ideas, to which the author later added a *Pasilalie* (1799), or phonetic transcription using an adapted Roman alphabet. For a year after its publication, Maimieux gave

[11] Pellerey and Eco use the English word 'cloak' (Pellerey, *Le Lingue perfette nel secolo dell'utopia*, 1992: 138).

public demonstrations every Friday at the Bibliothèque nationale, and for two years it was taught to secondary school children. He boasts in an advertisement of the 'beautés logiques' of his language, and that '[la Pasigraphie] s'apprend, sans maître, en 6 heures' (Maimieux, *Carte générale de pasigraphie*, 1808). Garat recognizes the political advantage of 'une invention extrêmement propre à rendre les révolutions plus sûres, plus faciles, plus générales' (Garat, *Discours sur [. . .] les caractères pasigraphiques*, 1799: 8).

Like Delormel's scheme, it is based on a functional nomenclature, 'une classification de pur sens-commun' with no claim to ontological significance (Maimieux, *Pasigraphie*, 1797: 5). In accordance with the principles of 'idéologie', however, the nomenclature is said to follow a heuristic order; it is 'une mappemonde intellectuelle' (p. 22 n.). There are twelve characters in his alphabet, which can be combined according to fixed rules to form words of either three, four, or five characters, each expressing a definite idea, and classified in a separate grammatical table. Other characters can be placed outside the 'corps' in order to modify the central idea. Words of three characters signify 'les termes sensibles', and are classified in the 'indicule'. Words of four characters stand for ideas in practical life, such as 'amitié, parenté, les affaires', and are classified in the 'petit nomenclateur'. Words of five characters stand for abstract ideas in religion, politics, science, and morality, and are classified in the 'grand nomenclateur'. Ideas are arranged in these tables in analogical sequence, which is the basis for Maimieux's heuristic claim that *Pasigraphie* functions according to a 'natural' order. In the 'indicule', for example, there are six groups of six ideas in the column headed 'Homme physique'. One of these groups is a list of different postures, ranging from seated to riding bareback and pillion, and each idea is represented by a single pasigraphic character: 'sur le séant; à genoux; à pied; à cheval; à crud; en croupe' (see Figure 5). The recourse to 'analogie' is a common ordering principle in eighteenth-century systematics, but instead of using it to describe existing language, Maimieux makes it the generative principle of a new, a priori language. The principle of analogy is reminiscent, for example, of Girard's dictionary of synonyms, but the intention and product of Maimieux's system are very different: in

(5)

DE SENS ENTRE LES AUTRES PARTIES DU DISCOURS. *Ier Cadre.*

IVe COLONNE. HOMME PHYSIQUE.	Ve COLONNE. HOMME SENSIBLE ET INTELLIGENT.	VIe COLONNE. HOMME PIEUX ET SOCIAL.
ʊ	ᴄ	ᴇ
Debout, droit, sur pied.	Ah! ahi! oh! hem!	Plaise -, s'il plaît à Dieu.
A tâtons, en bronchant.	Eh! eh bien! hoho! holà!	Dieu veuille, Dieu aidant.
A tort et à travers [3].	O! quoi! las! hélas!	Au nom, - de Dieu.
A part, en particulier.	Bah! bz, fi, ouf!	Dieu garde,-préserve,-sauve.
Sans, à défaut, manque.	Certes, comment? peste!	A la bonne heure.
A l'abandon, d dire.	Qu'est-ce?mal-peste!morbleu!	Ainsi soit-il, patience.
En présence, face à face.	De gré, volontiers.	De -, en bonne foi.
Tête à tête, à la tête.	De cœur, de bon cœur.	De -, en bonne part.
De front, de face.	Malgré, en dépit.	De -, en bonne grace.
De compagnie, côte à côte.	A contre-cœur, à regret.	De grace, en grace.
Avec, ensemble.	Au gré (de), à volonté.	Daignez, s'il vous plaît.
Par bande, en foule.	Comme, de même, en guise.	Graces, grand-merci.
Sur le séant, en (son) séant.	Et, aussi, et cetera.	Bonjour, bon matin.
A genoux, à deux genoux.	Ou, ou bien, soit [6].	Bon soir, bonne nuit.
A pied, à toutes jambes.	Concernant, touchant.	A vos souhaits, à (la) santé.
A cheval, à toute bride.	A propos, quant (à).	Au plaisir, à l'honneur.
A crud, à poil, en selle.	Mal à propos, à tort.	A revoir, au retour.
En croupe, en trousse.	A contre-sens, par -.	Adieu, portez-vous bien.
A pleine main, à poignée.	Pour, afin, pourquoi.	De la part, de part.
D'un tour de main.	A cause, attendu, vu.	A l'occasion, au sujet.
A tour -, à revers de bras.	Par, parce que, puisque.	Par rapport, eu égard, à l'-.
A bras tendus, - ouverts.	D'autant, - plus, - moins.	A titre, en qualité.
De force, de vive force.	Quoique [7], loin (de, que).	A juste titre, à bon droit.
En eau, en nage [4].	Excepté, hormis, sauf.	Pour, en faveur, envers.
Prêt (à), à même (de).	Si, sinon, au cas.	De manière, de façon.
Après (à), en train (de).	Mais, d'ailleurs.	En sorte, de sorte.
Au dépourvu, en sursaut.	A la vérité, au reste.	En -, par considération.
En butte, à la merci.	Car, cependant, pourtant.	A condition, à la charge.
En proie, à quia.	Néanmoins, nonobstant.	En forme, pour la forme.
A l'extrémité, sans retour.	En vain, vainement.	Sous prétexte (de, que).
Bien, mieux, au mieux.	Oui, soit, d'accord, tope.	De peur, de crainte.
Tant mieux, pour le mieux.	Exprès, à dessein.	Au risque, en danger.
De mieux en mieux.	Au vu, au su, de bon.	Malheur (à) ! contre.
Mal, au pis, au pis-aller.	Non, - pas, - point.	Gare, au secours, au feu.
Tant pis, pour le pis.	En conséquence, donc.	Pardon!merci!trêve!quartier!
Dommage, de mal en pis [5].	Encore, enfin, à la fin.	Tout beau, paix, silence.

IIe Partie.   B

Fig. 5. Joseph de Maimieux, extract from the 'Grand Nomenclateur' and 'Indicule', in *Pasigraphie* (1797: pp. 40, 5).

(40)

Iʳᵉ CLASSE. GRAND NOMENCLATEUR.

DIEU, ÊTRE, ESPRIT, NATURE, NOMBRE, CIEUX.	ASTRES, SIGNES, ÉLÉMENS.	SAISONS, MÉTÉORES.
— ou /	∾ ou ↗	ℒ ou ℒ
DIEU, divinité, divin.	SOLEIL, disque, rayon.	SAISON, température.
Cause, principe, origine.	Etoile, constellation.	Temps, il fait un-,intempérie.
Possibilité, pouvoir.	Voie lactée, ourse, pet-.,gr-.	Printemps, été, automne.
Puissance, toute-puissance.	Planète, satellite.	Arrière saison, hyver.
Suprême, sublime, - ité.	Comète, chevelure-, queue-.	Météore, aurore boréale.
Infinité, éternité, - nel [1 .	Apparition, disparition.	Parélie, feu folet, -St. Elme.
PROVIDENCE, toute-sagesse.	Saturne, anneau, Jupiter.	Aube, point du jour.
Préscience, prédestination.	Mars, Vénus, Mercure.	Anrore,crépuscule,-dumatin
Nécessité, fatalité, fortune.	Herschel, lune, lunaison.	Matin, matinal, matinée.
Destin, sort, destinée.	Nouvelle lune,quartier,plein	Midi, avant-, après-.
Cas, contingent, éventuel.	Phase, croissant, décours.	Soir, soirée,crépusculedusoir
Devenir, y avoir, faire [2].	Solstice,d'hyver,d'été; éclipse	Nuit, sombre, obscurité.
ÊTRE, existence, pré-.	Cercle, orbe, rotation.	Sérénité, beau-soleil.
Néant, cahos, ténèbres.	Hémisphère, climat.	Ombre, ombrage, ombragé.
Création, créature, faire.	Equateur, équinoxe, horison	Vapeur, fumée, brouillard.
Formation,auteur,rendre(tel)	Méridien, tropique, colure.	Rosée, serein, brume.
Opération, exécution.	Ecliptique, Zodiaque.	Bruine, pluie, ondée.
Acte, œuvre, ouvrage.	Pole,-arctique,-antarctique.	Déluge, cataracte, arche [4].
Substance, substantiel.	SIGNE, degré, nœud.	Vent, zéphir [5], bise.
Simple; composé, mixte.	Bélier, taureau, gémeaux.	Bouffée, coup de vent,rafale.
Modification, animation.	Ecrevisse [3], lion, vierge.	Vent coulis, vent alisé.
Parfaire, perfection, achevé.	Balance,scorpion, sagitaire.	Aquilon, autant, borée.
Accomplissem.t, consommation	Capricorne,verseau,poissons.	Tramontane, tourbillon.
Conservation, préserver.	Canicule. Ephémérides.	Rumb, maestral, siroc.
Esprit, spirituel, - tualité.	ELÉMENT, éther, vague.	Fraîcheur, froidure, refroidi.
Ange,arch-,chérubin,séraph.	Terre, terrestre, terraqué.	Froid, frimas, giboulée.
Démon, diable, Satan.	Eau, goutte, filet d'eau.	Gelée, congélation, figer.
Substance corporelle.	Source, ruisseau, torrent.	Givre, grésil, grêle, grêlon.
Nature,-rel,monde,univers.	Air, gas, phlogistique.	Verglas, glace, glaçon.
Nombre, numération, tout.	Feu,étincelle,flamme,flamber	Dégel, fonte, débacle.
Ciel, firmament, empirée.	Nord, septentrion.	Tiédeur, moiteur, chaleur.
Globe, boule, sphère.	Boréal, hyperborée.	Ardeur, hâle, brûlé, - lure.
Orbite, cours, révolution.	Sud, sud-est, sud-ouest.	Orage, ouragan, trombe.
Attraction, gravitation.	Midi, méridional, austral.	Eclair, éclat, coup.
Astre, corps céleste.	Est, orient, - tal, levant.	Foudre, tonnerre, carreau.
Lueur,lumière,-mineux,clarté	Ouest, occident, couchant.	Arc-en-ciel, iris.

accordance with the principles of 'idéologie', natural language is no longer the primary rational model. Perhaps, as in the case of Delormel's scheme, natural language contains too many indeterminable elements, such as metaphor or 'les accens de la passion', which do not conform to a nomenclaturist's view of language. Accordingly, *Pasigraphie* is an automaton language which avoids them completely: 'de bonnes tablatures mécaniques organisées feroient de l'ouvrier un émule d'Euclide et d'Archimède pour l'exécution. Dirigé par l'instrument, dès qu'il en connoit bien l'usage, il se méprend aussi peu que l'automate qui joue de la flute ou qui dessine' (Maimieux, *Pasigraphie*, 1797: 36). This is an odd idea of artistic creativity, that writing, drawing, and playing music can be preprogrammed, and are a matter of 'not making mistakes'. It only makes sense from the point of view of the 'idéologiste', whose primary concern is to follow rigorously a hypothetical conceptual order, a metalanguage more akin to algebra than natural language. The Euclidean apprentice follows the logical principles of 'pasigraphie', manipulates the discrete units of thought unambiguously defined in Maimieux's 'nomenclateurs', and thus effortlessly composes and decomposes language. Maimieux's automaton view of language makes sense also in the context of contemporary reform of scientific nomenclature and the predictive value it provided for a variety of disciplines. Linnaeus's binomial system of classification for natural history, or Lavoisier's descriptive nomenclature for chemical compounds were designed to standardize methodology.[12] *Pasigraphie*, similarly, is intended as an 'instrument' which 'directs' philosophical procedure, so that thinking is as predictable and faultless as an automaton musician. When the 'pasigrapheur' looks through Maimieux's tables for the word meaning 'god', for example, he is obliged to formulate it from the ideas 'infinity', 'supreme', and 'spirit'. *Pasigraphie* is designed to direct the thoughts and study of the metaphysician, as surely and consistently as scientific nomenclature directs the methodology of the chemist or the natural historian.

---

[12] For a discussion of eighteenth-century systems of taxonomy in natural history, see Simpson, *Principles of Animal Taxonomy* (1967).

5.3 L'Epée's sign language

Language can only work as a conceptual straitjacket if the idea of nomenclature is whole-heartedly embraced. The common characteristic of the post-Revolutionary language projectors is indeed a zealous pursuit of the ultimate 'grand nomenclateur' which would fix firmly all the ideas that could be expressed in language. In contrast, pre-Revolutionary thinkers in France were as resigned as Locke to the practical impossibility of such an exercise, and turned their interests to other things. The two approaches are nicely contrasted in the ground-breaking work on sign language for the deaf and dumb by the abbé de l'Epée in the 1770s, and by the abbé Sicard in the 1790s. The success of both is testimony to a particularly French perspective on language during the eighteenth century.[13] Other teachers of the deaf and dumb, in England and Spain, were not advocates of the same 'silent' method of visual signs; they taught either a manual alphabet or they forced the dumb to articulate 'the word of God'. French interest in Sensualism and in the origin of signs encouraged a more psychological approach; if language is a system of signs, any signs will do, as long as they represent ideas. Teaching the deaf to spell out words using a manual alphabet, or forcing them to articulate does not necessarily teach them to express ideas.[14] L'Epée died in 1789, and Sicard, his former pupil, took over the direction of what became two years later the *Institution nationale des sourds et muets*.[15] Despite their close collaboration, their published works

[13] Sicard gives examples of the occupations which his deaf and dumb pupils take up after leaving the Institute: two become teachers, two work in the administration of the Imperial lottery, another is a private tutor in grammar, many are typesetters at the Imprimerie impériale, and all are fervently religious (Sicard, *Théorie des signes*, 1808: Vol. I, p. lviii).

[14] In England, Johann Conrad Amman pioneered the oral method of teaching the deaf (*Dissertatio de Loquela*, 1700). L'Epée discusses the manual alphabet of the Portuguese teacher, Jacob-Rodriguez Pereire (*Mémoire que M. J.-R. Pereire a lu dans la séance de l'Académie Royale des sciences*, 1749). Seigel says of eighteenth-century teaching of the deaf and dumb: 'It is evident that there was in England throughout the 18th century little intellectual concern for the deaf and their culture; nothing comparable to that in France during the same period' ('The Enlightenment and the Evolution of a Language of Signs in France and England', 1969: 103).

[15] See Knowlson, *Universal Language Schemes* (1975): 220.

follow quite different courses, and the disparity illustrates the divergence in approaches to language discussed above.

L'Epée's intentions are apparent from the title of the book, published in 1776: *Institution des sourds et muets, par la voie des signes méthodiques; ouvrage qui contient le Projet d'une Langue Universelle; par l'entremise des Signes naturels, assujettis à une Méthode.* His interest is in pedagogy, 'institution', which means that his book contains more suggestions for classroom activities than discussion of sign language in the abstract. When he does discuss actual signs, it is in order to show what he means by 'signes méthodiques', which is the codification of instinctive gesture. He devotes one chapter to a discussion of signs as a universal language, which contains no extra material, and seems intended only to lend support to his key principle, that sign language is natural and universal. He believes there is a fundamental 'langage d'action' which allows man to express emotions: 'ses besoins, ses désirs, ses inclinaisons, ses doutes, ses inquiétudes, ses craintes, ses douleurs, ses chagrins &c &c' (L'Epée, *Institution des sourds et muets*, 1776: 37; Sicard says something similar in *Théorie des signes pour l'instruction des sourds-muets*, 1808: 10). The tutor's task is to teach the deaf and dumb how to harness this natural expression, how to expand upon and codify their instinctive ability to use gesture to communicate. In order to teach them tense, for example, l'Epée makes use of their instinctive gesture over the shoulder to refer to actions in the past. He teaches them to use one gesture for the imperfect tense (glossed as 'hier', i.e. Tuesday), two gestures for the perfect tense (glossed as 'avant hier', i.e. Monday), and three for the pluperfect (glossed as 'avant avant hier', i.e. Sunday; L'Epée, *Institution des sourds et muets*, 1776: 50). According to these principles, l'Epée says that the deaf and dumb can express any idea in sign language, even the most abstract. The sign 'je crois', for example, is composed of four parts: (1) point to the forehead (meaning 'l'esprit') and nod; (2) point to the heart (meaning 'j'aime') and nod; (3) point to the mouth (meaning 'je parle') and nod; (4) point to the eyes (meaning 'je vois') and this time shake the head. The gloss for the sign 'belief' would thus be: 'je pense que oui, j'aime penser que oui, je dis oui, je ne vois pas encore de mes yeux' (L'Epée, *Institutions des sourds et muets*, 1776: 80). The sign is quite long and involved, but in time and through ellipsis, it would be short-ened to something more manageable.

The analysis involved in producing and understanding these signs is such that they may, in fact, be better representations of ideas than spoken language. L'Epée says of the idea 'belief' expressed in sign language: 'on le comprend beaucoup mieux que la plupart de ceux qui parlent et qui entendent' (L'Epée, *Institution des sourds et muets*, 1776: 81). It is more universally understood, and hence a better basis for a universal language because it is both natural and rational, much in the sense that Condillac spoke of a 'second' nature.

L'Epée's main interest and talent, however, is pedagogical. He uses games, for example, in his classes. Pupils use a pack of cards which have the names of parts of the body written on them. On drawing a card, they must be able to make the sign for the word on the card, so that the others understand. Then they must use other cards, each with a letter of the alphabet written on it, to spell out the word. The game is designed to amuse, as well as instruct with minimum interference from the tutor, and maximum interaction between the pupils (L'Epée, *Institution des sourds et muets*, 1776: 42). As his title suggests, l'Epée's book really is 'une méthode de langue', an instruction manual for learning language and ideas. Using these tech-niques, l'Epée claims that he can teach the deaf and dumb all the niceties of eighteenth-century grammar in two months, by which time they are capable of writing down anything he dic-tates to them in sign language (L'Epée, *Institution des sourds et muets*, 1776: 68).

L'Epée does not concern himself with listing the signs of his language. The few that are included in his book are intended only to explain how it is possible to analyse ideas and teach them effectively to the pupil. He thinks that a dictionary of signs would be a lengthy and ineffective pedagogical tool: 'quelques personnes auroient désiré que je donnasse avec cette Méthode le détail de mes signes. Cela est impossible. Il faudrait plusieurs volumes, puisqu'il n'est aucun mot qui n'ait son signe partic-ulier, qui s'exécute en un instant, mais qui ne se décrit pas de même. Il en est plusieurs qui demanderoient des pages entières. C'est donc une chose qui ne peut s'apprendre que par tradition; & je suis au service de quiconque le désirera' (L'Epée,

Institution des sourds et muets, 1776: 177). Like Locke, he does not deny that it would be possible to produce such a dictionary, but thinks that the time would be better otherwise spent. A dictionary cannot convey the theory of language and the pedagogy that l'Epée thinks is so important, the 'art' of representation which l'Epée compares to painting: 'la peinture est un art muet, qui ne parle qu'aux yeux, & l'habilité de l'artifice consiste à scavoir attirer les regards des spectateurs, fixer leur attention sur son ouvrage [. . .] Le riche fond dans lequel la plupart des grands maîtres ont puisé les originaux de leurs portraits, nous annonce donc où nous devons chercher la matière la plus ordinaires des nôtre' (L'Epée, *Institution des sourds et muets*, 1776: 180). A dictionary would be a poor reflection of the painter's art; it would not explain the artist's 'inner eye', which focuses on a portrait in his imagination in order to paint the portrait on the canvas; nor would it explain the artist's ability to focus the viewer's attention on the resulting canvas. The successful portrait is a convergence of both perspectives, so that artist and viewer are, in a sense, sharing the same imagination. Sign language is based on the same principles: that the deaf and dumb naturally create portraits or signs of ideas in their minds, and that they can be taught to convert them into visual signs which communicate their feelings to others.

L'Epée developed the practical application of this theory of instinctive semiosis more than Condillac or Diderot, whose interests remained more theoretical. Nevertheless, l'Epée did not think that a real understanding of sign language could be grasped without an awareness of the principles involved, an awareness which would not be served by a dictionary format. To know the signs is insufficient; like an artist who paints noses, mouths, and eyes without ever painting a complete body, a language of isolated signs is not a complete picture of language (L'Epée, *Institution des sourds et muets*, 1776: 181). It is more important to understand the communicative theory of language, to teach ideas, how they are related by syntax and grammar, so that the mute can co-ordinate signs to paint a more complex semantic picture. As if pre-empting Lancelin's exclamation: 'il faut écrire un dictionnaire!', l'Epée says: 'il faut faire sortir les mots de leurs cases' (L'Epée, *Institution*, p. 183). In l'Epée's mind, nomenclature is secondary to the semiotics and pedagogy involved in learning language.

5.4 Sicard's sign language

Sicard's ideas are a continuation of l'Epée's theories presented in a very different manner. His published work is a two-volume dictionary of sign language called significantly, *Théorie des signes pour l'instruction des sourds-muets* (1808), with an introduction which apologizes for itself, since he thinks that a dictionary needs no explanation. A 'théorie des signes' is essentially the enumeration and systematic exposition of all the meanings that it would be possible to express in sign language. Sicard's introduction is imbued with the vocabulary of the 'idéologistes'. He speaks of composing and decomposing ideas according to the order in which they are 'generated' in the mind, of creating a natural 'tableau' of the intellect: 'on procédera à l'invention des signes, d'après la génération des idées [. . .] Imitez la nature, faites parcourir, dans l'ordre même de leur génération, le tableau de toutes les idées qui peuvent être du domaine de l'intelligence' (Sicard, *Théorie des signes*, 1808: Vol. I, 22–3). There is an 'order' in which ideas must be 'classified' in the mind of the mute, which is reproduced in the design of the dictionary. Volume I deals with things which can be pointed to, while Volume II deals with abstract concepts, 'des choses sensibles, idées morales, idées purement intellectuelles' (Sicard, *Théorie* Vol. I, lvi). There are evidently principles of the 'idéologistes' in this dictionary of sign language, because Sicard says it is designed to 'défricher les landes arides du pays de l'intelligence [. . .] ces vastes plaines entre les sensations et le raisonnement' (p. 23). Like Maine de Biran's image of the intellectual cartographer, whose elevated position provides a better understanding of the workings of the mind, Sicard's dictionary is intended to cultivate a new intellectual understanding, to reflect the generation of 'raisonnement' from simple ideas in sensation.

Sicard includes in his introduction a brief glossary of sign language devised by l'Epée, and sent to Sicard for his comments.

It is only a summary outline of a dictionary that l'Epée never realized, but Sicard finds it a useful starting-point to explain the merits of his own work. The glossary contains very little instruction in making signs, only precise definitions to be used as the first step in inventing them. Sicard imagines that such a dictionary, 'contiendra plus d'explications que de signes' (Sicard, *Théorie des signes*, 1808: Vol. I, p. li), and would be of no use for the way he teaches the deaf and dumb: 'il faudra nécessairement [enseigner] les noms de tous les objets qui s'offriront à ses regards [. . .] Il a fallu parcourir avec eux toutes les séries des êtres et des choses, tous les objets d'utilité journalière, tous les états de la société, enfin, tout ce qui s'offre sans cesse à nos regards' (pp. liii–liv). Volume I of Sicard's dictionary is this enumeration of all the signs necessary for day-to-day living, in which each 'pantomime', each 'scène mimique' is described in the most minute detail (p. lvi).[16] Inevitably, he does not share l'Epée's ludic principles of pedagogy, because he regards it as crucially important to teach signs according to a strict order. The names of the parts of the body are learnt in sequence, from head to toe: 'cette nomenclature, dont le front est le premier mot, et le pied le dernier' (Sicard, *Théorie des signes*, 1808: Vol. I, 11). To play wordgames introduces a random element into learning which does not suit Sicard's objectives. He, like Maimieux, is searching for a way to see through language to the heuristic order beneath. Sicard, in fact, writes the preface to *Pasigraphie*, in which he says that he collaborated with Maimieux in its early stages. Both, he says, have the same objective: 'ce grand nomenclateur [. . .] tendant à former de l'universalité des idées un systême clair' (Maimieux, *Pasigraphie*, 1797).

L'Epée's 'méthode' and Sicard's dictionary both have their uses for teaching sign language, but it is characteristic of the last decades of the eighteenth century that they should be regarded as mutually exclusive. In common with many of his contemporaries, l'Epée's study of language is coloured by an interest in natural semiosis and imitation; sign language is related to the painter's imagination and a natural 'langage d'ac-

---

[16] e.g., there are five parts to the sign for 'bread': 1) mixing flour with water; 2) putting the dough on a spade; 3) putting the dough into the oven; 4) taking it out of the oven; 5) eating. Sicard says that signs would in practice be shortened by ellipsis (Sicard, *Théorie des signes*, 1808: Vol. I, 27).

tion'. Sicard's 'idéologie' causes him to be less interested in the origin of signs, either in the painter's imagination or in natural imitation, and more interested in finding a programmable order of ideas. For this purpose, a dictionary is more useful than playing random language games. Sicard is obviously much more confident in the ability of nomenclature to explain language, and also more indifferent to the other side of language which it may 'cloak'.

5.5 Condillac's algebraic language

It is perhaps useful in this regard to consider Condillac's *La Langue des calculs*, his last and unfinished work, published for the first time posthumously in 1798 with a preface by Garat.[17] Condillac and the 'idéologistes' share certain principles, and it is no doubt significant that *La Langue des calculs* was published at the height of their intellectual reputation. As we have seen before, however, there is a danger in taking Condillac's ideas out of context.

La Langue des calculs opens with an inspiring sentence for contemporary 'idéologistes': 'toute langue est une méthode analytique, et toute méthode analytique est une langue', and it continues in terms no less in accord with 'idéologie'. What is known of the manuscript is divided into two parts: the first which demonstrates how arithmetic can be considered a language of signs, the second which seeks to discover the general properties or 'grammar' of mathematical signs. In the first place, algebraic signs have the advantage of functioning according to exact rules, 'l'analogie n'échappe plus, dès qu'une fois on l'a saisie' (Condillac, *La Langue des calculs*, 1981: 238). It would therefore be an advantage to discover the 'grammar' of algebraic signs in order to understand the general principles of analysis on which all languages are based. The analogy between grammar and algebra is based on the idea that there is a similar process of generalization at work: proper nouns are related to common nouns as numbers are related to algebraic symbols

---

[17] Chouillet judges that Condillac probably began *La Langue des calculs* after 1771, and abandoned it unfinished in 1779, a year before his death (Condillac, *La Langue des calculs*, 1981: p. xxxviii).

(Condillac, *La Langue des calculs*, 1981: 275). Condillac thinks there may be rewards in pursuing this analogy, because if it were possible to understand the grammar which links the ultimate generalization possible in any language, 'x', with the ultimate particularization, a number such as '1', then the procedure may be applicable to language in general. On the assumption that thinking relies upon exact signs and predictable operations, to discover the grammar of algebra would be to discover, also, the grammar of thought. Condillac makes the analogy between thinking and algebra that would have appealed to the 'idéologistes': 'je sens que, lorsque je raisonne, les mots sont pour moi ce que sont les chiffres ou les lettres pour un mathématicien qui calcule; et que je suis assujetti à suivre mécaniquement des règles pour parler et pour raisonner, comme il l'est lui-même à faire l'équation $x = b - a$, quand il a fait l'équation $x + a = b$' (Condillac, *La Langue des calculs*, 1981: 226). Although we do not understand the mechanism of thought, there is a consistent series of operations which is as inescapable as the logic of algebra. If discovered, it would provide the heuristic foundation to the ambition of the 'idéologistes' to create an a priori language that would be programmed according to universal intellectual principles.

'Idéologistes' often claim Condillac as an advocate for their language philosophy. Maine de Biran regards *La Langue des calculs* as a model of the 'elevated' thinking which he believes is characteristic of 'idéologie' (Maine de Biran, 'Note sur les rapports de l'idéologie et des mathématiques', 1988: 9). Destutt de Tracy cites Condillac in support of his idea that language and algebra are both ultimately reducible by analysis to discrete signs (Destutt de Tracy, *Elémens d'idéologie*, 1825: Vol. I, 236–7).[18] Yet their agenda is much more limited. Condillac is as interested in aesthetics, imitation, art, and literary style as he is algebra and heuristics. He regards them as different perspectives on the same fundamental object of study, which is the representation of ideas (Condillac, *Grammaire*, 1798: p. cxxxvii). Destutt de Tracy and Maine de Biran regard him as a prototypical 'idéologiste', but his perspective is much broader

---

[18] Some also disagreed. Condorcet thought that the mathematics were inaccurate, and Garat in his 'Avertissement' did not like the mechanical interpretation of arithmetic (Condillac, *La Langue des calculs*, 1981: xx).

than theirs. His theory of language includes primitivist ideas of holistic signs, aesthetic ideas of good literary style, as well as algebraic ideas of analytical language. A much more faithful interpretation of *La Langue des calculs* would be to understand his references to 'analogie', 'proportion', and 'rapport' in the light of his previous works. Only in this way would we do justice to the historical and intellectual continuity that is so important to Condillac's work.

In view of Condillac's other writings, *La Langue des calculs* cannot be said to 'cloak' language in a nomenclature which dissimulates its more nebulous, literary aspects. It is, rather, the final stage in a course of thinking which began with the *Essai sur l'origine des connoissances*, in which he discussed the origins of thought and signs, which continued with the *Art d'écrire*, the *Grammaire*, and other discussions of literary language, and ends with *La Langue des calculs*. At every stage, Condillac has been concerned to show how the primary intellectual impulse of sentient man, which is to compare perceptions and place them in analogical order, has been pursued by different means at different points during man's intellectual development. As a result, Condillac's theory of language takes into account the emblematic quality of poetry, the role of the painter's imagination, composition in prose writing, the use of metaphor and synonymy, all of which are aspects of his interest in the representation of ideas, and all of which are neglected by the 'idéologistes'. What fascinates Condillac in all these cases is the conceptual patterns which the mind has to find in the flux of mental activity in order to make some sense. It is always the 'rapports' which interests him. In the *Essai*, it was the 'rapports' which made sense of confusing sensations; in the *Art d'écrire*, it was the 'rapports' which provided the internal logic of a sentence; now, in *La Langue des calculs*, it is the 'rapports' in numerical progression that is the grammar of algebra. Much as the 'idéologistes' would like to claim him as their own, they can only do so on condition that they overlook the background to his thought. They do not see that when Condillac describes the 'rapports' in the sequence of real numbers, and the 'rapports' in arithmetical and geometrical progressions he is still wrestling with his favourite problem, but in a different context (Condillac, *La Langue des calculs*, 1798: 100–1).

These are key points in his semiotic theory, of which an algebraic language is only one, and indeed the last. The first key point is when his sentient statue learns to manipulate ideas by first comparing sensations. The next key point, is when he learns to represent these ideas to others, which leads eventually to the invention of language. The golden age of literature, is when ideas are marshalled to create a stylistic reflection of the statue's manipulation of ideas, 'la liaison des idées' which is a universal rational principle (hence Buffon's 'le style est l'homme même', because good style is as universal as human reason). The final stage is revealed in *La Langue des calculs*: 'nous [aurons à] substituer aux mots, des signes plus simples [. . .] des signes permanens [. . .] Voilà ce qu'il faut chercher, et ce que nous trouverons dans l'algèbre' (Condillac, *La Langue des calculs*, 1981: 110). Condillac would like to think that ultimately, it would be possible to define the *rapports* between linguistic signs as accurately and as 'simply' as they are defined in algebra. Perhaps even the most abstract words are only complex relations of simple ideas, like geometric progressions which depend ultimately on real number progressions.

Condillac has a much more varied agenda than the 'idéologistes', and his work is a further example of the different approach to language which separates the respective periods in which they were writing. Like the abbé de l'Epée, he does not abstract the semiotics of language from related questions in aesthetics and representation. His broad range of interests is an assumption of the eighteenth century sense of 'la philosophie', and it is perhaps the case that the eclectic 'philosophe' is beginning to seem like an outdated phenomenon by the time of the 'idéologistes'. Even if one can dispute the principle that algebra is a kind of language, the scale and optimism of his ambition is nevertheless typical of his generation of thinkers.

It may be the case, however, that he did not finish *La Langue des calculs* because he encountered conceptual incompatibilities between language and algebra. The editor of the first edition appends the following postface: 'ce qu'il avoit principalement en vue, ce qui avoit été le but constant des recherches d'une vie employée tout entière à perfectionner la raison, c'étoit de débrouiller le chaos où les abus et les vices du langage ont plongé les sciences morales et métaphysiques' (Condillac, *La*

Langue des calculs, 1981: 479). Perhaps he lost confidence in the ability of language to be clarified to the point where morality, metaphysics, and perhaps also aesthetics could be as impartial and exact as mathematics. Whatever misgivings he may have had, 'compromise' is probably an inappropriate term for the way he and his contemporaries would have understood the analogy between language and algebra. They may better be described as 'complementary', on the Enlightenment assumption that reason is universal, and informs all human activities. The confident eclecticism of the 'philosophe' is based on this principle, as is also the literary consensus which allowed mutual understanding between grammarians and creative writers. The complementary relation between the two breaks down by the time of the 'idéologistes' and the language projectors; from their point of view, part of the virtue of their theory is that it is abstracted from literary language and its inherently nebulous characteristics. It is a new, objective discipline. The wall that Lancelin thought should separate the language of the analyst from that of the poet does not trouble them, as it would have done Condillac and his contemporaries.

Nor, however, does it trouble the poet that his creative medium is now beyond the objective criticism of the grammarian. In the following discussion of Mercier and Maimieux the prevalent conception of literary genius and language is freedom from any objective standard or rationalizing principle, freedom to think and write subjectively and obscurely, freedom to recreate language according to unfettered inspiration. These writers cannot be told what and how to think by the 'idéologistes'. Their conception of genius is the second side to Lancelin's contrast between analyst and poet.

5.6 The literary aesthetics of 'impertinence'

Joseph de Maimieux is perhaps the best example of the extent to which the ideas of poet and analyst are distinct in this period, even within the mind of one person. Not only is he the inventor of *Pasigraphie*, but he is the author in 1788 of *Eloge philosophique de l'impertinence*, an uncompromising manifesto for a new aesthetic to replace all the traditional values of neoclassicism. His conception of literary genius is as far from neoclassicism as was 'idéologie' in its own way, and yet 'idéologie' and 'impertinence' are totally incompatible. In effect, Maimieux has built a wall in his own mind between poet and analyst, between 'impertinence' and 'idéologie'. From what we know of previous writers on language and aesthetics, the two interests lent each other mutual support, so the theories of thinkers such as Gébelin could be applied to aspects of literary debate without any ostensible incongruity. Maimieux, however, cannot, and the reason is only partly imputable to the departure in linguistic theories of the period. There is also a departure in aesthetic thinking which is just as radical.

Maimieux uses 'impertinence' to mean 'genius', creative freedom, or spontaneity and authenticity as opposed to subservience to artistic convention. As such, *Eloge de l'impertinence* restates the contention of the 'modernes' in the 'querelle des anciens et des modernes', and yet it is distinctive for its immoderate tone and fanatical sense of purpose. The aesthetic of 'impertinence' is a departure from traditional notions of the exalted, lofty, and harmonious qualities of genius, and has instead connotations of the extraordinary, strange, extravagant, and even mentally unbalanced.

The *Eloge* opens with an allegory to illustrate the worst excesses of intellectualism and intellectualizing literature, the tragic consequences which result, and therefore the desirability of finding a different approach to literature. The fictitious author, La Bractéole, decides to test his theories on the corporeality of knowledge by carrying out an experiment. He arranges a set of mirrors around his room, so that all the light entering through the window focuses on a single spot. Into one end of an ear trumpet he places the book whose knowledge he would like to absorb, while attaching the other end hermetically to his nose, via a rubber tube. He hopes that all the light entering the room will focus on the book and transmit to him the light of human knowledge. Unfortunately, all does not go to plan when the street lights outside come on at that very moment, which causes an excess of light in the room and a surfeit of enlightenment in the ear trumpet. La Bractéole dies, suffocated on his own intellect.

The story is meant to mock the worst excesses of Enlightenment philosophy, as Maimieux understands it, which is a reductive materialist doctrine that would pretend that the light of knowledge can be inhaled like philosophical pipe smoke. Maimieux would like to think that there is a more spiritual approach to literature which does not lead to the same base materialism as arises from excessive faith in philosophical doctrine. La Bractéole dies because he wants to understand too much. Maimieux's solution is to accept that enlightenment, especially taken literally, has its limits, and that some things should be valued for their very obscurity and the sense of mystery which they provoke.

Literature belongs to this realm of the mysterious: 'plus le sens est vague, plus on en tirera parti', and Maimieux suggests we should revel in the irrationality of language, the subjective nature of aesthetics, the richness of equivocation when objective interpretation of literature is impossible. Maimieux thinks that literature is by its nature an esoteric art, as opaque and confusing as the 'tables isiaques' or incomprehensible, mystical symbols of Egyptian priests which we are free to interpret at will, as long as we all finally exclaim 'Ah, que c'est beau!' (Maimieux, *Eloge*, 1788: 135). Literature is a matter of subjective interpretation, like Egyptian hieroglyphs which were only deciphered by Champollion forty years later. This sounds like a reflection of the idea of the literary hieroglyph, but it is at complete antipodes to Gébelin's version of the concept, and different, also, to Diderot's. Maimieux is more convinced than both of them that literature is permanently emblematic and that there is no way at all to resolve our aesthetic feeling in any rational manner. Accordingly, the *Eloge* is a celebration of literary freedom, even irresponsibility, and a denunciation of neoclassical rules and conventions: 'nous avons abrogé toutes les règles, afin de penser, de composer, d'agir & de juger plus librement, moins artificiellement, plus naturellement [...] Pourquoi s'imposeroit-on des privations, des gênes, des fatigues inutiles?' (Maimieux, *Eloge*, 1788: 132). Maimieux clearly favours modernity over tradition, free composition over 'la difficulté vaincue'. The 'gênes inutiles' have been fabricated by 'cette foule de rhéteurs qui alignoient leurs froides idées au

cordeau', who measure and standardize literary expression so
that it conforms to an a priori system of values (p. 134). Girard
is the target on several occasions of Maimieux's criticism. He
says that Girard's dictionary of synonyms is a typical example
of the sterile nature of the rational exercise to control literary
expression, to attempt to fix the use of language regardless of
its evident variability over time and between different authors
(Maimieux, *Eloge*, 1788: 6–8). The idea of 'im-pertinence' is an
emancipation from rational cohesion, from 'pertinence' which
Girard made the ordering principle of his dictionary. 'Impertinence' is therefore a celebration of incongruity and diversity
in composition: 'quelle non-convenance de chaque partie à
toutes, de toutes à chacune! quelle incohérence de notions
vagues & superficielles! quel chaos! quel oubli de tous les rapports!' (p. 83). 'La non-convenance' is the provocative transgression of all the conventional rules of literary practice, and
Maimieux says it is best illustrated by the 'calembour': 'quant
à l'esprit dont on raffole, un calembour peut seul le peindre
dignement' (Maimieux, *Eloge*, 1788: 233). Like Bièvre, his contemporary, Maimieux seizes on the frivolity of wordplay as the
best antidote to the limitations of established literary practice.
It disturbs the comfortable feeling that language will always
make sense, that it is a cohesive semantic system, because
'calembours' are incongruous semantic associations justified
only on the grounds of phonetic similarity. 'Impertinence'
means these leaps of the imagination, but also the imagination
completely free to explore the concealed order of dreams:
'un malade en délire ne peut rêver aucune absurdité', or the
opium-induced pleasures of the mind: 'que d'illusions ravis-
santes se succèdent dans un cerveau bien organisé! à l'opium
près, & si l'on admet quelques autres ressources de la sagesse à
la mode & de la pharmacie' (Maimieux, *Eloge*, 1788: 56, 187).
For these reasons, Maimieux thinks that creative genius has
some of the esoteric virtues of Mesmer or Caliostro, that he
is a magician who would wave a magic wand to turn barren
rock into a fertile garden: 'le génie créateur couvre [le] rocher
effrayant & stérile, des plus abondantes moissons; & d'un coup
de sa baguette enchantée le change en un second jardin des
Hespérides' (p. 7).

There is very little left of the 'analyst' in this idea of the poet, no balance between reason and imagination that was so characteristic of the earlier idea of genius. Maimieux demands the freedom to be subjective, to be extravagant, to abandon literary conventions which stifle the spontaneity of genius, the freedom to be a magician more than a philosopher. His basic contention, that literary conventions may suppress the creative imagination, is a well-worn issue in the eighteenth century. La Motte, Fénelon, Dubos, and Marivaux all make contributions which were considered influential in their time, and which are better known to posterity than Maimieux's 'impertinence'. The argument has moved on, however, since the 'querelle des vers'. Maimieux's generation is more iconoclastic, less compromising, and not as susceptible to reconciliation through innovative linguistic thinking. In the early part of the century, thinkers such as Girard and Dumarsais seem to extend literary licence in response to critics of convention. Dumarsais expands enormously the traditional range of tropes, and Girard standardizes the equivocal meaning of synonyms, and both arguably are reacting to contemporary appeals for freer expression in literature. They feel able to make a contribution to debate, because the innovators appeal only for a loosening of literary conventions, not a total abnegation. Fénelon, for example, thinks that 'il seroit à propos de mettre nos poëtes un peu plus au large sur les rimes, pour leur donner le moyen d'être plus exacts sur le sens et sur l'harmonie' (Fénelon, *Lettre à l'académie*, 1970: 67). His *Télémaque* is cited all through the eighteenth century as an example of poetic prose which gains by abandoning formal versification, and yet gains also by the wonderful use it makes of traditional 'harmonie imitative'. In effect, he discards one convention only to make better use of another. Similarly, Marivaux abandons one idea of 'clarté', only in order to embrace another more complex kind. As a result, 'le marivaudage' is not in principle incompatible with Girard's dictionary of synonyms, or Dumarsais's study of figurative language, because all assume that it is possible to discuss objectively the limits to literary expression. Even La Motte does not completely abandon conventional form in poetry. He prefers the ode to the epic because the ode has traditionally allowed more freedom of form and expression, but even in this case there are formal conventions which La Motte respects. The real targets of his criticism are the uninspiring 'malins rimeurs', who confuse versification with poetry, and who think that servile respect for convention is a substitute for talent. The tone of these neoclassical authors is generally transgression with the intention of reform, whereas with Maimieux, transgression leads to iconoclasm. There is no room for the reconciling influence of grammarians like Girard or Dumarsais. If there were any linguistic advocate of 'impertinence', it would surely be Maimieux himself. One could imagine him devising an obscure, cabalistic language, 'des tables isiaques', in fact, which might have some kind of suggestive, incantatory power. Yet, on the contrary, he devises an ideologically driven universal language, designed according to putative objective principles, and which in effect acts as an intellectual straitjacket. There is no reconciliation in his mind between poet and analyst, between artistic and philosophical genius. In the closing pages of the *Eloge*, for example, he apologizes to the reader in case his essay has seemed disorganized and frenzied, but feels justified because he is tired of the analytical and systematic treatment of ideas: 'nous pardonnera-t-il d'avoir cru l'intéresser sans de longs calculs, de l'algèbre, des équations, de la géométrie, des lignes ponctuées, des planches &c?' (Maimieux, *Eloge*, 1788: 233).

Maimieux is a curious Janus figure for whom there is no contradiction between 'les tables isiaques' of literary language, and the algebraic logic of *Pasigraphie*. He would presumably contend that each fulfils a different function, and yet it is this belief which sets him and his contemporaries apart from thinkers earlier in the century. It certainly distinguishes him from Gébelin, whose idea of the hieroglyph was merely a preliminary step towards completely resolving the mysteries which it comprised. It distinguishes him, also, from Diderot, whose characteristically sensitive argument gives an explanation of the literary hieroglyph only to say subsequently that few are in a position to understand it. In contrast with both Gébelin and Diderot, Maimieux has abandoned any pretence to making objective sense of what he calls 'les tables isiaques' of literature, and leaves it to the realm of drug-induced dreams and meaningless 'calembours'.

5.7 Mercier's literary aesthetics

Maimieux's creative writing is disappointingly conventional in comparison to his theory. It is sometimes remarked that the most adventurous aesthetic theorists in this period are also the least adventurous creative writers, and Maimieux for one follows the fashion for oriental and libertine stories without much attempt at innovation.[19] In contrast, Louis-Sébastien Mercier is both a radical theorist and practitioner of the new literary aesthetic.

He shares Maimieux's fundamental precepts, that a writer's vocation is to communicate a powerful and subjective literary aesthetic, unfettered by the conventions of established literary practice. He absolves himself of these literary conventions by reinterpreting them (or else creatively misunderstanding them!), so that they mean precisely the opposite of what they originally stood for. He is perhaps the first of many, for example, to confuse Buffon's famous maxim, that 'le style est l'homme même'. Buffon meant 'l'homme' in the universal sense of 'humanity', in order to suggest that style, too, could conform to universal principles: man is a rational being, and if language is intended to communicate rational thoughts, then there must be a universally acceptable form of language which does it best. It was on this basis that Buffon and Condillac proposed a renovated form of 'style coupé' as the best literary style. Mercier's interpretation is the reverse: 'le style est l'homme, & chacun doit avoir le sien bien & duement caractérisé' (Mercier, Du Théâtre, 1773: 330). He repeats the same dictum in his utopian novel L'An 2440, when the protagonist who has awoken after five hundred years asleep sets about discovering the new Paris. On visiting the 'Collège des nations', he is told that style is a matter of personal taste, and that French grammar can be modified according to the writer's needs: 'le style est l'homme, & l'ame forte doit avoir un idiome qui lui soit propre & bien différent de la nomenclature' (Mercier, L'An 2440, 1774: ch.

---

[19] Delon comments on the lack of innovation in L'Idée d'énergie au tournant des lumières (1988): 80. Examples of Maimieux's writing are Le Compte de Saint-Méran, ou les Nouveaux égaremens du cœur et de l'esprit (1788); L'Heureux jeune homme. Histoire orientale (1786).

XII). Not for the first time in his utopian novel his intuitions about the future prove correct: there will indeed be a radical divide between literary style and 'nomenclature'.[20]

In the same manner, he adapts an analogy which Batteux, Condillac, and others use to express the universality of style, in order to make it mean just the opposite. Condillac, for example, draws an analogy between walking and style in order to explain that rhythm, or poetic 'mesure' in language is a kind of 'langage d'action': sentiment is expressed by vocal modulation as inevitably as it is by a person's gait or posture (Condillac, *L'Harmonie du style*, 1798: 430).[21] He meant 'langage d'action' and 'sentiment' as universals; the first is an inevitable exteriorization of the second, which itself is a primary human faculty. Mercier uses a similar analogy, but this time to demonstrate that both style and the body are expressions of subjective personality: 'le style est à l'ame ce que la démarche est au corps. Chacun a son attitude propre. Cette attitude négligée convient à tel homme, à cause des graces qu'il y met. Cette grande figure longue a de la gravité, & elle lui sied. Ce petit homme gentil est froid & fat, & n'est pas tout-à-fait insupportable. N'allez donc pas soumettre votre ouvrage à ces gens qui tondent le style [. . .] C'est à l'Ecrivain à modifier la langue, & non à recevoir sa loi' (Mercier, *Du Théâtre*, 1773: 334–5). He discards the universal principles which support Condillac's 'langage d'action', because he is more interested in the writer's own contribution to style.

Even more fundamentally, he turns on its head the traditional metaphor for artistic imitation in which the artist is said to hold a mirror up to nature. In Mercier's version, the artist comes out from behind the mirror and becomes the centre of the mimetic process. He is the prism through which light must pass and be transformed before it emerges as the artwork. He says of the writer: 'tu seras, pour ainsi dire, le point vivant où viendront se réfléchir les merveilles diverses de la nature' ('Le Bonheur des gens de lettres', in *Mon bonnet de nuit*, 1784–5:

---

[20] *L'An 2440* arguably predicts other social and political changes, such as the demise of heriditary monarchy and the ruin, real or metaphorical, of the palace of Versailles. See Dorigny, 'Du "Despotisme vertueux" à la République' (1995), and Vidler, 'Mercier urbaniste: l'utopie du réel' (1995).

[21] See also the same analogy in Batteux, *Cours de Belles-Lettres* (1753): Vol. II: 116–17.

Vol. IV, 252).[22] Evidently Mercier dislikes the connotations of the traditional mirror analogy, because it relegates the artist to a subordinate role as a technical operator behind the mirror instead of the focal point of artistic creation.

As if this were not sufficient departure from the past, he later endorses the new Kantian aesthetic of the sublime and quotes Kant in preference to Condillac, Locke, and the Ideologues, whose intellectualism he finds unpalatable (Mercier, *Néologie*, 1801: Vol. I, preface: p. lvii). Even before he could have read Kant, however, he is already describing literary aesthetics in terms of the mountain sublime which Kant made an important example of aesthetic experience: 'je laisse s'élever mon imagination, je la laisse creuser l'univers; je tombe avec elle, je traverse les mondes, je tombe encore . . . ! je cherche en vain le point central [. . .] quel vuide immense!' (Mercier, *Mon bonnet de nuit*, 1784–5: Vol. IV, 83).[23] Mercier thinks that the emotional impact of art should be analogous to the feeling we have contemplating the vastness of the mountains: reason is powerless to measure the effect on our senses of the magnitude of a mountain view, only imagination can fly hither and thither in an attempt to find spatial limits with which to define our own relative position in space. It fails, and we are absorbed into the vastness, still retaining a feeling of incessant mental motion within us as the imagination continues its quest. The important analogies between Mercier's sublime and Maimieux's 'impertinence' are that both are non-rational, both refuse to tame an awesome experience, both are profoundly subjective, and both have a distinct feeling of the extraordinary, strange, or even mentally unbalanced. This demands creative freedom and the subjective conceptions of style which Mercier derives perversely from those objective principles of Condillac and Buffon mentioned above. And most tellingly, this aesthetic requires the

---

[22] See also *Mon Bonnet de nuit* (1784–5): Vol. IV, 267–8: 'active imagination [. . .] tu es le miroir heureux où se peignent, se multiplient, s'embellissent tous les objets de la nature'.

[23] See also *Néologie* (1801): Vol. I, preface, 57–8 for Mercier's references to Kant. For Kant's idea of the sublime, see *The Critique of Judgement* (1790; 1952: 117–30). Mercier and Kant make original use of the mountain sublime, but the experience in itself has an interesting history in the seventeenth and eighteenth centuries. See Nicolson, *Mountain Gloom and Mountain Glory* (1959), and Bouillier, 'Silvain et Kant, ou les Antécédents Français de la Théorie du Sublime' (1928).

reformulation of the traditional mirror image for artistic imitation. None of the old imitative categories fit anymore, neither naturalistic, typological nor idealizing, because Mercier claims a much more subjective aesthetic than his predecessors did. In addition, he puts it into practice in some extraordinary ways which even his most fanatical contemporaries like Maimieux did not.

5.8 Mercier and necrophilia

When Mercier draws together all the elements of the new aesthetic: subjectivity, subjective mimesis, the sublime, and the extraordinary or strange, he arrives at a poetic formula which produces such novel works as *Le Tableau de Paris, Mon bonnet de nuit*, and *Songes et visions philosophiques*. Perhaps the most interesting in this respect, however, is his necrophilic poem, *Lettre de Dulis à son ami* (1767), because it takes an otherwise conventional theme of frustrated love and deferred desire, and expresses it in a manner which hugely lacks 'bienséance', at the same time as it emphasizes all the notions of subjectivity, the sublime, and extraordinary that other contemporary poetic modes do not. In order to illustrate this, one can contrast Mercier's poem on necrophilia with a more conventional poetic mode for the expression of powerful emotions and frustrated desire. Below is an ode by Fontenelle which compares closely in some thematic ways with Mercier's poem, but instead of using necrophilia to figure frustrated desire, it uses the image of moonlight and the poetic mode of reverie.

> Quand l'amour nous fait éprouver
> Son premier trouble avec ses premiers charmes,
> Contre soi-même encor c'est lui prêter des armes
> Que d'être seul et de rêver.
> La dominante idée, à chaque instant présente,   5
> N'en devient que plus dominante,
> Elle produit de trop tendres transports,
> Et plus l'esprit rentre en lui-même,
> Libre des objets du dehors,
> Plus il retrouve ce qu'il aime.   10
> Je conçois ce péril, et qui le connaît mieux?

Tous les soirs cependant une force secrète
M'entraîne en d'agréables lieux
Où je me fais une retraite
Qui me dérobe à tous les yeux.   15
Là, vous m'occupez seule, et dans ce doux silence,
Absente je vous vois, je suis à vos genoux,
Je vous peins de mes feux toute la violence;
Si quelqu'un m'interrompt, j'ai le même courroux
Que s'il venait par sa présence   20
Troubler un entretien que j'aurais avec vous.
Le soleil dans les mers vient alors de descendre,
Sa sœur jette un éclat moins vif et moins perçant,
Elle répand dans l'air je ne sais quoi de tendre,
Et dont mon ame se ressent.   25
Peut-être ce discours n'est guère intelligible,
Vous ne l'entendrez point, je sais ce que j'y perds;
Un cœur passionné voit un autre univers
Que le cœur qui n'est pas sensible.
    (Fontenelle, 'Sur un Clair de lune' (c.1700), quoted
    in Finch, *French Individualist Poetry*, 1971: 100)

Les yeux toujours fixés, mes regards se troublerent,
Et bien-tôt par degrés mes esprits s'allumerent. . . .
Je me crus transporté dans un autre univers;
Là, j'apperçus Junie au sein de mille éclairs:
D'Archanges radieux elle est environnée,   5
Et d'immortelles fleurs sa tête est couronnée:
Je la vois qui sourit & qui me tend les bras,
Je m'élance. . . . Tout fond dans la nuit du trépas.
Je me leve agité, temblant, hors de moi-même,
Mes sens étoient glacés, pleins d'une horreur suprême;   10
L'œil égaré, j'errois d'un pas mal affermi.
Je vois à mes côtés ce Vieillard endormi.
Le flambeau va s'éteindre, il forme une ombre immense.
Me voilà seul, au sein d'un terrible silence.
Ce calme qu'interrompt l'airain retentissant.   15
Ce lit, ce lit funèbre & son voile effrayant.
Entouré de la mort & seul avec Junie,
Je crois encor répondre à cette ombre chérie. . . .
    (Mercier, extract from *Lettre de Dulis à son ami*, 1767:
    25)

The moment of the necrophilic act is unspoken, but unmistakable in line 8 of Mercier's poem: Junie's body lies veiled on the

bed, Dulis is overcome with an unspeakable desire, he loses his senses in a momentary fit of morbid passion, and 'dot, dot, dot'.

These poems are thematically quite similar: both are about unrequited love, the solitude of the lonely lover who nevertheless finds solace in his thoughts about love, melancholy, the feeling that the object of the lover's desire is somehow present even in its absence because desire endures separation, the consequent idea that the lonely lover is 'transported' to another world where his desires are somehow fulfilled and, finally, the potential danger that this altered state brings.

Yet they are quite different in the means by which they express these matters. Fontenelle's is a typical neoclassical ode in which the challenge is to versify an irrational, emotionally charged moment, precisely the kind of moment which in principle is least amenable to any intelligible expression at all. Hence the compromise between the structure of formal versification, which risks falsifying the emotional charge, and the formal variety of line length and rhyme scheme, both of which fluctuate quite unpredictably in this ode. The emotional moment in Fontenelle's poem is a feeling of unfulfilled desire which arises like the moonlight, a pale reflection of something far away and unobtainable which evokes absence by its very presence: 'Le soleil dans les mers vient alors de descendre, | Sa sœur jette un éclat moins vif et moins perçant' (ll. 22–3). Such is the lover's conflicting feeling of unrequited love which is nonetheless imminent in his overpowering desire: 'Absente je vous vois' (l. 17). From the ambient twilight ensues a mood of irrational reverie, an altered state in which the lover dreams his desires instead of satisfying them in the real world; 'être seul et rêver' (l. 4) 'transports' him (l. 7) to an inner world: 'l'esprit rentre en lui-même' (l. 8). The lover partly relishes the opportunity to indulge his feelings and revel in his desires, but realizes also the peril of giving in to 'une dominante idée' and abandoning reason to 'ce discours guère intelligible' (l. 5 and 26). He is in any case powerless to do otherwise, because he is driven by 'une force secrète' (l. 12).

Like the versification which remains formal despite its fluctuations, the peril of frustrated desire never really gets out of hand in Fontenelle's poem. The irrepressible 'dominante idée' has been kept within some bounds, at least, by the relatively tranquil image of 'tender' moonlight (l. 24) which points to something absent while at the same time alleviating distress. The state of reverie that this enduces causes the lover to withdraw within himself (or herself?), to feel detached from his circumstances, 'Libre des objets du dehors' (l. 9), and fall into a mood of listless meditation. There is none of the perpetual 'mental motion' which characterizes Mercier's Kantian feeling of the sublime, nor the mental unbalance which it gives rise to. On the contrary, Fontenelle's lover has quieted his mind by assuaging insatiable desire; insatiable because it is awakened by thoughts of love which can never satisfy it, it owes its existence to what is permanently unsatisfactory, and therefore as long as it exists, it will remain unsatisfied. Like the moonlight which brings light to the darkness while also signifying the absence of daylight. The desire of unrequited love is a malady with no cure, unless the lover falls out of love, but Fontenelle seems to find a cure in reverie which turns the lover's attention away from what is distant and unobtainable, and focuses his attention instead on himself.

From Mercier's point of view, moonlight and reverie are insufficient ways of expressing the potency of the idea of frustrated desire and the destructive potential which even Fontenelle admits it has. There are darker recesses to this emotion which Mercier expresses differently.

Mercier's poem is the story of a young man, Dulis, who falls in love with Junie, but for two years does not tell her of his feelings, by which time she is promised in marriage to another man. Dulis is distraught, leaves the family home and wanders aimlessly in the forest, where he hears a voice calling him to Junie's deathbed. He becomes still more distraught, but follows the voice's calling to the home of Junie's family where her body lies veiled on her bed. He is overcome with an unspeakable desire, loses his senses in a momentary fit of morbid passion, and commits an act of necrophilia. Miraculously, Junie awakens from death. There is no fairy-tale happy ending to the story, however, and Dulis is no Prince Charming because, just in case the reader is not quite sure whether the necrophilic act did in fact take place, it later transpires that Junie is pregnant. Given that she is an unmarried virgin promised in marriage, this is distressing to say the least. In order to save her honour, Dulis owns up to his terrible deed, and is sent to prison from which this tale is told (the title-page has an engraving in red ink of a woeful Dulis behind ivy-clad bars).

The necrophilic subject of the poem is unique in the eighteenth century, except perhaps for intimations in *Manon Lescaut* (1731), where the Chevalier spends forty days in the desert with his lips pressed tightly to those of the dead Manon, and more overtly in Sade's writings (although even here there is little actual necrophilia, since sexual pleasure is more often derived from inflicting death than abusing the corpse). And yet the general theme is anything but unique; unrequited love, the desperate response to an impossible desire and the temporary loss of reason is a topos of love poems like Fontenelle's and of the ode form in general. Mercier's poem stands out because the danger of unrequited love is unfettered by standards of universality, reason, and 'bienséance', and free to reflect the extreme emotions of a single mind.

The extreme emotions arise at the point where Dulis sees the object of his affections who has become doubly unobtainable, because Junie who was promised in marriage to another is now dead. The occasion for the feeling of unfulfilled desire is therefore not a pale reflection of something far away like Fontenelle's moonlight, but carnal remains which are more present and yet more absent than moonlight could ever be. The visionary state that Dulis falls into is correspondingly more extraordinary, even supernatural: Junie is bathed in light, surrounded by archangels and crowned in flowers (l. 4–6). In contrast, the object of affections in Fontenelle's poem scarcely appears; her body, dead or alive, is excluded along with some of the consequences of frustrated desire. Fontenelle leaves the consequences hanging menacingly at the end of his ode, the 'dominante idée' which the lover just about manages to repress. Dulis, on the other hand, is faced with a more frightening symbol of unobtainable love, and is lured by a beckoning, smiling vision of Junie to try to fulfil his impossible desire by a vain act of consummation. The vision is not a product of the mind, as in Fontenelle's poem: '*l'esprit* rentre en lui-même', but of the senses: '*mes esprits* s'allumerent' (l. 2), and its effects are consequently that much less rationally controllable. Dulis cannot, therefore 'retreat within his own mind', but feels 'hors de moi-même' (l. 10). Consequently, there is nothing of the meditative state of reverie in Mercier's poem; the 'transports' of emotion that Fontenelle's lover feels carry him no further than his own mind, whereas Dulis desires to be 'transported' almost from this world to the next, from life to death in order to be united with the object of his desires.

Necrophilia, then, is Mercier's way of dramatizing the anguish of an existential divide between the desiring lover and the unobtainable object of desire. The existential anguish, the desire to embrace, but the impossibility of consummation is an internalized version of the mountain sublime he describes elsewhere. Dulis contemplates something too great and too desirable to be rationally comprehended, so it is his senses which transport him to meet it. Like the viewer of an awesome mountain prospect who is transfixed by the vastness, Dulis is overcome with the image of his desire which lies across an impossible abyss between life and death. The subsequent act of attempted consummation is like the mountain viewer who desires to find the 'point central' in the emptiness with which to define his own relative position, discovers that this is not rationally possible, and throws himself into the abyss in a hopeless attempt to reach this point by other means. In the introduction to *Lettre de Dulis*, Mercier thinks that the state of mind which leads to this turmoil is an abyss in itself as awesome as any mountain prospect, and that it is the poet's vocation to stare into it. He distinguishes between the vocation of the poet and the scientist as two different ways of viewing the same awesome phenomenon: 'si le Physicien observateur s'assied, sans pâlir, sur les roches calcinées qui bordent les gouffres des Volcans, si plus intrépide il ose sonder l'ouverture de ces abîmes, où les Torrens embrasées des feux de la nature ont laissé les traces de leur fureur; le Poëte, à son exemple, fouille le cœur humain, abîme aussi vaste, aussi profond, aussi horriblement brûlé, aussi cruellement déchiré par le ravage plus funeste des passions' (Mercier, *Lettre de Dulis*, 1767: preface). His vision of the human soul is as unusual in the eighteenth century as a poem on necrophilia, and therefore very remote from Fontenelle's essentially enchanting picture of a lover's lament. The distinction between scientist and poet, however, is the same as Lancelin's, Maimieux's, and others in this chapter who contrast

two different kinds of exploration of the world, and two different kinds of language. Fontenelle's is probably the better poem
in terms of formal intricacy, and has its own depths of insight.
Perhaps it is also unfair to compare his poem to Mercier's,
because the former is addressed directly to the object of affections, while Dulis addresses his poem to a third party, 'à son
ami', and therefore does not in the least intend that it should
woo Junie. Nevertheless, the major difference lies in Mercier's
intention to 'fouiller' the dark recesses of the emotion of unrequited love which he says in his preface is 'le plus intarissable,
le plus violent, le plus difficile à peindre [. . .] aliment nécessaire & destructeur du cœur de l'homme'. Although it is difficult to 'paint', Mercier goes about mimesis essentially in the
Aristotelian manner of finding an 'action' which is an appropriate vehicle for the emotion (Aristotle, *Poetics*, 6; 1995, Vol.
II: 2320). His choice is less shocking when we remember the
case of Sophocles' *Œdipus Rex* which Aristotle cites repeatedly.
Yet the relation to Aristotle ends here, because Mercier's poem
also has Kantian overtones of the sublime and therefore a
subjective aesthetic which has repercussions in the narrative.
Unlike *Œdipus Rex*, the action which Dulis commits cannot be
blamed on the Gods or any other universal principle, only on
his mad momentary vision of Junie. The difference between the
two is perhaps an illustration of what Mercier meant when he
adapted the conventional mirror analogy for imitation, to say
that the artist does not seek to create a quasi-objective universal image of 'nature' by hiding behind the mirror he holds up
to nature, but to be the prism through which nature is
refracted. The representation is correspondingly more subjective, and Mercier is more free to explore the limits of subjective responses to extreme emotions.

5.9   *Mercier's* Tableau de Paris

Lettre de Dulis is exemplary of Maimieux's 'impertinent' aesthetic and all the subjective, sublime, and extraordinary qualities that it presupposes, but the whole range of Mercier's writing
is remarkable for the extent to which it employs this aesthetic

in different contexts. The *Tableau de Paris* is a very different work to his necrophilic poem, yet it is complementary in many ways, and a departure from contemporary literary aesthetics for all the same reasons. In order to experience the same feeling of immensity which Mercier sees in a mountain prospect or in the abyss of the soul, he need go no further than the streets of Paris and the minor incidents which kindle the imagination. Together, the long digressions and over a thousand articles in the *Tableau de Paris* inspired by these incidents constitute a rich compendium of the author's thoughts and an immense tableau of Paris from an avowedly subjective perspective. The most fleeting moment reveals to him a giddying perspective into the dark recesses of the soul. He watches the faces in the crowd as a funeral procession passes by, and is almost lost for words to describe the profundity that each reveals:

Vous verrez des visages tels qu'aucun peintre n'en a imaginé [. . .] Une succession instructive de figures que ma plume ne saurait exprimer. Ainsi les plus petites choses, pour qui sait les examiner, jettent une lueur vive et rapide dans l'horizon vaste et ténébreux de l'ame; le rideau se tire en un instant indivisible; c'est à l'œil d'être tout aussi prompt pour saisir ce qui se passe à travers ces nuages ouverts et refermés. (Mercier, 'Layetiers', in *Tableau de Paris*, 1994: Vol. II, 1096)

The *Tableau de Paris* is disconcerting because behind every detail there is an unexpected grand vista, sometimes so grand that Mercier can only hint at it. There is a feeling of unforeseen and uncontrollable vastness in the day-to-day episodes that we take for granted. He watches the rich client of a cobbler as she tries on an expensive shoe, and he comments: 'quelle distance entre la chaussure d'une femme de qualité et celle d'une maîtresse de pension?' (Mercier, 'Cordonnier', in *Tableau de Paris*, 1994: Vol. I, 1045). The episode is brief, but leads him to discuss the problem of rising prices, the inequities of the wealthy who demand credit from the poor, the virtues of the god-fearing artisans who indirectly maintain the monks in their solitary lives. There is no fleeting moment which escapes Mercier, no detail so small that it cannot be magnified into the portrait of a moment.

The fleeting moments are sometimes signs of absence which provoke emotional turmoil, like Dulis who feels the presence of Junie all the more for her death. Mercier visits a disused prison and is overcome with a morbid fascination of the idea that the walls were witness to the agonies of their inmates: 'répondez, murailles, rapportez à mon oreille les gémissements dont vous avez été témoins. Que d'angoisses! L'ennui, le désespoir ont habité ces lieux' (Mercier, 'Donjon de Vincennes', *Tableau de Paris*, 1994: Vol. II, 592).

Like Maimieux who refuses any artificial marshalling of these experiences of the imagination, Mercier also rejects any putative intellectual order to his fragmented vision of Paris. Each experience stands isolated as a product of an individual perspective on a unique moment, and it is for this reason that the *Tableau de Paris* is a collection of articles in no particular order. He finds the alternative approach deeply uninspiring. A visit to the 'Cabinet du roi' gives him a headache because the natural history collection is arranged according to taxonomic principles:

Rien ne me paraît plus désordonné que cet assemblage savant, fait pour être dispersé sur la surface de la terre. Toutes ces différentes espèces qui se touchent et qui ne sont pas crées pour se toucher réunies en un seul point, forment une dissonance en mon cerveau [...] Cet ordre symétrique [...] a quelque chose de factice et de bizarre qui blesse mon sens moral et intime. Ce n'est pas l'ordre dont j'ai l'image en moi. (Mercier, 'Cabinet du roi', *Tableau de Paris*, 1994: Vol. II, 1414–15).

There is something absurd about taxonomic principles which place the skeleton of an elephant alongside the bones of a whale. The order he prefers is the sequence arising from personal observation, because the observer is not excluded, and the vision thus concurs more closely with his prism metaphor for representation.

Conclusion

Mercier's poet cannot be an analyst, just as Lancelin's analyst cannot be a poet. It is interesting that both claim to occupy a 'high point', but with very different intentions. Maine de Biran's 'idéologiste' occupies an intellectual vantage point over the other sciences in order to draw an intellectual map of the world of knowledge, to encompass all that he surveys with a powerful heuristic theory. Mercier's sublime poet stands on a mountain top in order to feel lost in the immensity, to experience the moment when reason is powerless to measure the emptiness, and imagination alone provides the vision. Both the analyst and the poet can devise a tableau, but of very different kinds. The analyst invents a nomenclature, a system of names for all the ideas that he surveys from his commanding position over the rational world. For the poet there is no nomenclature which can translate the immensity of what he sees into a universal language of the imagination. All he has is the order of subjective perception.

The debate on language is polarized in a way it never was earlier in the century, when philosopher-grammarians and creative writers were untroubled by a dual perspective on language. Condillac's 'langage d'action', Buffon's objectification of style or the 'nuances' metaphor in general all look out of date by the end of the century. At best, these are attempts to understand how literary language could be explained in relation to broader questions of art, representation, and the nature of knowledge. At worst, however, they come to be considered by later creative writers as a limitation on their creative freedom.

The breakdown of the consensus at the end of the century is arguably not a failure, but a quite radical shift of priorities. The demands on the one hand for a language with more scientific, methodological aptitude, and on the other for a language which engages with the ineffable, subjective nature of art makes it inappropriate to attempt a reconciliation between the two.

CONCLUSION

Eighteenth-century language debates are a rich source of theories about imitation in the arts and a remarkable attempt to answer the 'what' and 'how' questions to which it gives rise. They are also a symptom of an era which is trying to stretch the notion of imitation as far as it will go to include a wide range of quite different approaches. Imitation in language includes the naturalistic theories of onomatopoeia of Gébelin and de Brosses, the typological theories of Girard's synonyms, and the idealizing theories of Condillac's 'liaison des idées'. The consequence of this is that a wide variety of different literary writing is also regarded as imitative, from Diderot's hieroglyph, to Marivaux's preciosity, to Buffon's idea of universal style. Imitation means all these things in the eighteenth century, but after having been stretched so far, it reaches breaking-point with the theory of 'idéologie' and Maimieux's subjective aesthetic of 'impertinence' in the latter part of the century. It cannot include them both, and the theory of representation in language polarizes with at one extreme the putatively universal mathematical symbols of Lancelin's 'analyste', and at the other extreme the reputedly subjective expression of Mercier's sublime poet. Language, therefore, is no longer a good model of the theory of imitation in the arts, and the theory thus loses a major pillar which supported it.

Before this happens, the process of stretching imitation to include such diverse literary styles and theories of language draws on a medley of potentially conflicting intellectual sources which are only made compatible by the overarching aim of sustaining the traditional theory of artistic imitation. Cartesian rationalism is combined with Sensualism and Empiricism to show that artistic representation works in many ways, but always according to the principle of imitation. Castel's colour harpsichord, and especially Diderot's interpretation of it, is the best example of this. The nuances of colour are empirically identifiable because we can literally put our finger on them; they are also the evidence of a rationalist 'distinct' idea, and they are also the sensual stimuli which cause ideas to arise in the mind of the spectator. We need a large measure of Hume's 'honest' philosophy to accept this hybrid or else, as Diderot's deaf mute implies, we should simply exclaim, 'ah! this is the language of poetry!'.

Castel's harpsichord is a characteristic answer to the 'what' and 'how' questions of imitation. 'What' because art imitates 'nature' in all its empirico-naturalistic, rational-idealizing, and typological-psychological richness; and 'how' because all the arts imitate in the same way. The latter is admittedly a circular argument, but the synaesthetic principles of Castel's harpsichord lend such strong support to the sister-arts theory that it suddenly looks capable of being extended to all the arts. As a result, there are more than two 'sister' arts in the eighteenth century, a fact which transforms a circular argument into an appealingly self-sufficient system.

Despite the constant doubts raised about the theory of imitation in the eighteenth century, therefore, for many it is the best working hypothesis available. The blend of different intellectual influences we find in Castel's harpsichord, Diderot's hieroglyph, Gébelin's symbolism, or any of the language theories discussed in this book are perhaps not as distilled as we have since come to expect of the discipline of 'aesthetics', but they are nevertheless examples of an intellectual search for a theory of art which is more rigorous than taste and less abstract than rationalistic philosophy. In this sense, they are instances of what Cassirer meant when he said that 'eighteenth-century aesthetics called for a Newton of art' (Cassirer, *The Philosophy of Enlightenment*, 1951: 280). They are also reminders that the frequent modern tendency to trace the history of aesthetics to Sensualism and Baumgarten's re-evaluation of 'sensate knowledge' is only part of a more complex picture which includes a variety of Empirical and Rationalist elements. It is probably more apt to trace aesthetics back to a more general loosening of the idea of 'reason' to include 'poetic reason'. It is in this sense that the language theories discussed in this book are 'aesthetic', despite their varied background.

APPENDIX

La Motte, *Œdipe, tragédie*, Act III, scene vi (*Œuvres*, 1754:
Volume IV, 497–9), extract.

JOCASTE. Ah! ne m'accablez plus.
Je ne connois que trop le malheureux Laïus.

ŒDIPE. Je l'ai donc dévoilé ce terrible mystere!
La Haine de Jocaste est déja mon salaire.
Que deviens-je à vos yeux! & quel objet pour vous
Qu'un Epoux tout soüillé du sang de votre Epoux!
Vous ne me voyez plus que comme un parricide,
Comme un monstre cruel, sacrilege, perfide. . . .

JOCASTE. Seigneur, ces noms affreux ne sont dûs qu'aux forfaits.
Respectez vos vertus: respectez mes regrets.
Tout accablé qu'il est du malheur qui l'opprime,
Mon cœur sçait en gémir, sans vous en faire un crime.
Je vois toûjours en vous ce Héros adoré,
A qui seul pour jamais tout ce cœur fut livré.
Je n'impute qu'au sort mes mortelles allarmes,
Et je vous doit toûjours mon amour & mes larmes.

ŒDIPE. Et moi, quand votre cœur craint de me condamner,
Le mien désespéré ne peut se pardonner.
Je sçais qu'en ce combat je ne fus point coupable;
Mais je suis de vos maux la source déplorable:
Et malgré ma raison, mon trouble plus puissant
Me défend en secret de me croire innocent.
J'entends déja Laïus: & je crois voir son ombre
Sortir, pour se venger, de la demeure sombre,
Me venir demander un sang que je lui doi,
Et retracter les vœux qu'il avoit faits pour moi.

JOCASTE. Vous le deshonorez par ce triste présage.
Non, non, calmez, Œdipe, un trouble qui m'outrage.
Le sort impitoyable a seul conduit vos coups;
J'en accuse les Dieux; & j'en pleure avec vous.

ŒDIPE. Mais, Madame, malgré ce pardon magnanime,
Le Ciel toûjours armé demande sa victime.
Voilà ce criminel, ce cœur qu'il faut frapper,
Et que Thébe a laissé trop long-tems échaper.

JOCASTE. Seigneur, s'il faut des Dieux appaiser la colere,
Attendons, en tremblant, que leur voix nous éclaire.
D'un des Fils de Jocaste ils veulent le trépas.
Peut-être votre mort ne les sauveroit pas.
Allons encor au Temple implorer leur clémence;
Nous les désarmerons; j'en crois votre innocence;
Mais si rien ne fléchit leur barbare courroux,
Je ne m'y soumettrai qu'en mourant avec vous.

ŒDIPE. Jocaste, épargnez-moi cette horrible menace.
Mais, j'y consens, aux Dieux venez demander grace,
Tandis qu'impatient de sauver mes Etats,
Je vais les conjurer d'accepter mon trépas.
Fin du troisiéme Acte.

La Motte, *Œdipe, tragédie en prose*, Act III, scene v (*Œuvres*, 1754: Volume V, 43–6), extract.

JOCASTE. Arrêtez, Œdipe. Je ne reconnois que trop le malheureux Laïus.

ŒDIPE. Affreuse vérité! me voilà donc devenu l'objet de la haine de Jocaste! elle ne verra plus dans Œdipe que le coupable meurtrier de son époux.

JOCASTE. Que dites-vous, Œdipe! ces noms odieux sont-ils faits pour la vertu; je gémis, je suis accablée de mon infortune: mais elle ne me rend pas injuste. Vous êtes toujours ce Héros à qui j'ai donné mon cœur; & je vous dois encore & mon amour & mes larmes.

ŒDIPE. Et moi je ne me pardonne pas mon malheur. Je ne puis soutenir l'idée de vous avoir été funeste. Je sçais que je ne suis pas coupable; & cependant une horreur secrete me défend de me croire innocent. Il me semble que je vois l'ombre de Laïus retracter la priere qu'il faisoit aux Dieux de ne me point imputer sa mort. Eh bien, Ombre sacrée, vous serez satisfaite. Je ne vois refuserai point votre victime.

JOCASTE. Seigneur, l'amour de Jocaste vous est-il cher encore?

ŒDIPE. S'il m'est cher! c'est le seul bien que jaye jamais craint de perdre.

JOCASTE. Ne le blessez donc plus par un desespoir que m'outrage. Non, vous n'êtes point le meurtrier de Laïus: Vous avez vaincu des ennemis. La fortune seule a fait tomber mon époux sous vos mains innocentes. Les dernieres paroles de Laïus ne m'apprennent que trop mon devoir. Il a loüé votre courage; mais c'est assez pour moi de vous le pardonner.

ŒDIPE. Je connois votre vertu, Madame, vous vous faites un devoir de me cacher l'impression que ce malheur vous cause: mais vous l'éprouvez malgré tous vos efforts. Non, vous ne me verrez plus des mêmes yeux. L'horreur & le tendresse vont se confondre dans vôtre ame; & vos larmes ne m'avertissent que trop que je vous suis devenu moins cher. Trop malheureuse Jocaste! à quel point vos sentimens m'interessent, puisque je m'en occupe encore au milieu des horreurs qui m'environnent! Voilà le coupable découvert. Voilà du moins l'auteur de cette mort dont les Dieux poursuivent la vengeance. Allons, c'est trop leur refuser le sacrifice qu'ils demandent.

JOCASTE. Ah, seigneur, s'il faut subir un arrêt si cruel, attendons du moins que le Ciel s'explique clairement; il a demandé la mort d'un de mes fils; peut être la votre ne les sauveroit pas. Attendez. . . .

ŒDIPE. Qu'attendre, Madame? & c'est le sang d'un de mes fils qu'ils demandent! ah, Dieux cruels, vous sçavez trop que la mort ne peut m'allarmer; & vous voulez que je sente le coup que vous me portez! que devenir! que résoudre! mon incertitude même est un crime. A combien de mes sujets mes délais coutent-ils la vie! juste Ciel, faut il que je porte, malgé moi, le coup mortel à tout ce que je veux sauver!

JOCASTE. Je sens que, je me meurs, Œdipe, si votre fermeté ne soutient la mienne. Supportez vos malheur par pitié pour votre épouse. Allons encore implorer les Dieux. Votre innocence m'en fait esperer des ordres plus favorables.

ŒDIPE. Allons, Madame: mais, pour prix de cette innocence, je ne leur demande que la mort.

Fin du troisiéme Acte.

BIBLIOGRAPHY

Whenever possible, dates of first editions are given in parentheses before the semi-colon.

BOOKS AND ARTICLES FIRST PUBLISHED BEFORE 1820

'Extrait d'une lettre écrite de Londres, le 27. Mars 1721', *Le Journal des sçavans* (28 Apr. 1721), 256.

'Lettre écrite de Londres sur les Estampes colorées, l'université d'Oxford, & autres curiositez, &c.', *Le Mercure* (December 1721), 29–37.

'Lettre écrite de Londres par M. Des-Maiseaux, Membre de la Société Royale, à M. l'Abbé de Veissiere, Censeur Royal des Livres, à Paris, touchant l'Art d'imprimer des Tableaux & des Portraits en couleur, &c.', *Le Journal des sçavans* (18 May 1722), 316–18.

Alembert, Jean Le Rond d', *Discours préliminaire* (1751), in *Encyclopédie ou Dictionnaire raisonné des sciences, des arts et des métiers* (17 vols): Vol. I.

—— *Réflexions sur l'usage et sur l'abus de la philosophie dans les matières du goût* (1766), in *Œuvres philosophiques, historiques et littéraires* (Paris: Bastien, 1805), Vol. IV.

—— 'Suite des réflexions sur la poésie, et sur l'ode en particulier' in *Œuvres*, 5 vols (Paris: Martin Bossange et Col, 1822), Vol. IV: 299–304.

André, Père, *Essai sur le Beau, où l'on examine en quoi consiste précisément le Beau dans le Physique, dans le Moral, dans les Ouvrages de l'Esprit et de la Musique* (Paris: H.-L. Guérin et J. Guérin, 1741).

Aristotle, *Poetics*, in *The Complete Works of Aristotle*, ed. Jonathan Barnes, 2 vols (Princeton: Princeton University Press, 1995), Vol. I.

Batteux, Charles, *Cours de Belles-Lettres, ou Principes de la littérature*, 3 vols (Paris: Desaint et Saillant, 1753).

—— 'Harmonie' in *Cours de Belles-Lettres, ou Principes de la littérature*, 6 vols (Lyon: Amable Leroy, 1802), Vol. V.

—— *Les Beaux-Arts réduits à un même principe*, ed. Jean-Rémy Mantion (1746; Paris: Aux Amateurs de Livres, 1989).

Beaumarchais, Pierre-Augustin Caron de, *Essai sur le genre dramatique sérieux* in *Œuvres*, ed. Pierre Larthomas (1767; Paris: Gallimard, 1988).

Bernis, François Joachim de Pierres, cardinal de, *Œuvres* (Paris: N.

Delange, 1825): 'Epitre sur le goût. A M. le duc de Nivernois'; 'Ode IV. Les Poëtes lyriques'; 'Réflexions sur la métromanie'.

Bertière, Simone, and Vidal, Lucette (eds.), *Anthologie de la littérature du XVIIe siècle* (Paris: Livre de Poche, 1993).

Bertin, Théodore Pierre, *Système universel et complèt de Sténographie, ou maniere abregée d'écrire applicable à tous les idiomes. Et fondée sur des principes si simples et si faciles à saisir, qu'on peut connoître en un jour les élémens de cet art et se mettre en état dans très peu de tems, de suivre la parole d'un orateur* (Paris: P. Didot l'ainé, L'An 4. de l'Ere françoise [1795]).

Bièvre, Georges Mareschal, marquis de, *Lettre écrite à madame la Comtesse Tation, par le Sieur de Bois-Flotté, étudiant en droit-fil.* (Amsterdam: Compagnie de Perdreaux, 1770).

——— *Vercingentorixe* (n.p., 1770).

——— 'Kalembour', in *Supplément à l'Encyclopédie, ou Dictionnaire raisonné des sciences, des arts et des métiers*, 4 vols (1777), Vol. III, 680–1.

Blanc, Honoré, *Okygraphie, ou L'Art de fixer, par écrit, tous les sons de la parole avec autant de facilité, de promptitude et de clarté que la bouche les exprime [. . .] Présentant des moyens aussi vastes, aussi surs que nouveaux d'entretenir une correspendance secréte dont les Signes seront absolument indechiffrables* (Paris: Bidault, 1801).

Bouhours, père Dominique, *Entretiens d'Ariste et d'Eugène* (1671; Paris: G. Desprez, 1771).

——— *Doutes sur la langue françoise* (Paris: S. Mabre-Cramoisy, 1675).

——— *La Manière de bien penser dans les ouvrages de l'esprit* (Paris: La Veuve de Sébastien Mabre-Cramoisy, 1687).

Brosses, Charles de, *Traité de la formation méchanique des langues et des principes physiques de l'étymologie* (1765; Paris: Terrelonge, 1800).

Buffon, Georges Louis Leclerc, comte de, *Le Buffon de Benjamin Rabier* (Paris: Gallimard, 1917).

——— *Œuvres philosophiques de Buffon*, ed. Jean Piveteau (Paris: Presses universitaires de France, 1954), Vol. XLI,1: 'De l'Art d'écrire'; 'De la Nature de l'homme'; *Discours sur le style.*

——— 'Le Cheval' in *L'Histoire naturelle (extraits)*, (Paris: Le Tresor des Lettres françaises, 1975).

——— *Discours sur le style*, ed. Cedric Pickford (Hull: Hull University Press, 1978).

——— *Histoire naturelle*, ed. J. Varloot (Paris: Gallimard, 1984).

Castel, père Louis-Bertrand, 'Nouvelles expériences d'optiques & d'Acoustique: adresseés à M. le Président de Montesquieu. Par le P. Castel, Jesuite', *Journal de Trévoux, ou, Mémoires pour servir à l'histoire des sciences et des arts* 35 (Aug. 1735), 1444–82.

——— 'Coloritto, or the harmony of colouring &c. C'est à-dire, l'harmonie du Coloris dans la Peinture, réduite en Pratique mechanique, & à des regles sûres & faciles, avec des figures, en couleurs &c', *Journal de Trévoux, ou, Mémoires pour servir à l'histoire des sciences et des arts* 37 (Aug. 1737), 1435–44.

—— *L'Optique des couleurs, fondée sur les simples observations, & tournée sur-tout à la pratique de la peinture, de la teinture & des autres arts coloristes* (Paris: Briasson, 1740).

Catullus, *Carmen*, ed. John Ferguson (Kansas: Colorado Press, 1985).

—— *Carmen*, ed. C. J. Fordyse (Oxford: Oxford University Press, 1990).

Cerutti, J-A-J., *De l'intéret d'un ouvrage, Discours prononcé par le P. Cerutti, Jésuite, à sa réception à l'Académie Royale des Sciences & Belles-Lettres de Nancy* (Nancy: La Veuve & Claude Leseure, 1763).

Chabanon, Michel-Paul Guy de, *Observations sur la musique, et principalement sur la metaphysique de l'art* (1779; Geneva: Slatkine Reprints, 1969).

Chénier, André, *Œuvres*, ed. Gérard Walter (Paris: Gallimard, 1950).

Cherrier, Claude, *L'homme inconnu, ou les équivoques de la langue, dédié à Bacha Bilboquet* (Paris: J. Quillau, 1713).

—— *Polisonniana ou recueil de Turlupinades, Quolibets, Rebus, Jeux de mots, Allusions, Allégories, Pointes, Expressions extraordinaires, Hyperboles, Gasconades, espèces de bons mots et autres plaisanteries. Avec Les Equivoques de l'Homme Inconnu et la liste des plus rares curiosités* (Amsterdam: Henry Desbordes, 1722).

Condillac, abbé Etienne Bonnot de, *Œuvres*, 23 vols (Paris: Ch. Houel, 1798): *Essai sur l'origine des connoissances humaines* (1746), Vol. I; *Traité des Sensations* (1754), Vol. III; *Grammaire*, Vol. V; *Art d'écrire*, Vol. VII; 'Dissertation sur l'Harmonie du style', in Vol. VII.

—— *Dictionnaire des synonymes*, in *Œuvres philosophiques de Condillac*, ed. Georges Le Roy (Paris: Presses universitaires de France, 1951), Vol. III.

—— *La Langue des calculs*, eds. Sylvain Auroux and Anne-Marie Chouillet (Lille: Presses Universitaires de Lille, 1981).

Condorcet, 'Langue universelle et formalisation des sciences', see Granger, Gilles-Gaston.

Cooper, Anthony Ashley, 3rd earl of Shaftesbury, *The Moralists, A Philosophical Rhapsody. Being a Recital of certain Conversations on Natural and Moral Subjects* (1709), in *Characteristicks of Men, Manners, Opinions, Times &c.* (London, 1733), 181–443.

Crousaz, J. P. de, *Traité du Beau. Où l'on montre en quoi consiste ce que l'on nomme ainsi, par des Exemples tirez de la plûpart des Arts & des Sciences* (Amsterdam: François L'Honoré, 1715).

Dacier, Anne, *L'Iliade d'Homere, traduite en françois, avec des remarques* (1699; Amsterdam: Compagnie, 1712).

Dagen, Jean and Janine (eds.), *Anthologie de la littérature du dix-huitième siècle* (Paris: Livre de Poche, 1994).

Delille, Jacques, *Œuvres*, 10 vols (Paris: Furne, 1832): *Les Georgiques* (1769), Vol. I; *L'Imagination* (1794), Vol. VIII.

Delon, M., ed., *Anthologie de la poésie française du XVIIIe siècle* (Paris: Gallimard, 1997).

Delormel, Jean, *Projet d'une langue universelle, présenté à la Convention nationale* (Paris: n.p., 1795).

Descartes, René, *Œuvres*, eds. C. Adam and P. Tannery (Paris: Vrin/CNRS, 1964–76), 12 vols.

Desfontaines, Pierre-François Guyot, *Dictionnaire néologique. A l'usage des beaux Esprits du Siécle. Avec l'Eloge Historique de Pantalon-Phoebus* (1726; Amsterdam: Michel Rey, 1731).

——— [review of Olivet's *Prosodie*], *Observations sur les écrits modernes* VII (Paris: Chaubert, 1736), 145–68.

——— 'Portrait du Roi' [by Le Blon], *Obervations sur les écrits modernes* XIX (Paris: Chaubert, 1739), 70–2.

Destutt de Tracy, Antoine Louis Claude, *Elémens d'idéologie*, 4 vols (Paris: Lévi, 1825).

Devismes, Anne-Pierre-Jacques, *Pasilogie, ou de la musique considérée comme langue universelle* (Paris: Prault, 1806).

Diderot, Denis, *Lettre sur les sourds et muets à l'usage de ceux qui entendent et qui parlent. Où l'on traite de l'origine des inversions, de l'harmonie du style, du sublime de situation, de quelques avantages de la langue française sur la plupart des langues anciennes et modernes, et, par occasion, de l'expression particulière aux beaux-arts*, in *Diderot Studies* VII, ed. Otis Fellows (1751; Geneva: Droz, 1965).

——— *Œuvres*, 14 vols (Paris: Le Club français du livre, 1969–72): *Les Bijoux indiscrets* (1749), Vol. I; *Discours sur la poésie dramatique* (1758), Vol. III; *Eloge de Richardson* (1762), Vol. V; *Entretiens sur le Fils naturel* (1757), Vol. III; *Le Fils naturel* (1757), Vol. III; *Leçons de clavecin* (1771), Vol. IX.

——— *Salon de 1767*, ed. Jean Seznec (Oxford: Clarendon Press, 1983): Vol. III.

——— *Recherches philosophiques sur l'origine et la nature du beau* in *Œuvres esthétiques* (1751; Paris: Garnier, 1988).

Dubos, abbé Jean-Baptiste, *Réflexions critiques sur la poésie et sur la peinture* (Paris: Jean Mariette, 1719).

Dumarsais, César Chesneau, *Des tropes, ou des différents sens* (1730; Paris: Flammarion, 1988).

Faiguet, 'Langue Nouvelle', in *Encyclopédie ou Dictionnaire raisonné des sciences, des arts et des métiers*, 17 vols (1765), Vol. IX, 268–71.

Félibien, André des Avaux et de Javercy, *Entretiens sur les vies et sur les ouvrages des plus excellens peintres anciens et modernes; avec la vie des architectes* (1666; Farnborough: Greff Press, 1967).

Fénelon, François de Salignac de la Mothe, *Lettre à l'Académie. Avec les versions primitives*, ed. Ernesta Caldarini (1714; Geneva: Droz, 1970).

——*Les Aventures de Télémaque*, ed. Jacques Le Brun (1699; Paris: Gallimard, 1995).

Ferrein, M., 'De la formation de la voix de l'homme' in *Mémoires de l'Académie royale des sciences* 57 (15 Nov. 1741), 409–32.

Fontenelle, Bernard le Bovier de, *Préface de la tragédie et des six comédies* in *Œuvres*, 10 vols (Paris: B. Brunet, 1758), Vol. VII.

——*Lettres galantes*, ed. Daniel Delafarge (1683; Paris: Les Belles Lettres, 1961).

——*Entretiens sur la pluralité des mondes habités*, in *Œuvres*, 6 vols (1686; Paris: Fayard, 1991), Vol. II.

Fréron, Elie-Catherine, 'Lettres sur quelques écrits de ce temps', IV, 1 (1751), 3–24.

Gaillard, *Poëtique françoise, à l'usage des dames. Avec des exemples* (Paris: Le Clerc, 1749).

Gamaches, père Etienne-Simon de, *Les Agréments du langage réduits à leurs principes* (Paris: Guillaume Cavelier et al, 1718).

Garat, Dominique Joseph, *Discours sur l'hommage fait au Conseil des Anciens des premières strophes du Chant du Départ écrites avec les caractères pasigraphiques* (Paris: n.p., 1799).

Gébelin, Antoine Court de, *Monde primitif, analysé et comparé avec le monde moderne*, 9 vols (Paris: Boudet et al, 1773–84): Vol. I: *considéré dans son génie allégorique et dans les allégories auxquelles conduisit ce génie, précédé du plan général des diverses parties qui composeront ce monde primitif*; Vol. II: *considéré dans l'histoire naturelle de la parole, ou Grammaire universelle et comparative*; Vol. III: *considéré dans l'histoire naturelle de la parole: ou origine du langage et de l'écriture*; Vol. V: *considéré dans les origines françoises; ou dictionnaire étymologique de la langue françoise*; Vol. VI: *considéré dans les origines latines; ou dictionnaire étymologique de la langue latine.*

Girard, abbé Gabriel, *La Justesse de la langue françoise, ou les différentes significations des mots qui passent pour synonymes* (Paris: Laurent d'Houry, 1718).

——*Synonymes françois, leurs différentes significations, et le choix qu'il en faut faire pour parler avec justesse* (Amsterdam: J. Wetstein & G. Smith, 1737; and Paris: Vve d'Houry, 1740).

[review of Girard's *Synonymes françois*], *Journal encyclopédique* (Feb. 1770), 384–93.

Goethe, Johann Wolfgang von, *Goethe's Colour Theory*, trans. Herb Aach (1810; London: Studio Vista, 1971).

Granger, Gilles-Gaston, 'Langue universelle et formalisation des sciences. Un fragment inédit de Condorcet', *Revue d'histoire des sciences et de leurs applications* VII (1954), 197–219.

Grimm, Friedrich Melchior, *Correspondance littéraire, philosophique et critique* (Paris: Garnier frères, 1877–82).

Hérault de Séchelles, *Voyages à Montbard* (Solvet, an VIII).

Hogarth, William, *The Analysis of Beauty* (1753; New Haven: Yale University Press, 1997).

Hourwitz, Zalkind, *Polygraphie, ou l'art de correspondre à l'aide d'un dictionnaire dans toutes les langues, même celles dont on ne possède pas seulement les lettres alphabétiques* (Paris: chez l'auteur, 1800).

Hugo, Victor, *Les Contemplations*, in *Œuvres* (Paris: Seuil, 1972), Vol. I.

Hurtaut, Pierre-Thomas-Nicolas, *L'Art de péter, essay théori-physique et méthodique* (En Westphalie: Florent-Q., 1751).

——*Dictionnaire des mots homonymes de la langue française, c'est-à-dire dont la prononciation est la même et la signification différente, avec la quantité sur les principales syllabes de chaque mot, pour marquer la durée de leur prononciation: prouvée par des Exemples agréables, tirés des Auteurs & des Poëtes Latins & François, tant anciens que modernes. Ouvrage Nécessaire aux Etrangers, & à la Jeunesse Françoise des deux Sexes, &c. Par M. Hurtaut, Maître-ès-art & de Pension de l'Université de Paris; Ancien Professeur de l'Ecole-Royale-Militaire, & Pensionnnaire de Sa Majesté* (Paris: P.-D. Langlois, 1775).

Kant, Immanuel, *The Critique of Judgement*, trans. James Creed Meredith (1790; Oxford: Oxford University Press, 1952).

Kratzenstein, C. G., 'Sur la naissance de la formation des voyelles' in *Journal de Phys. Chim. Hist. Nat. Arts* 21 (1780).

L'Epée, abbé Charles Michel de, *Institution des sourds et muets, par la voie des signes méthodiques; ouvrage qui contient le Projet d'une Langue Universelle; par l'entremise des Signes naturels, assujettis à une Méthode* (Paris: Nyon l'Aîné, 1776).

La Bruyère, Jean de, *Les Caractères*, ed. R. Garapon (Paris: Garnier, 1990).

La Faye, Jean-François Lériget de, 'Epitre sur les avantages de la rime' (c. 1725), in La Motte, *Œuvres*, Vol. I.

La Motte, Antoine Houdard de, *Œuvres*, 10 vols (Paris: Prault, 1754): Vol. II: *L'Iliade, poëme* (1714), *Discours sur Homere*; Vol. IV: *Discours à l'occasion de la Tragédie d'Œdipe; Œdipe, Tragédie; Suite des Réflexions sur la tragédie, où l'on répond à M. de Voltaire*; Vol. V: *Œdipe, Tragédie en prose*.

Lancelin, P. F., *Introduction à l'analyse des sciences, ou la Génération des fondemens, et des instrumens de nos connaissances* (Paris: Firmin Didot, 1801).

Landois, Paul, *Silvie, tragédie, en prose, en un acte* (Paris: Prault Fils, 1742).

Le Blon, Jakob Christoph, *L'Harmonie du coloris dans la peinture; réduite en pratique mecanique et à des regles sures & faciles: avec des figures en couleur, pour en faciliter l'Intelligence, non seulement aux PEINTRES, mais à tous ceux qui aiment la Peinture.* (np: 1725).

—— *Coloritto. By J. C. Le Blon. Inventor ad Developer of the RED-YELLOW-BLUE Theory of Color Printing (Ca 1720)*, ed. Faber Birren (New York: Van Nostrand Reinhold Company, 1980).

Le Bossu, *Traité du poème épique* (Paris: M. Le Petit, 1675).

Le Brun, Ponce Denis Ecouchard, *Sur la différence des vers et de la poésie, à M. de Buffon*, in *Œuvres*, 4 vols (Paris: Gabriel Warée, 1811), Vol. III.

Le Gros, Jean-Charles-François, *Analyses des ouvrages de J. J. Rousseau, de Genève. Et de M. Court de Gébelin, Auteur du Monde Primitif* (Geneva, Paris: Barthelemy Chirol, Veuve Duchesne, 1785).

Lessing, Gotthold Ephraim, *Laocoön*, transl. William A. Steel (1766; London: Dent, 1966).

Locke, John, *An Essay Concerning Human Understanding* (1690; London: Dent, 1977).

Maimieux, Joseph de, *L'Heureux Jeune Homme. Histoire orientale* (London, Paris: Thomas Hookham, la Veuve Duchesne, 1786).

—— *Eloge philosophique de l'impertinence. Ouvrage posthume de M. de La Bractéole* (Abdère, Paris: Maradan, 1788).

—— *Le Compte de Saint-Méran, ou les Nouveaux égaremens du cœur et de l'esprit* (Paris: Leroy, 1788).

—— *Pasigraphie, ou Premiers élémens du nouvel art-science d'écrire et d'imprimer en une langue de manière à être lu et entendu dans toute autre langue sans traduction* (Paris: Bureau de la Pasigraphie, 1797).

—— *Pasigraphie et pasilalie; méthode élémentaire* (Paris: Bureau de la Pasigraphie, 1799).

—— *Carte générale de pasigraphie* (Paris: Bureau de pasigraphie, 1808).

Maine de Biran, Marie François Pierre Gontier de Biran, dit, 'Note sur les rapports de l'idéologie et des mathématiques' in *Mémoire sur la décomposition de la pensée*, ed. François Azouvi (Paris: Presses universitaires de France, 1988).

Marivaux, Pierre Carlet de Chamblain de, 'Le Cabinet philosophique; sixième feuille, Du Style' in *Journaux et Œuvres diverses de Marivaux*, ed. F. Deloffre (1734; Paris: Bordas, 1988).

—— 'Sur la clarté du discours' in *Journaux et Œuvres diverses*, ed. F. Deloffre (1719; Paris: Bordas, 1988).

—— *La Vie de Marianne*, ed. Jean Dagen (Paris: Gallimard, 1997).

Marmontel, Jean-François, 'INTERET (Belles Lettres, Poèsie)', in

Supplément à l'Encyclopédie, ou Dictionnaire raisonné des sciences, des arts et des métiers, 4 vols (1777), Vol. III, 628–9.

Marmontel, Jean-François, *Elémens de littérature* in *Œuvres*, 18 vols (Paris: Amable Costes et compagnie, 1819): Vol. XII: 'Analogie du style'; Vol. XIV: 'Harmonie du style'.

Mercier, Louis Sébastien, *Du Théâtre, ou Nouvel essai sur l'art dramatique* (Amsterdam: E. van Harrevelt, 1773).

——*L'An 2440* (London: 1774).

——*Mon bonnet de nuit* (Lausanne: Jean-Pierre Heubach et Comp., 1784–5).

——*Songes et visions philosophiques* (Amsterdam: Garnier, 1788).

——*Néologie, ou vocabulaire de mots nouveaux, à renouveler, ou pris dans des acceptions nouvelles* (Paris: Moussard, 1801).

——*Tableau de Paris*, ed. Jean-Claude Bonnet, 2 vols (1781–8; Paris: Mercure de France, 1994).

Moissy, Alexandre Guillaume Mouslier de, *Le Vertueux mourant, Drame en trois actes et en prose* (Paris: Bailly, 1770).

——*La Vraie mère, drame didacti-comique* (Paris: Bailly, 1771).

Mondorge, 'Lettre & Mémoire sur la Gravure colorée, nouvellement inventée par M. le Blond', *Le Pour et le contre* XVI (1738), 41–5.

Montaigne, Michel de, *Essais*, ed. A. Micha, 2 vols (Paris: Garnier-Flammarion, 1969).

Necker, Suzanne Curchod, *Mélanges extraits des manuscrits de Mme Necker* (Paris: C. Pougens, An VI [1798]).

Olivet, Pierre-Joseph Thoulier, abbé de, *Traité de la prosodie françoise* (1736; Amsterdam: J. Wetstein, 1737).

——*Prosodie de la langue françoise*, in *Remarques sur la langue françoise* (Paris: Barbou, 1767).

Parny, vicompte Evariste-Désiré Desgorges de, *Les Poésies érotiques*, in *Œuvres* (Paris: Hardouin et Gattet, 1778).

Piis, Pierre-Antoine-Auguste, chevalier de, *Recueil de poésies fugitives, et Contes nouveaux* (Paris: Ph.-D. Pierres, 1781).

——*L'Harmonie imitative de la Langue Française—poème en quatre chants* (Paris: Ph.-D. Pierres, 1785).

Piles, Roger de, *Cours de peinture par principes* (1708; Paris: Gallimard, 1987).

Pons, abbé Jean-François de, *Dissertation sur les langues en général et sur la langue françoise en particulier; Réflexions sur l'éloquence* (Paris: Prault, 1738).

Prévost, Antoine François, abbé, 'Progès [*sic*] du nouvel art de la Gravure colorée, inventé par M. le Blon', *Le Pour et le contre* XVII (1739), 265–70.

Racine, Louis, *Réflexions sur la poésie*, in *Œuvres* (Paris: Dessaint & Saillant, 1747), Vol. III, IV.

—— *Œuvres*, 6 vols (Amsterdam: Marc Michel Rey, 1750): Vol. V: 'Harmonie imitative'; Vol. IV: 'Odes sur l'Harmonie'.

Rameau, Jean-François, *Complete Theoretical Writings*, ed. Erwin R. Jacobi (n.p.: American Institute of Musicology, 1968–9).

Rémond de Saint-Mard, Toussaint, *Sur les petits poëmes* in *Œuvres mêlées*, 3 vols (Hague: Jean Neaulme, 1742), Vol. III.

Reynolds, Sir Joshua, *Discourses on Art*, ed. Robert R. Wark (San Marino, Calif.: Huntington Library, 1959).

Roucher, Jean-Antoine, *Les Mois, poëme, en douze chants* (Paris: Quillau, 1779).

Rousseau, Jean-Jacques, *Œuvres* (Paris: Gallimard, 1959–95): Vol. I: *Les Confessions*; Vol. II: *Julie, ou la Nouvelle Héloise*; Vol. III: *Discours sur l'origine et les fondemens de l'inégalité parmi les hommes*; Vol. V: *Essai sur l'origine des langues*.

—— Correspondence, ed. R. A. Leigh (Geneva: Institut et Musée Voltaire, 1965–71, Vols. I–XV; Oxford: Taylor Institution, 1975–91, Vols. XVI–L; Oxford: Voltaire Foundation, 1995, Vol. LI).

Scoppa, Ant., *Les Vrais Principes de la versification, développés par un examen comparatif entre la langue italienne et française. On y examine et l'on y compare l'accent qui est la source de l'harmonie des vers, la nature, la versification, et la musique de ces deux langues [. . .] Et, en relevant dans la langue française les beautés qui la rendent susceptible de tous les charmes de la Poésie et de la Musique, on la venge des imputations de ceux qui lui refusent de la douceur et de l'harmonie* (Paris: Courcier, 1811).

Shaftesbury (see Cooper).

Sicard, abbé Roch-Ambroise Cucurron de, *Théorie des signes pour l'instruction des sourds-muets*, 2 vols (Paris: Imprimerie de l'Institution des Sourds-Muets, 1808).

Staël, Germaine, baronne de, *De la Littérature, considérée dans ses rapports avec les institutions sociales* in *Œuvres*, 17 vols (Paris: Treuttel et Würtz, 1820), Vol. IV.

Sulzer, Johann Georg, 'INTERESSANT (Beaux-Arts)', in *Supplément à l'Encyclopédie, ou Dictionnaire raisonné des sciences, des arts et des métiers*, 4 vols (1777), Vol. III, 627–8.

Swift, Jonathan, *Gulliver's Travels* (Oxford: Oxford University Press, 1971).

Turgot, *Sur la Prosodie de la langue française et la Versification métrique* in *Œuvres*, 9 vols (Paris: Delance, 1810), Vol. 9.

Vattel, Emmerich de, *Poliergie, ou Mélange de littérature et de poësie* (Amsterdam: Arkstée et Merkus, 1757).

Vaugelas, Claude Favre, seigneur de, *Remarques sur la langue françoise* (Paris: La Veuve Camusat et P. le petit, 1647).

Virgil, *Ecloga*, ed. H. Rushton Fairclough (Cambridge, Mass.: Loeb Classical Library, Harvard University Press, 1972).

Virgil, *Eclogues*, ed. Robert Coleman (Cambridge: Cambridge University Press, 1977).

Voltaire, François Marie Arouet, dit, *L'Œdipe de Monsieur de Voltaire. Avec une préface dans laquelle on combat les sentiments de M. de la Motte sur la Poësie* (1719; Paris: La Veuve de Pierre Ribon, 1730).

—— *Œuvres*, ed. Moland, 50 vols (Paris: Garnier, 1877–9): Vol. 34: 'Lettre à M. Rameau', pp. 437–40; Vol. 10: *Le Mondain*; Vol. 8: *Le Temple du goût*; Vol. 17: 'Anciens et modernes', 'Art dramatique' and 'Art poétique' in *Dictionnaire philosophique*; Vol. 14: 'Des beaux-arts' in *Siècle de Louis XIV*; Vol. 18: 'Epopée' in *Dictionnaire philosophique*; Vol. 19: 'Esprit' and 'Langue' in *Dictionnaire philosophique*; Vol. 3: 'Réponse à M. de Lindelle'; Vol. 23: *Connaissance des beautés et des défauts de la poésie et de l'éloquence dans la langue française*.

Warburton, William, *The Divine Legation of Moses demonstrated on the principles of a religious deist, from the omission of the doctrine of a future state of reward and punishment in the Jewish dispensation* (London: 1738–41).

—— *Essai sur les hiéroglyphes des Egyptiens Où l'on voit l'origine et le progres du langage et de l'écriture, l'antiquité des sciences en Egypte, et l'origine du culte des animaux*, trans. Léonard Des Malpeines (1744; Paris: Aubier Flammarion, 1977).

BOOKS AND ARTICLES FIRST PUBLISHED AFTER 1820

Aarsleff, Hans, 'The History of Linguistics and Professor Chomsky', in *From Locke to Saussure: Essays on the Study of Language and Intellectual History* (London: Athlone, 1982).

Abrams, M. H., *The Mirror and the Lamp: Romantic Theory and the Critical Tradition* (Oxford: Oxford University Press, 1971).

Andersen, Wilda C., *Between the Library and the Laboratory: The Language of Chemistry in Eighteenth-century France* (London: Johns Hopkins University Press, 1984).

Aquien, Michèle, *Dictionnaire de poétique* (Paris: Livre de poche, 1993).

Auroux, Sylvain, *La Sémiotique des encyclopédistes* (Paris: Payot, 1979).

—— 'D'Alembert et les synonymistes', *Dix-huitième siècle* 16 (1984), 93–108.

Baker, Keith Michael, *Condorcet: From Natural Philosophy to Social Mathematics* (London: University of Chicago Press, 1975).

Baldensperger, Fernand, 'Court de Gébelin et l'importance de son *Monde primitif* in *Mélanges de Philologie et d'histoire littéraire offerts à Edmond Huguet* (Paris: Boivin, 1940), 315–30.

Barasch, Moshe, *Modern Theories of Art, 1: From Winckelmann to Baudelaire* (New York: New York University Press, 1990).

Bennington, G. P., 'Les Machines de l'Opéra: le, jeu du signe dans *Le Spectateur français* de Marivaux, in *French Studies* (1982), 155–70.

Bouillier, Victor, 'Silvain et Kant, ou les Antécédents Français de la Théorie du Sublime', *Revue de Littérature Comparée* VIII (1928), 242–57.

Branca, Sonia, ' "L'Art d'écrire" de Condillac (1775). A propos de quelques règles prescriptives: traitement des ellipses et des anaphores', *Langue française* 48 (1980), 44–56.

Bray, René, ed. *Anthologie de la poésie précieuse, de Thibaut de Champagne à Giraudoux* (Paris: Nizet, 1946).

Bruneau, Charles, 'Buffon et le problème de la forme', in *Œuvres philosophiques de Buffon,* ed. Jean Piveteau (Paris: Presses universitaires de France, 1954), Vol. XLI, 1, pp. 491–9.

Brunot, Ferdinand, *Histoire de la Langue française des origines à 1900* (Paris: Armand Colin, 1932).

Cannone, Belinda, *Philosophies de la musique, 1752–1789* (Paris: Aux Amateurs de Livres, 1990).

Cassirer, Ernst, *The Philosophy of Enlightenment* (Princeton: Princeton University Press, 1951).

Chevalier, J.-Cl., 'Note sur la notion de synonymie chez trois grammairiens des XVIIIe siècles', *Langages* 24 (1971), 40–7.

Chomsky, Noam, *Cartesian Linguistics* (Lanham, Md.: University Press of America, 1966).

Ciardi, John, *How Does a Poem Mean?* (Boston: Houghton Mifflin, 1960).

Clayton, Vista, *The Prose Poem in French Literature of the Eighteenth Century* (New York: Columbia University, 1936).

Croce, Benedetto, *Aesthetic as Science of Expression and General Linguistic,* trans. by Douglas Ainslie (London: Macmillan, 1922).

Darnton, Robert, *La Fin des Lumières: Le Mesmérisme et la Révolution,* trans. Marie-Alyx Revellat (Paris: Librairie Académique Perrin, 1984).

Davie, Donald, *Articulate Energy* (London: Penguin, 1955).

Decker, Ronald, Thierry Depaulis, and Michael Dummett, *A Wicked Pack of Cards: The Origins of the Occult Tarot* (London: Duckworth, 1996).

Deloffre, Frédérique, *Marivaux et le Marivaudage* (Paris: Armand Colin, 1971).

Delon, Michel, *L'Idée de l'énergie au tournant des Lumières* (Paris: Presses universitaires de France, 1988).

Derrida, Jacques, *De la Grammatologie* (Paris: Editions de Minuit, 1967).

——'La Loi du genre', in *Parages* (Paris: Galilée, 1986).

Dorigny, Marcel, 'Du "despotisme vertueux" à la République', in *Louis-Sébastien Mercier: Un hérétique en littérature*, ed. Jean-Claude Bonnet (Paris: Mercure de France, 1995).

Droixhe, Daniel, 'L'Orientation structurale de la linguistique au XVIIIe siècle', *Le Français Moderne* 39 (1971), 18–32.

——*La Linguistique et l'appel de l'histoire (1600–1800): Rationalisme et révolutions positives* (Geneva: Droz, 1978).

Finch, Robert, *The Sixth Sense: Individualism in French Poetry, 1686–1760* (Toronto: University of Toronto Press, 1966).

——and Eugène, Joliat, eds., *French Individualist Poetry, 1686–1760* (Toronto: University of Toronto Press, 1971).

France, Peter, *Rhetoric and Truth in France: Descartes to Diderot* (Oxford: Clarendon Press, 1972).

François, Alexis, *La Grammaire du purisme et l'Académie française au XVIIIe siècle. Introduction à l'étude des commentaires grammaticaux d'auteurs classiques. Suivi de Les Origines lyriques de la phrase moderne. Etude sur la prose cadencée dans la littérature française au XVIIIe siècle* (Geneva: Slatkine Reprints, 1973).

Gaiffe, Félix, *Le Drame en France au XVIIIe siècle* (1910; Paris: Armand Colin, 1971).

Genette, Gérard, 'La rhétorique restreinte', *Communications* 16 (1970), 158–71.

——*Mimologiques: Voyage en Cratylie* (Paris: Seuil, 1976).

——'Genres, "types", modes', in *Poétique* 32 (Nov. 1977), 389–421.

Ghil, René, *Traité du verbe: états successifs (1885, 1886, 1887, 1888, 1891, 1904)*, ed. Goruppi Tiziana (Paris: Nizet, 1978).

Gombrich, E. H., *Art and Illusion: A Study in the Psychology of Pictorial Representation* (London: Phaidon Press, 1996).

Grammont, Maurice, 'Le rythme et l'harmonie chez quelques prosateurs du XVIIIe siècle', in *Le Français moderne* (Jan. 1938), 1–16.

Grente, cardinal Georges, *Dictionnaire des lettres françaises: Le XVIIIe siècle*, édition revue et mise à jour sous la direction de François Moureau (Paris: Fayard, 1995).

Guitton, Edouard, 'Les Tentatives de libérations du vers français dans la poésie de 1760 à la révolution', in CAIEF 21 (1969).

Guthrie, W. K. C., *A History of Greek Philosophy*, 4 vols (Cambridge: Cambridge University Press, 1965).

Hausmann, F. J., 'Le "Dictionnaire" de Condillac', *Le Français moderne* 46 (1978), 226–49.

Hazard, Paul, *La Crise de la conscience européenne* (Paris: Fayard, 1961).

Head, Brian W., 'The origin of "idéologue" and "idéologie"', *Studies on Voltaire and the Eighteenth Century* 183 (1980), 257–64.

Hobson, Marian, *The Object of Art: The Theory of Illusion in Eighteenth-century France* (Cambridge: Cambridge University Press, 1982).

Jakobson, Roman and Waugh, Linda, *The Sound Shape of Language* (Brighton: Harvester Press, 1979).

Jespersen, Otto, *Language, its Nature, Development and Origin* (London: Unwin, 1922).

Joly, André, 'La linguistique cartésienne: une erreur mémorable', in *La Grammaire générale, des modistes aux idéologues* (Lille: Presses universitaires de Lille, 1977).

Kemp, Martin, *The Science of Art: Optical Themes in Western Art from Brunelleschi to Seurat* (New Haven: Yale University Press, 1990).

Kibédi Varga, Aron, *Les Constantes du Poème: Analyse du langage poétique* (Paris: Picard, 1977).

Knight, Isabelle F., *The Geometric Spirit: The Abbé de Condillac and the French Enlightenment* (London: Yale University Press, 1968).

Knowlson, James, *Universal Language Schemes in England and France, 1600–1800* (Toronto: Toronto University Press, 1975).

Larousse Encyclopedia of Mythology, transl. by Richard Aldington and Delano Ames (London: Hamlyn, 1990).

Lecercle, Jean-Louis, *Rousseau et l'art du roman* (Paris: Armand Colin, 1969).

Le Flamanc, Auguste, *Les Utopies prérévolutionnaires et la philosophie du 18e siècle* (Paris: Librairie philosophique J. Vrin, 1934).

Lichtenstein, Jacqueline, *La Couleur éloquente* (Paris: Flammarion, 1989).

Lote, Georges, *Histoire du vers français*, eds. Joëlle Gardes-Tamine and Lucien Victor, 8 vols (Aix-en-Provence: Université de Provence, 1992), Vol. VII, VIII.

Marcos, Jean-Pierre, 'Le Traité des sensations d'Etienne Bonnot, abbé de Condillac', *Corpus, revue de philosophie* 3 (1986), 41–3.

Mason, Wilton, 'Father Castel and His Color Clavecin', *Journal of Aesthetics and Art Criticism* 17 (1958), 103–16.

Mazon, Paul, *Madame Dacier et les traductions d'Homère en France*, The Zaharoff Lecture for 1935 (Oxford: Clarendon Press, 1936).

Mercier, Roger, 'La Querelle de la poésie au début du XVIIIe siècle', *Revue des Sciences Humaines* (Jan.–June 1969), 19–46.

Moriarty, Michael, *Taste and Ideology in Seventeenth-century France* (Cambridge: Cambridge University Press, 1988).

Mortier, Roland, 'Unité ou scission du siècle des lumières?' in *Clartés et ombres du siècle des lumières* (Geneva: Droz, 1969).

Mortier, Roland, and Hasquin, Hervé (eds.), *Autour du Père Castel et du clavecin oculaire* (Brussels: Editions de l'Université de Bruxelles, 1995).

Münch, Marc-Matthieu, *Le Pluriel du beau. Essai sur sa genèse au XVIIIe siècle et sur l'émergence du principe de rélativité dans l'esthéthique littéraire. Allemagne, Angleterre, France* (Lille: Presse universitaire de Lille, 1988).

Naves, Raymond, *Le Goût de Voltaire* (Paris: Garnier, 1938).

Nicolson, Marjorie Hope, *Mountain Gloom and Mountain Glory: The Development of the Aesthetics of the Infinite* (New York: Cornell University Press, 1959).

Pellerey, Roberto, *Le Lingue perfette nel secolo dell'utopia* (Rome/Bari: Laterza, 1992).

Prynne, J. H., 'Stars, Tigers and the Shape of Words': The William Matthews Lectures 1992, delivered at Birkbeck College, London (London: Birkbeck College, c.1993).

Ricœur, Paul, *La Métaphore vive* (Paris: Seuil, 1975).

Roudaut, Jean, 'Les Inconnues poétiques du XVIIIe siècle', *Cahiers du Sud* 48 (1959), 10–32.

——*Poètes et grammairians au dix-huitième siècle* (Paris: Gallimard, 1971).

Saussure, Ferdinand de, *Cours de linguistique générale*, ed. Rudolf Engler (Wiesbaden: Harrossovitz, 1967).

Scott, Clive, *French Verse-Art: A Study* (Cambridge: Cambridge University Press, 1980).

Seguin, Jean-Pierre, *La Langue française au XVIIIe siècle* (Paris: Bordas, 1972).

Seigal, G. P., 'The Enlightenment and the Evolution of a Language of Signs in France and England', *Journal of the History of Ideas* XXX (Jan.–March 1969), 96–115.

Simpson, G. G., *Principles of Animal Taxonomy* (New York: Columbia University Press, 1967).

Soublin, Françoise, '13→30→3', *Langages* 54 (June 1979), 41–64.

Spire, André, *Plaisir poétique et plaisir musculaire: Essai sur l'évolution des techniques poétiques* (Paris: Corti, 1986).

Spitzer, Leo, *Linguistics and Literary History* (New York: Princeton University Press, 1948).

Stevens, Jane R., 'The Meanings and Uses of *Caractère* in Eighteenth-Century France' in *French Musical Thought, 1600–1800*, ed. Georgie Cowart (London/Ann Arbor: U.M.I. Research Press, 1989), 23–52.

Starobinski, Jean, *Les Mots sous les mots: Les anagrammes de Ferdinand de Saussure* (Paris: Gallimard, 1971).

Sully-Prudhomme, René François Armand Prudhomme, dit, *Testament poétique* (Paris: Lemerre, 1901).

Teyssèdre, Bernard, *Roger de Piles et les débats sur le coloris au siècle de Louis XIV* (Paris: Bibliothèque de l'art, 1957).

——'Peinture et musique: la notion d'harmonie des couleurs au XVIIe siècle français', from the proceedings of *Stil und Uberlieferung in der Kunst des Abendlandes. Akten des 21. Internationalen Kongresses für Kunstgeschichte*, 4 vols (Bonn: Verlag Gebr. Mann, 1967), Vol. III, 206–14.

Thomas, Downing A., *Music and the Origins of Language: Theories from the French Enlightenment* (Cambridge: Cambridge University Press, 1995).

Thompson, W. R., 'The Philosophical Foundations of Systematics', *Canadian Entomology* 84 (1952), 1–16.

Todorov, Tzvetan, *Théories du symbole* (Paris: Seuil, 1977).

Verba, Cynthia, *Music and the French Enlightenment: Reconstruction of a dialogue, 1750–1764* (Oxford: Clarendon Press, 1993).

Vidler, Anthony, 'Mercier urbaniste: l'utopie du réel', in *Louis-Sébastien Mercier: Un hérétique en littérature*, ed. Jean-Claude Bonnet (Paris: Mercure de France, 1995).

Wandruszka, Mario, 'La Nuance', *Zeitschrift für romanische Philologie* LXX (1954), 232–48.

Waerden, B. L. van der, *A History of Algebra* (Berlin: Springer-Verlag, 1985).

Zumthor, Paul, 'Etymologie (essai d'histoire sémantique)', in *Etymologica: Walther von Wartburg zum siebzigsten Geburtstag 18. Mai 1958* (Tübingen: Keller, 1958).

Zweig, Stefan, *La Guérison par l'esprit* (Paris: Livre de poche, 1991).

INDEX